POLITICAL ROCK

Political Rock

Edited by
MARK PEDELTY and KRISTINE WEGLARZ
University of Minnesota, USA

ASHGATE

Published by
Ashgate Publishing Limited
Wey Court East
Union Road
Farnham
Surrey, GU9 7PT
England

Ashgate Publishing Company
110 Cherry Street
Suite 3-1
Burlington, VT 05401-3818
USA

www.ashgate.com

British Library Cataloguing in Publication Data
Political rock. – (Ashgate popular and folk music series)
  1. Rock musicians–Political activity.
  I. Series II. Pedelty, Mark. III. Weglarz, Kristine.
  782.4'2166'0922-dc23

The Library of Congress has cataloged the printed edition as follows:
Political rock / edited by Mark Pedelty and Kristine Weglarz.
    pages cm. – (Ashgate Popular and Folk Music Series)
  Includes index.
  ISBN 978-1-4094-4622-4 (hardcover) – ISBN 978-1-4094-4623-1 (ebook) – ISBN
978-1-4094-7305-3 (epub) 1. Rock music – Political aspects. I. Pedelty, Mark, editor. II.
Weglarz, Kristine, editor.
  ML3918.R63P65 2013
  306.4'8426–dc23

2012044680

ISBN 9781409446224 (hbk)
ISBN 9781409446231 (ebk – PDF)
ISBN 9781409473053 (ebk – ePUB)

MIX
Paper from
responsible sources
FSC
www.fsc.org **FSC® C013985**

Printed in the United Kingdom by Henry Ling Limited,
at the Dorset Press, Dorchester, DT1 1HD

Contents

Notes on Contributors

Douglas M. McLeod is the Evjue Centennial Professor in the School of Journalism and Mass Communication at the University of Wisconsin. He specializes in political communication, persuasion, and public opinion. He has published more than 100 articles. His research interests focus on social conflict and social protest and the role that mainstream media play in such conflicts. His forthcoming book, *Framing the War on Terror: The Struggle Over Civil Liberties in the Age of Terrorism*, is being published by Cambridge University Press. He is also a practicing rock musician and has long been a fan of political rock.

Michael LeVan is Senior Instructor in Communication and Affiliated Assistant Professor in Humanities and Cultural Studies at the University of South Florida. He is co-founder and general editor of *Liminalities: A Journal of Performance Studies*.

Kristine Weglarz is an Assistant Professor of Telecommunications and Film at the University of West Florida's Department of Communication Arts. Her dissertation and research focuses on the political economy of live rock performance, constructions of authenticity, protest rock, mediaphemes, and "liveness" as cultural constructions. She teaches courses on multi-camera electronic video production, popular music and media studies, introduction to mass media, and the political economy of media.

Marcy R. Chvasta is a Lecturer in Communication Studies at the California State University, Stanislaus. Marcy specializes in performance studies but teaches a variety of courses across the communication studies curriculum. Her published work includes philosophical treatments of "liveness" and "mediation," reality television, online journaling, and social activism. Currently, she is working on a consideration of risk as an essential feature of performance. She is a co-founding editor of *Liminalities: A Journal of Performance Studies*, the first online, open-access, multimedia journal of performance practices and theories. Marcy has also written, performed, and directed numerous stage and screen productions. She is a member of Underscore, a digital performance collective. And, unlike Sinéad O'Connor, Marcy sometimes wants what she hasn't got.

Mark Pedelty is an Associate Professor of Mass Communication at the University of Minnesota. He received his Ph.D. in Anthropology from UC, Berkeley, in 1993. He is the author of *War Stories: The Culture of Foreign Correspondents* (Routledge,

1995), *Musical Ritual in Mexico City: From the Aztec to NAFTA* (University of Texas Press, 2004), and *Ecomusicology: Rock, Folk, and the Environment* (Temple University Press, 2012). Pedelty has also published a number of journal articles dealing with popular music, including "Woody Guthrie and the Columbia River: Propaganda, Art, and Irony," in *Popular Music and Society* 31(3): 329–55 (2008). Dr. Pedelty is currently conducting applied research concerning music as environmental communication.

Keith Nainby is an Associate Professor of Communication Studies at California State University, Stanislaus. His primary areas of expertise are critical communication pedagogy and philosophy of communication, and he regularly teaches courses in communication and instruction, communication theory, and performance studies. His research explores constitutive models of selfhood and identity, especially the implications of these models for understanding pedagogical relationships. Significant recent publications on these topics include "Philosophical and Methodological Foundations of Communication Education," in *The SAGE Handbook of Communication and Instruction*, and "Effacement and Metaphor: Searching for the Body in Educational Discourse," in *Liminalities: A Journal of Performance Studies*.

Mark Mattern is Professor of Political Science at Baldwin Wallace University in Berea, Ohio, where he teaches political theory and political economy. He is the author of *Acting in Concert: Music, Community, and Political Action* (Rutgers University Press, 1998), and other articles and chapters on music, art, and popular culture. He is co-editor, with Nancy S. Love, of *Doing Democracy: Activist Art and Cultural Politics* (in review). He currently serves as co-editor, with Nancy S. Love, of *New Political Science: A Journal of Politics and Culture*. He is currently working on a manuscript tentatively entitled *Anarchism and Art: Democracy in the Cracks and on the Margins*.

Nancy S. Love is Professor of Government and Justice Studies at Appalachian State University in Boone, North Carolina. Professor Love received her AB degree from Kenyon College and her MA and Ph.D from Cornell University. She is the author of *Musical Democracy* (SUNY Press, 2006), *Marx, Nietzsche, and Modernity* (Columbia University Press, 1986; reissued 1996), and *Understanding Dogmas and Dreams*, 2nd edition (CQ Press, 2006), a companion text to her edited reader *Dogmas and Dreams: A Reader in Modern Political Ideologies*, 4th edition (CQ Press, 2010). Her articles and chapters on critical theory and feminist theory appear in numerous journals and anthologies. She is co-editor with Mark Mattern of *Doing Democracy: Activist Art and Cultural Politics* (under review at SUNY Press). She and Mattern currently co-edit *New Political Science: A Journal of Politics and Culture*.

Aaron S. Allen teaches in the School of Music, Theatre, and Dance at the University of North Carolina at Greensboro, where he also serves on the faculty committee for the Environmental Studies Program. After receiving a B.S. in environmental studies and B.A. in music at Tulane University, Aaron earned a Ph.D. at Harvard with a dissertation on the nineteenth-century Italian reception of Beethoven. He co-founded and currently chairs the Ecocriticism Study Group of the American Musicological Society and the Ecomusicology Special Interest Group of the Society for Ethnomusicology, and he is a Fellow of the American Academy in Rome. Aaron has published and presented papers on campus environmental issues, Beethoven, and ecomusicology.

Mark Andersen has done outreach, advocacy, and organizing in inner city DC since the late 1980s. He is the co-author of *Dance of Days: Two Decades of Punk in the Nation's Capital*, author of *All The Power: Revolution Without Illusion*, and a contributor to *We Owe You Nothing: Punk Planet/The Collected Interviews, Sober Living For The Revolution: Hardcore Punk, Straight Edge, and Radical Politics*, and *Rad Dad: Dispatches From The Frontiers of Fatherhood*. He was a co-founder of punk activist collective Positive Force DC in 1985, the Arthur S. Flemming Community Center in 2003, and senior outreach network We Are Family in 2004. He remains active with those groups and also works with the Justice & Service Committee of St Aloysius Catholic Church, the Social Justice Committee of Sacred Heart Catholic Church, and on the board of directors of the grassroots community organization Northwest One Council. He lives with his beloved Tulin Ozdeger, their son Soren Huseyin, and their two cats Spaatz and Seker in the Columbia Heights neighborhood of Washington DC.

Norma Coates is an Associate Professor with a joint appointment in the Don Wright Faculty of Music and the Faculty of Information and Media Studies at the University of Western Ontario. Her publications in journals and anthologies explore a wide range of popular music topics, including gender, television, and age.

An Introduction to Political Rock: History, Genre, and Politics

Mark Pedelty and Kristine Weglarz

This book is about *Political Rock*, the kind of music made by artists like Bruce Springsteen, Rage Against the Machine, and Rise Against. Granted, political rock is relatively rare. For every "Biko," by Peter Gabriel (1980), "War All the Time," by Thursday (2003), or "Let's Impeach the President," by Neil Young (2006), there are thousands of party tunes like Nickleback's "Bottoms Up" (2011) or LMFAO's "Party Rock Anthem" (2011). The big rock party saves little room for politics. The last thing most fans want to hear while working away the day or ending a long week is a song about human rights, presidential politics, or climate change. Life is hard enough already.

Nor have music scholars taken much interest in political rock. Practically every time the topic is raised, someone asks, "Isn't all rock political?" The answer, of course, is "yes." All *music* is political. However, there are already plenty of popular music scholars rethinking Michael Jackson's moonwalk, plumbing the depths of Britney Spears' outfits, or analyzing heavy metal performance for clues into our cultural psyche. These critics might be able to tell us how Lady Gaga's meat-based clothing challenges heteronormativity or how Metallica relates to middle age. Good stuff, but not what we are interested in here. We are much less interested in what party rock says about society than what politicized music means to rock artists, fans, and movements. This book is about explicitly *political rock*, not the *politics of rock* writ large. It is about Rage Against the Machine, not Florence and the Machine, Michael Franti, not Michael McDonald, The Indigo Girls and Riot Grrrl, not Boys Like Girls or the Spice Girls. You get the idea.

For some reason, explicitly political rock has been ignored by academics. In a 277-page book dedicated to *Popular Music and Society*, Brian Longhurst dedicates less than six pages to "Pop and Politics," with only a few mentions of explicitly political songs and singers (2007, 115–20), let alone a specific focus on rock artists. Despite a wealth of rock research, relatively few music researchers have examined songs or singers with political repertories or reputations. Yet, it seems almost obligatory to delve into politics when writing about hip-hop (Ogbar 2007, Spence 2011), reggae (King et al. 2002, Lewis and Gregg 1993), or folk (Ingram 2008, Reuss and Reuss 2000). There are rich literatures about politics in these and other popular music traditions. If there is consensus in the literature it is this: given the right historical circumstances, cultural conditions, and aesthetic qualities, popular music can help bring people together to form more effective political communities

(Mattern 1998). That statement is as true for rock as other styles of popular music (Garofalo 1992, Garofalo et al. 2005, Pedelty 2009, Pratt 1994).

Perhaps Longhurst and other musicologists downplay political rock because so little of it exists. Political bands like Anti-Flag, Fugazi, and Green Day are the exception to rock's apolitical rule. Nevertheless, such bands continue a political tradition that goes back to the beginning of rock, if not long before. The political tradition in American popular music links contemporary artists like Eddie Vedder and Zack de la Rocha to older generations of rockers like Bruce Springsteen (Pratt 1994) and Neil Young (McDonough 2002), on back to pre-rock figures like Woody Guthrie (1912–67), Paul Robeson (1898–1976), and Joe Hill (1879–1915). To ignore political rock is to ignore that long tradition of musicianship, a tradition of artistry that breaks cultural taboos and refuses to ideologically confine popular music to romance, intoxication, and revelry. Although such topics are essential to popular music, and always have been, they are not the totality of the human experience. One thing all politically critical musicians share, regardless of genre or historical era, is rejection and dismissal by mainstream critics and musicologists.

Not that rock fans, musicians, or critics care what music researchers do or think. Rock musicians keep performing political songs and fans keep listening to them, even when told to *Shut Up and Sing* (Ingraham 2003). This book is written for those fans, musicians, and activists, as well as students of rock history, culture, and music.

Although relatively few books have been dedicated to explicitly political rock, several authors have written about the political contexts of rock writ large. Foremost among them is Lawrence Grossberg. Grossberg devotes much of his effort to debunking the notion that rock is inherently resistant. He argues that there are several orientations to rock beyond opposition: alternative, independent, and "co-opted" (1983, 110). Grossberg argues that rock "can be used in radically different ways by different fans" (1983, 140). A fine point: rock has fueled peace movements, but is also used to promote war. Rock can sell high-consumption lifestyles or promote sustainability. The same song can serve different political ends. Rock has no singular essence, fixed politics, or social purpose. In a word, rock is polysemic. It can carry water for anyone, from environmental activists (Ingram 2010) to drill sergeants. The meanings of rock are as varied as political culture itself; rock belongs to no single ideology, institution, or group.

A brief survey of six decades of song titles, charts, and demographic sales data demonstrates what we all already know: that rock is, above all, a sensual soundtrack for youth. It has been the music of youthful discovery more than anything else. For over five decades, rock'n'roll has served as a rite-of-passage for teens and young adults who use it to learn the cultural ropes of subcultures (enculturation), communicate with each other, and express themselves. Rock is the soundtrack for discovery as young people explore adult possibilities and dangers. It is a ritual outlet, medium of collective expression, and means of forming identity. As rockers age, the music of their youth converts into a nostalgia soundtrack, cuing recollections of the listener's earlier age of discovery. Of course, rock is not the only popular music to serve that purpose, but it is surprisingly enduring.

Despite rock's rite-of-passage proclivities and pop sensibilities, there are nevertheless political dimensions worth exploring in specific songs, performers, fans, movements and moments. At various times and places, rock has been, and is, rebellious. *Political Rock* engages that more rebellious side of rock, rather than dismiss or ignore it. *Political Rock* is about that rare part of the popular music world where musicians, fans, and critics operate in the belief music can do more than express teen angst, sell mini vans, or evoke nostalgia. Rock is, among other things, a medium for political communication.

There have always been strains of politically charged rock, music that challenges powerful institutions and social mores. For some bands and fans, political rock matters a great deal. Consider The Clash. In 1979 a sticker appeared on the cover of their double album, London Calling (1979), boldly proclaiming that they were "The only band that matters." The Clash were calling attention to the relatively rarity, and significance, of political rock.

As Mark Andersen makes clear in Chapter 1, The Clash are an excellent example. Young rock fans often assume The Clash were more typical for their time (1976–86) and genre than political artists are today. They were not. Like all political rock bands, The Clash had to break through a sticky din of popular, less socially and politically challenging rock and pop in order to be heard and remain sustainable financially. Throughout The Clash's ten years of existence, the rock charts were, and are, dominated by anything put political rock. From The Bay City Rollers' "Saturday Night," the most popular song of January 1976, to The Bangles' "Walk Like an Egyptian," the most popular song in December 1986, the charts were, as always, dominated by youth-oriented party music. Somehow, amidst that spectacular taffy, The Clash managed to succeed while singing about Sandinistas, the CIA, and "Washington Bullets" (1980). Of course, those were not The Clash songs that hit the charts, but it is fair to say that the band communicated in a sonic vernacular both new and familiar to the time, appealing to a mass audience as well as a more politicized fan base. The Clash were bona fide rock, featuring genre-defining electric guitars, bass, and drum kit. However, The Clash added critical lyrics and integrated sounds relatively new to rock at the time, including reggae beats, ska stylings, and dub elements borrowed from Kingston, Brixton, and the neighborhood record shop. The idea that rock could be about more than sex, romance, and celebration was new to the bored youth who made up The Clash's fan base, from White kids stuck in Kent and rural Kansas to hip rock audiences in suburban Sydney and New York City, not to mention activists around the Anglophone world hungry for music that might speak more directly to their lives. Despite their bold claim (and marketing ploy), The Clash were not, and are not, "the only band that matters." They just seemed like it at the time. Every moment in the rock era has indulged at least a few political performers like The Clash.

Throughout the history of rock, musicians have ventured beyond socially safe parameters to create what Peter Blecha calls *Taboo Tunes* (2004), songs that "dare to question authority" (ibid., 137). Although rock is neither intrinsically nor typically rebellious, a select few rock musicians challenge dominant perspectives, despite the loud laughs and occasional bans of detractors. From Dylan and Donovan to DiFranco and Death By Stereo, some musicians have managed to burst out of pop's gilded cage of cool, parlaying popular music into political critique.

The disinclination toward politics is not just a problem in music. American art, in general, tends to remain safely ensconced in individual and interpersonal matters. Take American stagings of Hamlet. The play is as much about statecraft, governance, and power as it is about the young protagonist's existential dilemma, yet American dramaturges and directors tend to downplay those larger scale questions. When cutting the text to a more manageable three-hour play, the first cuts usually involve scenes and dialogue about international intrigue. Forget Norway and Poland, the play is *really* about Hamlet. The more complete work of art is reduced to psychodrama revolving around an immature youth's existential struggles and interpersonal entanglements. Like the character of Hamlet himself, American art has a hard time getting beyond self-reflective psychology.

When art limits itself to micro-scale matters, artistic potential is lost. Shakespeare knew that. He wrote about powerful institutions, ideologies, and international matters for a reason. So have the musicians profiled in this book: Bob Dylan, Peter Gabriel, Bruce Cockburn, The Clash, Billy Bragg, Sinéad O'Connor, Steve Earle, Kim Gordon, Ani DiFranco, Fugazi, Rage Against the Machine, and Pearl Jam. These are the type of rock musicians who have refused to be confined ideologically or artistically, and their musical stories are well worth telling.

As fans of popular music, their stories are our stories. Political rock matters a great deal to those who are inspired, motivated, and perhaps even informed by it. This book is for such people: fans, critics, musicians, scholars who believe political rock matters, and audiences for whom political rock performers have made a difference. It is also written by such people, scholar-critic-fans of political rock.

The authors have at least two traits in common. First, each is a fan of at least one political rock musician or band. Second, each author has studied and written about music, from scholars who have made it their life's work to others for whom it is a passionate side interest. However, don't worry; the book is not about its authors. Instead, the focus remains on the musicians who move us. Each author chose to write about one iconic rock musician or band. A few autobiographical details are included by each author as an interlocutor, a way to better explain the influence these musicians have had on fans' political lives.

We argue that political rock is a subgenre, a recognizable category within the wider world of rock. For example, when surveyed, political activists mentioned these musicians repeatedly (Pedelty 2009) and fans of political rock artists appear to blog more often about political issues than fans of other popular musicians (Pedelty and Keefe 2010). Each musician profiled here has crafted politically charged lyrics, spoken up in public, and lent support to political movements with their music. As Diane Weinstein reminds us, that is a rare set of traits (2006). Although the boundary distinguishing political rock from the rest of pop is somewhat blurry and is certainly porous, the conditions listed above do not apply to most popular performers.

All music is political, in social context, but only a "much-smaller subset of songs," explains Blecha, "contain overtly political lyrics" (2004, 137). A generation of music scholars has steered away from lyrical analysis, overreacting to Simon Frith's warning that there is much more to rock music than lyrics (1996, 158–82). Once again we see how the study of political rock has been dominated by voices emphasizing what political rock *is not* rather than examining what explicitly political songs, musicians, fans, and movements are about in a proactive sense. Inevitably, the examination of political rock steers us back to lyrics. Although lyrics are just part of what defines the political rock subgenre, as Frith pointed out, lyrics are central signifiers, one of the main ways composers and performers communicate political messages. The artists represented in *Political Rock* combine lyrical messages, innovative sound techniques, performance, visual cues, and spoken word to communicate political messages.

However, by no means do the twelve acts profiled in this book capture the entirety of political rock history. Therefore, the rest of the Introduction will be dedicated to providing a bit of historical context, while filling in some of the inevitable gaps in the narrative. Giant gaps will remain, of course. You might be wondering "Where is Neil Young (McDonough 2003), U2, David Crosby (1988), Frank Zappa (1989), Michael Franti, Midnight Oil, Joey 'Shithead' Keithley and DOA (Keithley 2003), Bruce Springsteen (Pratt 1994), Sex Pistols (Savage 2001), the Indigo Girls, or (insert your favorite political rock musician here)?" Our answer: they are waiting for you, the reader, to write about them. Submit an entry on the Political Rock blog at Wordpress.com. With your participation, this book will grow online.

Not only is this book limited in terms of the Anglophone world, but our need to focus thematically has led to neglect of political rock in other parts of the globe: for example, biographic studies of Mexico's politicized rockers—Alex Lora and El Tri, Café Tacuba, Maná, Tijuana No, and Ely Guerra, and many more—could fill volumes. However, *Political Rock* is just the start of a discussion we hope to see grow as each new reader/listener/fan/author contributes to the *Political Rock* blog.

A History of Political Rock

History tends to work backwards, finding origins and creating linear narratives to fit present needs and desires. In truth, there is no beginning to any musical trend, but rather continuities, revivals, syntheses, and innovations drawing on historical antecedents. Origin stories are always part myth. Before Bob (Dylan) came Woody (Guthrie), and before Woody, Paul (Robeson), and before Paul, Joe (Hill), and so on. Yet such nicely linear narratives obfuscate the more complex origins, developments, and influences of the political popular music tradition in America. Fainter traces might lead the curious fan of political rock back to influential folk and blues artists like Odetta and Lead Belly (often mistakenly spelled as "Leadbelly"). These performers drew audiences despite Left reputations, the critical barbs of mainstream critics, and lyrics that delve into political controversy. Or, maybe that is one of the reasons they drew listeners, audiences hungry for something more filling than mainstream musical fare. Each has been supported by a faithful core audience: political fan-activists whose connection to the music represents "homology" (Hopkins 1977). Such audiences not only love the music, they relate to the artist's political message as well, and integrate it into their political lives. Life, lyric, sound, and movement are integrally connected. If we ignore any of those elements, we fail to properly "decode" the meaning of the music, much less its social functions.

This retelling of political rock starts in the political ferment of the mid-1960s. During the 1960s rock first became explicitly articulated with political movements. A small branch of rock left its Oedipal underground to launch a more overt challenge to powerful political ideologies, policies, and institutions. Some bands, such as the MC5, were closely associated with antiwar and human rights movements. Others were one-hit wonders, such as Barry McGuire, whose "Eve of Destruction" hit the top of the Billboard Hot 100 the week of September 25, 1965. Perhaps what made the 1960s most remarkable, however, was the fact that even chart-topping rockers like The Beatles, The Rolling Stones, The Doors, and Creedence Clearwater Revival contributed political songs to the mix.

The 1960s colored how rock is conceived to this day, at least as an ideal type. Protest politics became inextricably articulated with rock in the public imaginary, albeit not in practice. Rock-as-rebellion is the type of story Marshall Sahlins describes in *Historical Metaphors and Mythical Realities* (1981), a mythic narrative that guides meaningful action in the world even if it is not empirically verifiable, explanatory, or accurate in a scientific sense. Music is myth, and myth matters. Successive generations of rock performers have evoked the myth of rock rebellion, kept it alive, and used it to inspire art.

Granted, political rock has never taken center stage for long. For example, just one week after "Eve of Destruction" hit the top of the pop charts in 1965, The McCoy's "Hang on Sloopy", released on the same label, took over first place. The McCoy's party rock was more typical for that and every other year, before and since. Nevertheless, rare as they are, political rock songs like "Eve of Destruction" have had a disproportionate influence on the rock imagination. The mythical ideal of rock as a political force endures.

1960s' activism ended in frustration, political passions dampened by war without end, the failure of movements to evidence immediate results, and a growing sense of environmental calamity. In the early 1970s a new wave of political rockers took stage while the old guard changed tune. As David Ingram notes, there was a pastoral strain to early 1970s' rock. Rock outsiders-turned-millionaires moved their studios to the countryside and began taking on environmental issues. Neil Young's "After the Gold Rush" (1970) led the charge and a number of 1960s' stalwarts followed suit. New bands like The Eagles took up the environmental challenge as well, while antiwar anthems became less common. While rock's nascent human rights movement was getting underway—most visibly in the form of George Harrison's Concert for Bangladesh—the early to mid-1970s would become known for a mellow turn toward country rock, production-heavy supergroups, and environmental songs like Joni Mitchell's "Big Yellow Taxi" (1970). Even the Beach Boys took their turn at environmental critique, releasing "Don't Go Near the Water" in 1971.

The mid-1970s witnessed the rise of punk, a musical movement that both challenged and embraced the 1960s' political rock tradition. Britain's "Revolution of '76" drew mostly on American influences—The Velvet Underground, The New York Dolls, The Stooges, and The Ramones—but added an explicitly political element, more in line with proto-punk rockers like the MC5 than the theatrical rock of America's East Coast acts. Most early American punks had little to say politically beyond simple parody. British punks—bands like the Stranglers, The Clash, Crass, and even the agitprop anarchist Sex Pistols—made political messages central to their music. These British bands would influence the rise of political punk throughout Europe, North America, and Australia. From Los Angeles' Bad Religion to Canadian Joey Shithead's D.O.A., London's Revolution of '76 represented ground zero for a political rock revival whose influence continues to this day. Although British punks were quite fond of desecrating the 1960s' sacred cows—passively resistant flower power, movement-oriented optimism, and drugged out psychedelia—punk did more to shepherd rock politics through the 1970s than any other style.

Meanwhile, in terms of movement politics, the 1970s witnessed as many or more gains than the 1960s. Gender equity, gay rights, reproductive rights, and global human rights experienced major leaps forward. These issues were reflected in protest rock, but somewhat less so than class-based labor politics, anti-war sentiments, environmental concerns and other issues associated with the New Left. A "new" New Left, more concerned with identity-based movements (or, more aware of the identity-biases of the Old and New Left) were much less represented in 1970s' and even 1980s' rock. Rock music and politics continued to be dominated by White male performers, producers, fans, and interests. As the world was changing rapidly, so was rock, but the rock world was largely ignoring women's issues, gay/lesbian/transgender rights, and other civil rights movements. All of these issues would be reflected in the wider world of rock. "Girl groups" of the 1950s, 1960s, 1970s, and 1980s (Gaar 2002) would give rise to the more explicitly feminist Riot Grrl rock movement of the 1990s (Gottlieb and Wald 2006, 355–61). Likewise, the 1970s' Glam trend brought rock's sublimated, yet potentially revolutionary, transgenderism to the surface, where it could more openly challenge heterosexual norms and assumptions. Movements like Rock Against Racism (RAR) allied mostly White male rockers with anti-racist movements (Frith and Street 1992).

Nevertheless, even in its most explicitly political forms, rock would continue to be dominated by White male performers throughout the 1970s and 1980s. The musicians featured in this book complicate that notion. However, a racial and gender bias to White males in rock is as undeniable as its proclivity toward youthful discovery and indulgence of sex, drugs, and other adult prohibitions. Although the ethnic articulations performed by critics and scholars tend to overly simplify how musicians and fans perform and experience music, the dominance of White male voices in rock is as obvious as the centrality of Black men in hip-hop, the role of women in pop, and so on. Although "the respective contributions of white and black musical traditions are nearly impossible to measure," the White male bias of rock is as evident in its politics as its performers and playlists (Frere-Jones 2007).

Britain's pale White punks—young men The Clash describe as looking "sick in the sun" (The Clash 1979)—redefined rock politics in the 1970s and on through the early 1980s. Punk exploded onto world consciousness and seemed to die almost as suddenly. Following Neil Young's ironic advice, most punks burned out rather than faded away. As a musical movement, punk went back underground (that is, became less popular, more avant-garde, and increasingly niche-specific in terms of audience). Less self-destructive punk came along in the likes of Fugazi, Propagandhi, and Anti-Flag, directly fueling political movements and inspiring new generations of activist fans. They no longer grabbed headlines, but their relative obscurity had some benefits. Political action and rhetoric came down to earth. Movements became less revolutionary in a millenarian sense and more sustainable at the grass roots. Today, the social and even physical distance between bands like Fugazi and political activists is much less than was the case for high-flying bands like The Clash and their activist fans in the 1970s and 1980s. Like all living traditions, punk remained alive by adapting, by being reborn for new purposes. In the 1990s, punk melded with other styles and produced more focused musical politics. The cultural war on everything declared by the Sex Pistols, Fear, and angry young men throughout the punk world burned twice as bright, but only half as long as most musical movements.

Meanwhile, an even more influential, politically charged, and lasting pop phenomenon arose around the same time as punk: hip-hop. Although mainstream hip-hop, like rock, does more to reflect hegemony than oppose it, rap artists like Public Enemy, KRS-One, and Mos Def became known for their lyrical critiques of powerful institutions, injustices, and individuals. The lyrical depth of hip-hop allows for rappers to craft more nuanced and complex political messages. Not surprisingly, political rock eventually turned to hip-hop for inspiration. Hip-hop, punk, and politics combined in 1990s' bands like Rage Against the Machine (see Chapter 11), The Beastie Boys, and hundreds of indie bands.

Meanwhile, Seattle-centered grunge was drawing from Americana punk progenitors like the Meat Puppets, Sonic Youth, and Butthole Surfers to craft a new sound and politics. Kurt Cobain and other early grunge rockers were more wary of political posturing than preceding generations of rock artists. Cobain took punk nihilism to the extreme, pointing the finger at himself more than any external institution, political class, or policy. Rock fans are often categorized according to a love for Beatles-like bands or those more in the mold of The Rolling Stones.

Perhaps punks can be put into two camps as well: The Clash or The Sex Pistols. Cobain favored the latter, and it showed in his life, music, and death. However, although Cobain's songs, guitar, and voice became seminal influences, the political rock tradition found its way into grunge nonetheless, most visibly in the form of Eddie Vedder and his band Pearl Jam. Krist Novoselic, Nirvana's bassist, became a tireless crusader on and offstage, campaigning for instant run-off voting and a fundamental transformation of America's electoral system. His book *Of Grunge and Government* (2004) is part political road map and memoir.

Throughout the 1990s, Vedder, Novoselic, and other alt-rockers saw less and less need to retain the fourth wall separating performers from politics. Grunge music was well represented in the heralded "Battle in Seattle" of 1991, a political watershed in the anti-corporate movement. Although 9/11 and the Bush years erased much of the momentum gained throughout the 1990s (Klein 2007), the spirit of the anti-corporate movement has been revived in the recent Occupy movement.

Grunge and other alt-rockers were more wary of stardom than their predecessors, less willing to put forth political absolutes and anthems. Yet, they tended to be more willing to engage in political organizing and policy-oriented details. Theirs was a more engaged, yet in many ways, more humble political orientation than that taken by rock gods of the 1960s or political punks of the 1970s and early 1980s. The Occupy movement shows many of the same traits, tracing a line of development back to the late 1990s' decentralized and broadly coalitional anti-corporate movement.

Growing nihilism and disillusionment failed to kill off political rock in the late 1960s, late 1970s, and early 2000s. In fact, each wave of political rock seems to only strengthen the articulation between popular music and politics. By 1998, even rock critic Richard Meltzer had bought into the end-of-days scenario for rock, arguing that what "was once liberating" about rock had "become irredeemably oppressive" (in McDonough 2002, 708). Each generation of aging fans, critics and scholars views rebellious rockers as a vanishing breed, ignoring the industrious young musicians and audiences who are busy remaking it in the underground. The young musicians' avant-garde rock might serve as the R&D of culture industries, but that inevitable dialectic—between revolution and re-incorporation—is no more reason to give up on rock than it is to give up on political organizing itself. It is the price of doing business, politics, and art.

Despite exaggerated claims of oppositional rock's death, by the 1990s "alternative" rock was partly defined by politics. Even relatively apolitical acts like Soundgarden seemed obligated to do at least some political work to boost their "alternative" bona fides. The closest Soundgarden's lyrics get to politics are relatively vague references to colonial oppression and environmental degradation in "Hands All Over" (1990). However, Soundgarden has lent support to a number of causes and political figures. In fact, lead guitarist Kim Thayil joined forces with the Dead Kennedys' Jello Biafra, Novoselic, and Gina Mainwal to create the No WTO Combo, a band that performed live at the Battle in Seattle, while

Chris Cornell worked with the members of Rage Against the Machine to form a politicized rock group, Audioslave. Meanwhile, perennial rock stars from the 1980s, from Bruce Springsteen to U2, continued to press their wildly popular music into political service throughout the 1990s and into the present.

By the 1990s, politics was so thoroughly associated with alternative rock that nearly all performers at least genuflected in a political direction. This was in part due to the success and florescence of rights-oriented "mega-events" in the 1980s (Garofalo 1992). Thanks to Bob Geldof (1986), Sting, Peter Gabriel, and Bono's pioneering work in the 1980s, popular music's progressive affiliations had become an assumption by the early 1990s. Alt-rockers were starting to view themselves as part of an established rock tradition, a political strain of rock, rather than something altogether new and revolutionary. Rather than the radical breaks imagined and promoted by earlier generations of avant-garde rockers, grunge was among the 1990s movements that viewed contemporary performance as an extension of an ongoing rock tradition rather than its undoing. Unlike the punks of the Revolution of '76, politicized grunge rockers often paid homage to their musical ancestors.

Political rock has become more conscious of itself as a distinct cultural tradition. Much as "I Dreamed I Saw Joe Hill Last Night" has been performed for decades by generations of labor-oriented folk musicians, code for allegiance to the labor-oriented Left, starting in the 1990s, politicized rock musicians increasingly made explicit references to iconic songs and singers from rock's political past. Neil Young, the "Godfather of grunge," became the living representative of a political rock tradition spanning half a century. Young continued performing alongside and supporting new generations of political rockers. Whereas The Clash, in their day, did everything they could to distance themselves from their political rock predecessors (hippies were anathema to punks), contemporary bands like Anti-Flag have performed entire sets made up of songs by The Clash. The somewhat illusory search for innovation has been matched, perhaps even assisted, by a complimentary search for historical roots among new generations of rock.

Eddie Vedder and Pearl Jam were among those who radically revived and revised the political rock tradition in the 1990s. From the start, Vedder was willing to engage directly in movement politics, lending much more than vocal support, vague musical references, or occasional benefit appearances. A particularly poignant reminder of this was Vedder's scrawling of "pro-choice" on his arm during Pearl Jam's MTV Unplugged appearance. In a similar vein, Vedder wore a "No Bush 92" shirt during one of Pearl Jam's earliest appearances on Saturday Night Live.

Where Vedder and Pearl Jam really carved out their niche as political engaged musicians was in the realm of the touring industry. In addition to bringing in booths promoting voter registration, pro-choice resources, and so forth, Pearl Jam worked hard very early on in their career to keep ticket prices low, often trying to stage large outdoor shows for free. This, of course, culminated in their anti-trust complaint against Ticketmaster, directly challenging the dominant political economy of live performance.

Several political bands from the 1980s and 1990s continued on into the new century. Rage Against the Machine, Propagandhi, Fugazi, Pearl Jam, Billy Bragg, Ani DiFranco, Bruce Cockburn, and others continued to inspire activist fans through the Bush era and on into the era of post-prosperity America (or so it must appear to the first American generation to slide backward). Perhaps no performer has had a greater influence in the last quarter century, however, than Michael Franti. His influence among human rights, peace, environmental and economic justice activists is perhaps unequaled. While Franti has had much less chart success than most of the other performers mentioned here, his direct influence among activists might surpass them all. While Franti and his band, Spearhead, produce music that is equal parts hip-hop, reggae, jazz, funk, folk and rock, there is perhaps no better representative of the path that movement music and political rock has taken in the new century. Canonically rock-centered acts like Anti-Flag continue apace, but style and genre divisions are more porous and recombinant than ever.

What's Left?

Readers may protest that the above examples are all from the Left. What about racist skinheads' Oi! music (Hamm 1993) or conservative musicians like Kid Rock and Ted Nugent? These artists are also worthy of examination. However, if Left-leaning political songs are relatively rare in comparison to mainstream songs extolling the virtues of parties, sex, romance, and conspicuous consumption, then Right-Wing rock barely registers at all. Although rock is politically polysemic, politicized rock has been much more connected to the Left than the Right. When conservative columnists like Laura Ingraham tell musicians to *Shut Up and Sing* (2003), she, like almost everyone else, is assuming that the main thrust of politicized rock leans toward the Left. However, hearing a conservative columnist telling popular musicians to shut up and sing might tell us something about the political tendencies of ostensibly apolitical rock. Perhaps mainstream rock fulfills the interests of conservative politics most effectively: *Shut up, have fun, buy stuff, don't question authority*. From providing a soundtrack to violence (Johnson and Cloonan 2008) to assisting the sale of unsustainable consumer goods, mainstream rock might be more hegemonic than often admitted. What we have called political rock here might, in fact, be dialectically related to mainstream rock: "Eve of Destruction" (1965) as the opposite of "Hang on Sloopy" (1965), The Stranglers versus Aerosmith, Ani DiFranco as the antithesis of AC/DC, and so on. Critical political rock is as different ideologically from mindless party music as it is from explicitly conservative art, texts, and rhetoric.

Of course, political rock is also polysemic, but less so than more easily co-opted music. Although The Clash's "London Calling" was converted into an advertisement for Jaguar automobiles, it is unlikely that their explicitly political tunes will do sales duty any time soon. Rock that contains explicitly political messages tends to be critical of dominant institutions, policies, and ideologies.

Rare as it is, explicitly political rock tends to proffer peace, human rights, social justice, and environmental messages as opposed to more conservative policies, themes, and values. As Ingraham makes clear, *Shut Up and Sing* (2003) is a conservative value statement.

As for resistant rock, we have barely scratched the surface here. The following chapters will take us much further into the political regions of rock. These profiles represent several different ways of looking at, and performing, political rock. Some of the artists featured here perform rock politics in a very literal way, as an act of direct confrontation with traditional forms of power. In this vein, we see the anti-Bush statements of Pearl Jam and the pro-union work, musically and otherwise, of Billy Bragg. The Clash, Fugazi, Rage Against the Machine and its guitarist Tom Morello offer no less pointed critiques of systemic problems regarding power relations, post-industrial capitalism, and class relations in the UK and USA. Some of the profiled artists have taken on specific issues and causes, including the anti-apartheid artistry of Peter Gabriel and Bruce Cockburn's concern with environmental degradation. Others have gone beyond political artistry and advocacy to model new *ways-of-being*. For example, the critical successes of Sonic Youth's Kim Gordon, Ani DiFranco, and Sinéad O'Connor have challenged the inequitable elements of rock culture itself, while engaging in larger movements and debates as well. As feminist rockers operating in a male-centered genre, their politics are personal as well as systemic. Lastly, we've featured a musician, Bob Dylan, who might quibble with his inclusion. Dylan continues to represent an important, perhaps even archetypal, model of political musicianship, despite his protestations to the contrary.

We hope that this book will just be the start of a long and interesting conversation. After or while reading it, please write your own contribution to the *Political Rock Blog* on Wordpress. Perhaps you would like to critique something written here or tell the world about a political musician who has inspired you. As with rock itself, this is a collaborative enterprise. So let's get started...

Bibliography

Blecha, Peter. *Taboo Tunes: A History of Banned Bands & Censored Songs*. San Francisco, CA: Backbeat Books, 2004.

Crosby, David, and David Bender. *Stand and be Counted: Making Music, Making History: The Dramatic Story of the Artists and Causes that Changed America*. San Francisco: Harper San Francisco, 2000.

Crosby, David, and Carl Gottlieb. *Long Time Gone: The Autobiography of David Crosby*. 1st ed. New York: Doubleday, 1988.

Frere-Jones, Sasha. "A Paler Shade of White." *New Yorker* 83, no. 32 (10/22, 2007): 176–81.

Frith, Simon. *Performing Rites: On the Value of Popular Music*. Cambridge, MA: Harvard University Press, 1996.

Frith, Simon, and John Street. "Rock Against Racism and Red Wedge: from Music to Politics, from Politics to Music." In *Rockin' the Boat: Mass Music and Mass Movements*, edited by Reebee Garofalo, 67–80. Boston, MA: South End Press, 1992.

Garofalo, Reebee. "Understanding Mega Events." In *Rockin' the Boat: Mass Music and Mass Movements*, edited by Reebee Garofalo, 15–35. Boston, MA: South End Press, 1992.

Garofalo, Reebee. *Rockin' the Boat: Mass Music and Mass Movements*. Boston, MA: South End Press, 1992.

Garofalo, Reebee, Billy Bragg, Tiffiniy Cheng, Susan Fast, Simon Frith, Holly George-Warren, Karen Pegley, and Will Straw. "Who is the World?: Reflections on Music and Politics Twenty Years After Live Aid." *Journal of Popular Music Studies* 17, no. 3 (2005): 324–44.

Gaar, Gillian G. *She's a Rebel: The History of Women in Rock & Roll*. Expanded 2nd ed. New York, NY: Seal Press, 2002.

Geldof, Bob. *Is That It?* New York: Weidenfeld & Nicolson, 1986.

Gottlieb, Joanne, and Gayle Wald. "Smells Like Teen Spirit: Riot Grrrls, Revolution and Women in Independent Rock." In *Microphone Fiends: Youth Music and Youth Culture*, edited by Tricia Rose, and A. Ross, 250–74. London: Routledge, 1994.

Grossberg, Lawrence. "The Framing of Rock: Rock and the New Conservatism." In *Rock and Popular Music: Politics, Policies, Institutions*, edited by Tony Bennett, Simon Frith, Lawrence Grossberg, John Shepherd, and Graeme Turner, 193–209. New York: Routledge, 1993.

Grossberg, Lawrence. "The Politics of Youth Culture: Some Observations on Rock and Roll in American Culture." *Social Text* 3, no. 2 (Winter, 1983): 104–26.

Grossberg, Lawrence. *We Gotta Get Out of this Place: Popular Conservatism and Postmodern Culture*. New York: Routledge, 1992.

Hamm, Mark S. *American Skinheads: The Criminology and Control of Hate Crime*. Praeger Series in Criminology and Crime Control Policy. Westport, CT: Praeger, 1993.

Hopkins, Pandora. "The Homology of Music and Myth: Views of Lévi-Strauss on Musical Structure." *Ethnomusicology* 21, no. 2 (May 1977): 247.

Ingram, David. "'My Dirty Stream': Pete Seeger, American Folk Music, and Environmental Protest." *Popular Music & Society* 31, no. 1 (2008): 21–36.

Ingram, David. *The Jukebox in the Garden: Ecocriticism and American Popular Music Since 1960*. Amsterdam: Rodopi, 2010.

Ingraham, Laura. *Shut Up & Sing: How Elites from Hollywood, Politics, and the UN Are Subverting America*. Washington, DC: Regnery Publishing, 2003.

Johnson, Bruce, and Martin Cloonan. *Dark Side of the Tune: Popular Music and Violence*. Ashgate Popular and Folk Music Series. Burlington, VT: Ashgate, 2008.

King, Stephen A., Barry T. Bays, and P. Rene Foster. *Reggae, Rastafari, and the Rhetoric of Social Control*. Jackson: University Press of Mississippi, 2002.

Keithley, Joey. *I, Shithead*. Vancouver, BC: Arsenal, 2003.

Klein, Naomi. *The Shock Doctrine: The Rise of Disaster Capitalism*. New York: Metropolitan Books, 2007.

Lewis, William F., and Joan Young Gregg. *Soul Rebels: The Rastafari*. Prospect Heights, IL: Waveland Press, 1993.

Longhurst, Brian. *Popular Music and Society*. 2nd ed. Malden, MA: Polity, 2007.

Mattern, Mark. *Acting in Concert: Music, Community, and Political Action*. New Brunswick, NJ: Rutgers University Press, 1998.

McDonough, Jimmy. *Shakey: Neil Young's Biography*. New York, NY: Random House, 2002.

Novoselic, Krist. *Of Grunge and Government: Let's Fix this Broken Democracy!* New York: RDV Books, 2004.

Ogbar, Jeffrey, and O.G. *Hip-Hop Revolution: The Culture and Politics of Rap*. CultureAmerica. Lawrence: University Press of Kansas, 2007.

Pedelty, Mark. "Musical News: Popular Music in Political Movements." In *The Anthropology of News and Journalism: Global Perspectives*, edited by Elizabeth Bird, 215–37. Bloomington, IN: Indiana University Press, 2009.

Pedelty, Mark, and Linda Keefe. "Political Pop, Political Fans?: a Content Analysis of Music Fan Blogs." *Music and Politics* 4, no. 1 (2010): 1–11.

Pratt, Ray. *Rhythm and Resistance: The Political Uses of American Popular Music*. Washington: Smithsonian Institution Press, 1994.

Reuss, Richard A., and JoAnne C. Reuss. *American Folk Music and Left-wing Politics, 1927–1957*. Lanham, MD: Scarecrow Press, 2000.

Sahlins, Marshall David. *Historical Metaphors and Mythical Realities: Structure in the Early History of the Sandwich Islands Kingdom*. ASAO Special Publications. Vol. 1. Ann Arbor: University of Michigan Press, 1981.

Savage, Jon. *England's Dreaming: Anarchy, Sex Pistols, Punk Rock, and Beyond*. New York: St Martin's Griffin, 2002; 1992.

Spence, Lester K. *Stare in the Darkness: The Limits of Hip-Hop and Black Politics*. Minneapolis: University of Minnesota Press, 2011.

Weinstein, Deena. "Rock Protest Songs: So Many and So Few." In *The Resisting Muse: Popular Music and Social Protest*, edited by Ian Peddie, 3–16. London: Ashgate, 2006.

Zappa, Frank. *The Real Frank Zappa Book*. With Peter Occhiogrosso. New York: Simon and Schuster, 1989.

Discography

Beach Boys. "Don't Go Near the Water." *Don't Go Near the Water*. New York: Brother Records, SSI2194, 1971.

The Clash. *The Clash*. New York: Epic, WJE36060, 1979.

The Clash. *London Calling*. New York: CBS, 8087, 1979.

The Clash. "Washington Bullets." *Sandinista!* New York: CBS, E3X37037E37037, 1980.

Gabriel, Peter. "Biko." *Peter Gabriel.* Los Angeles: Geffen, 20352, 1980.

Ke$ha. "Tik Tok." *Tik Tok.* New York: RCA, 2009.

LMFAO. "Party Rock Anthem." *Sorry for Party Rocking.* Santa Monica, CA: Interscope, B0015678-02, 2011.

McCoys. "Hang on Sloopy." *Hang on Sloopy.* New York: Bang Records, B506, 1995.

McGuire, Barry. "Eve of Destruction." *Eve of Destruction.* New York: RCA Victor, 45N1461, 1965.

Mitchell, Joni. *Big Yellow Taxi.* Burbank, CA: Reprise, 0906, 1970.

Nickleback. "Bottoms Up." *Here and Now.* New York: Road Runner, RR77092, 2011.

Soundgarden. "Hands All Over." *Louder than Love.* Hollywood, CA: A&M, CS5252, 1990.

Thursday. "War All the Time." *War All the Time.* New York: Island, B000029301, 2003.

Young, Neil. *After the Gold Rush.* Burbank, CA: Reprise, RS6383, 1970.

Young, Neil. "Let's Impeach the President." *Living With War.* Burbank, CA: Reprise, 443352, 2006.

Chapter 1
The Clash and Fugazi: Punk Paths Toward Revolution

Mark Andersen

Punk rock has always been about more than music. Born largely as a reaction to the self-indulgent excesses and perceived failure of the Sixties rock/revolution, punk offered a blistering critique of idealism sold out or gone bad. This stance was a double-edged sword. Punk's "ruthless criticism of everything existing" (Tucker 1978, 13) spared no one, and could slip towards nihilist extremes. As such, it made the idea of harnessing music for radical change an ever more perilous venture, where only angels or fools might dare to tread. Beneath noisy blasts of illusion-shattering negation, however, an unbending belief in the power of music to generate transformation still lurked. This sense of mission defined no band— punk or otherwise—more profoundly than The Clash. Dubbed "The Only Band That Matters" by record company PR, the moniker nonetheless accurately evoked the risk-taking heroic spirit the band sought to embody.

If the early Clash track "Hate And War" encapsulated the band's dismissal of the 1960s, they nonetheless borrowed freely from certain currents of that era. Indeed, their jagged, relentless music, close-cropped hair, quasi-military garb, and fierce sense of purpose suggested nothing less than a marriage of Detroit agit-rock legends MC5 with the Chinese Cultural Revolution. If their embrace by the punk underground proved short-lived as the band stretched towards broader horizons, The Clash never fully forsook that initial commitment or community.

Many bands rose in the wake of The Clash also willing to risk the ridicule that might come with marrying rock to the pursuit of revolution. Of this hardy breed, the DC punk juggernaut Fugazi was perhaps the most worthy of The Clash mantle. Fugazi would likely not have existed without The Clash before them, but in many ways they lived out the band's rhetoric in a much more consistently convincing manner. Joe Strummer would essentially acknowledge this in the last years of his life, offering them accolades on several occasions, even going so far to identify Fugazi as the single band who best exemplified "the spirit of punk" in a *Rolling Stone* interview in 2000 (Andersen and Jenkins 2003, 411).

The two bands both shone with a sense of defiant grandeur, and their sound often shared a similar anthemic roar, freely mixing dub and raw rock power. Nonetheless, their respective paths could hardly have been more different. Indeed, in certain ways The Clash provided an object lesson to Fugazi on what *not* to do. Tracing the divergent trajectories of The Clash and Fugazi can sketch the wide parameters of possibility that punk facilitated. Together, they suggest both the power and pathos of seeking to promote revolution within a system of, by, and for multinational corporations, while utilizing an artistic form that many look to simply for entertainment.

The Clash: The Power of Revolutionary Contradiction

From the beginning, The Clash were a vibrant, fascinating—and often infuriating— mix of contradictions. No band was more associated with punk's "Year Zero" stance, blithely dismissing rock icons The Beatles, the Rolling Stones and Elvis Presley in "1977," the b-side of their debut single, "White Riot." But if the songs warned of class war, suggesting that racial and generational differences be set aside for a more fundamental confrontation, this incendiary piece of art was made possible through the largesse of CBS Records, then one of the massive behemoths dominating the rock music industry.

"Punk died the day The Clash signed to CBS"—fiery punk scribe Mark Perry famously declaimed in his flagship fanzine *Sniffin' Glue* in 1977 (Echenberg and Perry 1996, 51). Proved demonstrably false by the decades that followed, Perry's words nonetheless suggested both the immense meaning and deep contradiction fixed from birth at the heart of The Clash: they wanted to be the biggest rock band in the world while somehow still remaining "death or glory" heralds of revolution. If their inability to live this paradox on a lasting basis would bring the band crashing to earth within a decade, it also could not erase the genuine idealism and undeniable vision that The Clash brought to their art.

Lead singer/lyricist Joe Strummer was not only the eldest member of the band, but also its soul. Rising out of the British squat scene, he was fascinated by American folk radical Woody Guthrie as well as the dwindling embers of late 1960s' revolt. Already active with a rising roots rock band, The 101ers—named after the ramshackle squat where the band mostly lived and practiced—Strummer was wrenched out of his backward gazing by a blistering Sex Pistols show in April 1976. Shortly thereafter, he was poached from The 101ers by guitarist Mick Jones and bassist Paul Simonon to front their nascent punk unit. This gifted pair had fallen under the spell of agitator/sometime-manager Bernie Rhodes who played a catalytic role in not only assembling the band, but in encouraging them to write about urgent sociopolitical issues.

If the Sex Pistols lit the fuse of the punk explosion, The Clash sought to guide the movement's subsequent momentum in a constructive direction, making the implicit affirmation behind "no future" rants more explicit and convincing. "We never came to destroy," Strummer noted to *Melody Maker* in 1978 (Jones 1978), adding years later in a punk retrospective, "We had hope in a sea of hopelessness" (Haimes 1995). After the collapse of 1960s' rock idealism, however, this was a tricky line to walk. Strummer captured the ambivalence well in a March 1977 interview with *Melody Maker* journalist Caroline Coon, later reprinted in her landmark book, *1988: The New Wave Punk Rock Explosion*. Asked how potent a rock band can be in making political change, Strummer responded, "Completely useless! Rock doesn't change anything. But after saying that—and I'm just saying that because I want you to know that I haven't got any illusions about anything, right—having said that, I still want to try to change things" (Coon 1977, 74).

Although The Clash were careful never to accept a narrow ideological label, they stood on the revolutionary socialist Left, as Strummer acknowledged elsewhere. Given this anti-capitalist stance, Strummer admitted to Coon—who later would briefly manage the band—that, "signing that contract (with CBS) did bother me a lot" (Coon 1977, 79). However, despite their roots in the emergent punk underground, The Clash were not interested in being captured by a narrow subculture; no, world conquest was their aim. If the Top Ten beckoned, it was ostensibly in the hopes of bringing a message of radical change to the broadest possible segment of the population.

In retrospect, The Clash signing to a major label like CBS seems preordained. Simply put, capitalism would provide the avenue for reaching the masses that then, in principle, could be mobilized to overturn that same system and build something better. CBS, of course, had been home to Bob Dylan, Janis Joplin, and other 1960s' countercultural heroes, and the label put out an ad in the tumultuous year of 1968 that promised "The Man Can't Bust Our Music" (Andersen and Jenkins 2009, xiv). Such stretches of rhetorical audacity seemed thinly disguised folderol then; by the mid-1970s, such pretensions sounded dubious indeed.

Not surprisingly, new bands arose, inspired by The Clash, yet as hostile to the band's compromises as punk had been to those of the hippie generation. Among them was anarchist trailblazer Crass. In 1978 Crass co-founder Penny Rimbaud acidly noted that "CBS promotes the Clash—but it ain't for revolution, it's just for cash" (MacKay 1996, 91). For his part, Strummer dismissed Crass as "a storm in a teacup," critiquing their DIY self-sufficiency as "self-defeating, 'cos you've got to be heard" (Crassical Collection, *Penis Envy* 2010, back cover).

If some of this was self-serving, Strummer's words also offered a valuable corrective. Their third album, *London Calling*, pushed back against a version of punk that was growing ever narrower. As Strummer groused in 1979:

> I don't want to see punk as another slavish image and everything is pre-planned and pre-thought out for you to slip into comfortably like mod or hippie music or Teddy Boy rock'n'roll. In '76 it was all individual. There was a common ground, it was punk, but everything was OK. Punk's now become 'he's shouting in Cockney making no attempt to sing from the heart and the guitarist is deliberately playing monotonously and they're all playing as fast as possible so this is punk' … God help us, have we done all that to get here? (Andersen 1981, 4)

To Strummer, punk was a spirit, an attitude and approach to life, not a set of clothes, a haircut, or even a style of music (Andersen and Jenkins 2009, 415).

If this was, once again, possibly convenient for the band's commercial aims, the critique rang true. Soon many of The Clash's hardcore underground punk critics would find themselves striving to transcend self-made straitjackets. In this way, the revolutionary political ambition of The Clash was matched with a parallel all-encompassing musical openness.

With *London Calling* the Clash began to stake its claim not only on underground insurgency, but also on the broader arena of mainstream rock'n'roll. In so doing, they abandoned their disavowal of pre-punk sounds for a fervent embrace of the many forms and faces of rebel music. While the album quickly rose into the American Top Twenty, the full measure of its success came ten years later when the record was honored as "The Album of the Eighties" by *Rolling Stone* (Gray 2010, 479). This global vision was made even clearer by the following triple album set *Sandinista*. This album sought to articulate—with wildly varying degrees of success—a world music that spanned jazz, salsa, reggae, funk, rap, folk, steel drum, disco, and rock tied together only by a common grass-roots focus and a radical political commitment. The latter was made obvious by the album's title, an approving nod to victorious Central American Marxist revolutionaries then bedeviling the Reagan Administration. The band itself created anguish for its corporate sponsors in certain ways. This began as early as 1977 with their third single "Complete Control" which lambasted record company machinations in savagely direct terms. Likewise, the band won few friends in the CBS boardrooms with their insistence on first putting out the double LP *London Calling* for the price of a single album, only to then up the wager with the three-for-the-price-of-one *Sandinista*. In the end, however, the band was playing the rock industry game, one arguably as fixed as any casino. In 2001, Strummer offered a sober assessment that The Clash had become "corporate revolutionaries," acknowledging that the band's success spread their message, but also made mountains of money for its corporate overlord, all at tremendous cost to their humanity:

> (I was) professionally paid to be a rebel, which is truly insane. And it was only going to get worse. Say we'd gotten as big as U2 … life would only be—"Photo shoot. Do the interview. Go to the video shoot. Go do another interview. Fly to Rio. Play the Asshole Stadium. Come back in a helicopter." And all the time you're supposed to try and write something real, or think real, or get through to real people—to "keep it real," as they say. Im-fucking-possible. (Mills 2001)

Seen from a 21st-century vantage point, CBS seems the victor over The Clash in practical political terms; far more corporate profit than revolution resulted from the uneasy marriage. Still, a fair observer would grant that the band wanted it both ways, to be stars *and* revolutionaries, much like the failed effort by protest folkie-gone-rocker Phil Ochs to revolutionize America by developing a hybrid of Elvis Presley and Che Guevara (Eliot 1989, 190).

Fortunately, The Clash had the artistic gifts to walk that fine line, at least for a time. Surely songs like "Clampdown," "Guns Of Brixton," "Lost In The

Supermarket," and "Death Or Glory" (from *London Calling*), or "The Magnificent Seven," "The Call Up," "Charlie Don't Surf," "The Equaliser," and "Washington Bullets" (from *Sandinista*) packed as much radical punch as any of their early work, albeit in more diverse and accessible musical forms. Articulating an internationalist anti-capitalist, anti-imperialist, anti-war vision amidst the dark days of Reagan and Thatcher, The Clash created tunes that could move millions of units in stores, but also move bodies into action in the streets.

Their mission to bring "revolution rock" to the mainstream seemed to be succeeding when the band broke through to Top Ten acclaim in 1982 with their fifth album *Combat Rock* and embarked on a stadium tour with none other than 1960s' icon The Who. Skeptics, however, pointed out that the songs—*London Calling*'s "Train In Vain" and *Combat Rock*'s "Should I Stay or Should I Go"—that brought the Clash mass acclaim were anything but insurrectionary calls to arms. If the third of their hit singles—"Rock The Casbah"—had more depth musically and lyrically, its liberatory message was undermined by the silliness of its companion MTV video. Moreover, it faced swift co-optation for reactionary ends, especially as radical Islam became the latest "free world" bogeyman, replacing Red Scare anti-communism. Strummer was said to have burst into tears years later upon hearing that the song's name was painted on American bombs used in the Persian Gulf War, thus becoming a tool of the militaristic imperialism the band had always opposed (Temple 2007).

This ugly turn suggested the dangers and limitations of revolution through consumption. But if The Clash's politics were becoming a bit muddled or watered down by 1983, personal affairs within the band were even dodgier. First, gifted drummer Topper Headon was ejected from the band because of his heroin addiction, and then co-founder and musical mainstay Mick Jones was kicked out due to rock star tendencies. Remaining originals Strummer and Simonon soldiered on with returned manager Rhodes, assembling a new Clash with relative newcomers: guitarists Nick Sheppard and Vince White, and drummer Pete Howard. Meanwhile, rumors of lawsuits over the band's name swirled and Clash bank accounts were frozen in the subsequent disputes with Jones (Lacey 1984, E3).

The rhetoric of this revamped Clash suggested that Strummer had been listening to his underground critics. The band disavowed their mainstream path and moved back towards raw rebel punk. For a time this leap seemed like it might succeed; the "revolution rock" banner flew boldly once again in new songs such as "The Dictator," "Are You Ready For War?," "North And South," "Three Card Trick," "Sex Mad Roar," and "This Is England." However, behind-the-scenes chaos and internal contradictions within the unit—exacerbated by Strummer's depression after the death of his father and his mother's subsequent terminal illness—crushed the promise of the moment. As a result, this latest Clash stab at cultural revolution flamed out prematurely not long after a risky but bracing "busking tour" in mid-1985. "We made all the rock band mistakes in the book," Strummer conceded ruefully later, "And maybe even invented a few of our own" (Letts 2000).

From London to Washington, DC

While this drama was playing out, the reverberations of The Clash's music and politics had been rippling out across the globe. In late 1978, an unlikely but ferocious new band rose from the African-American communities of Southeast, Washington, DC, and neighboring Prince George's County, Maryland. While dubbed Bad Brains—an obvious reference to NYC punks, The Ramones—this imposing all-black quartet drew much of its inspiration from one-time Clash manager Caroline Coon's seminal punk book, *1988*, and in particular its sections on The Clash.

A local 1979 feature on Bad Brains noted that the band had been energized by "the example of The Clash playing for free in disadvantaged areas of London," an approach they had read about in *1988* and also in *Overthrow*, the newspaper of the 1960s' holdover Youth International Party, more commonly known as the Yippies, who were still active in DC and a few other locales (Andersen and Jenkins 2009, 44). In part, this was a reference to one of the most successful mixing of music and politics in the punk-era UK: the Rock Against Racism campaign, instigated and influenced by members of the Socialist Workers Party, among others (Widgery 1986, 42). The Clash stood right at the nexus of rock and reggae that gave this movement its artistic force as well as its cachet in youth culture circles, bringing black, brown, and white together in a concerted, creative effort to turn back the then-rising tide of neo-fascism in Britain.

Together with other punk-related artists such as X-Ray Spex, Stiff Little Fingers, Tom Robinson Band, and The Specials, The Clash were early supporters of Rock Against Racism, and essentially headlined their largest and most celebrated event, the massive outdoor concert and rally at Victoria Park in 1978. While the unique conditions that generated the potency of this movement were not easily replicable outside of Britain, its example did help spur Clash fans such as Bad Brains into action. Given that Washington, DC, was partly built by slave labor and suffered decades of segregation and racial tension, Rock Against Racism seemed particularly relevant. When Bad Brains performed their own audacious Rock Against Racism concerts in the notorious Valley Green public housing complex in 1979 and 1980, they drew a committed knot of their mostly white fan base across DC's volatile racial dividing lines. Among those electrified by the music and audience at the first Valley Green show—and performing at the second via the band Teen Idles—was a white teenage punk named Ian MacKaye.

A long-haired skater kid into Ted Nugent and other hard rock luminaries, MacKaye had been initially exposed to the punk rebellion through listening to Georgetown University radio station WTGB. After experiencing punk live for the first time—a chaotic, mind-blowing performance by The Cramps at a February 3rd, 1979 benefit protesting the closing of WGTB—the 16-year-old MacKaye cut off his shoulder-length locks in preparation for his second show two weeks later: The Clash at Ontario Theatre on their first US tour. That evening served to cement his new path (Andersen and Jenkins 2009, 34).

Shortly thereafter, MacKaye was bushwhacked by the staggering power of Bad Brains opening for British band The Damned. The energetic youngster was transfixed and transformed that day, as by subsequent Bad Brains' shows at the Valley Green complex and a ramshackle row house called Madams Organ that was an art-collective-turned-Yippie-commune. If MacKaye would absorb The Clash's burning sense of mission mostly secondhand through Bad Brains, he nonetheless exemplified the band's single-minded belief in rock music as a communal force for transformation—be it personal or political—with possibilities far transcending mere entertainment. This sense of purpose shone from his new band Minor Threat, which debuted in late 1980. While deeply influenced by the precision and velocity of Bad Brains, Minor Threat blazed its own trail as a progenitor not only of hardcore punk but also of anti-drug "straight edge." With Minor Threat joining Bad Brains and others in igniting an unprecedented and massively influential scene—HarDCore, as it came to be known—Washington, DC, assumed an unfamiliar role. Long derided as a cultural wasteland where people imported art rather than created it, DC began to be seen as perhaps the single most significant cutting-edge punk underground in the USA, contending with much larger scenes such as New York and Los Angeles for influence.

But while NYC and LA—like London—were also entertainment industry strongholds, DC came to represent just the opposite: the embodiment of the DIY punk ideal. It was no accident that Crass co-conspirator John Loder made an alliance with Minor Threat and MacKaye's related Dischord independent record label in 1983. Indeed, while Minor Threat and Crass seemed nearly universes apart in subject matter, the shared spirit was palpable. As DC rock critic (and early punk) Mark Jenkins noted in 1992: "This second generation of bands took the rhetoric of early bands like The Clash and Sex Pistols seriously ... In some cases, far more seriously than the original bands themselves."[1] As a result, a version of punk unimaginable without the vision of The Clash, but utterly at odds with its corporate compromises began to take root, flourish, and blossom, germinating similar scenes. While Minor Threat splintered in late 1983 thanks to musical and philosophical differences, MacKaye soon found himself jolted back into action by a galvanizing new band, Rites of Spring. Now branded the originator of "emo," Rites of Spring sparked a rousing reinvention of the DC punk underground as part of what would be labeled "Revolution Summer."

As the final version of The Clash slowly, sadly disintegrated over that summer of 1985, something new was rising across the Atlantic, something that shared that idealism, but sought to go beyond, to more consistently live the life punks were singing about in their songs. In part, Revolution Summer was simply a nudge between friends, gently pressing towards renewed action after the crash of HarDCore on the shoals of its own contradictions. At the same time, Revolution Summer became a bold expansion of the emotional, musical, and political commitments implicit in the original hardcore scene, a re-creation of punk, more

---

[1]   Mark Jenkins, interview by Mark Anderson, Washington, DC, March 12, 1992.

artistically open, while still defiantly anti-commercial. This moment would spark another influential passel of DC bands and a long-lasting punk activist collective: Positive Force DC. Unlike outside politicos like the Yippies or the Revolutionary Communist Party, organizations that sought to harness punk for pre-existing agendas, Positive Force was an expression from within the scene.

Having felt exploited by outside groups, MacKaye sought more collaborative alliances. When his new band Embrace played its third show as a Positive Force benefit, the seeds were sown for a lasting partnership. I was able to witness this evolution firsthand, as a co-founder and organizer of Positive Force, first drawn into activism by the message and energy of punk, particularly The Clash.

Ironically, I had come to DC in 1984 not to pursue revolution, but for graduate studies and a lucrative career. I stood uncomfortably at the cusp of the lower echelons of the global political/economic elite, seeking to complete an odd decade-long transformation. Somehow I had gone from an alienated rural working-class punk to a college student/radical activist to an upwardly mobile "young urban professional" studying at The Johns Hopkins School of Advanced International Studies on Embassy Row while working part-time on Capitol Hill.

The rhetoric of the revamped Clash crashed harshly against my mainstream trajectory,, blunting its momentum. Strummer's doubts about the cost of the band's success resonated in personal terms, pointing me back towards the underground. This sense of failure-disguised-as-victory drove my role in co-founding Positive Force while still attending graduate school. In the process, I encountered the rising tide of Revolution Summer, and punk turned my life upside down/right side up for the second time. I found particular inspiration in Embrace, in Ian MacKaye's conflicted, starkly personal anthems of recommitment and persistence. Tragically, Embrace self-destructed after less than a dozen performances. MacKaye retreated, weary but wiser, determined to make sure that his next effort would not share the internal contradictions that had brought untimely demise to both of his last bands. While MacKaye did not turn his back on the "straight edge" idea—which now had expanded past a simple anti-drug stance to include vegetarianism and animal rights—he wanted a militant band where all of the members were deadly serious about its music and its message, seeking to be widely heard while repudiating the corporate rock circus.

The entity that resulted was named Fugazi, after Vietnam-era GI slang signifying "a fucked up situation," which, as MacKaye explained, "is kind of how I view the world" (Andersen and Jenkins 2009, 242). Fugazi included not only MacKaye but also Guy Picciotto and Brendan Canty of the now-defunct Rites of Spring as well as Joe Lally, roadie for fellow Revolution Summer stalwart, Beefeater. Debuting at another Positive Force-organized benefit in September 1987, Fugazi would ultimately broadcast the Revolution Summer spirit to the world.

If The Clash were a band founded on fundamental contradictions, always close to splitting under pressure, Fugazi was more self-consciously aware of such dangers. If the band might appear, on paper, to be a punk "super group"—that dreaded 1960s' rock Frankenstein—Fugazi was actually built from long-time friends who shared a deep commitment to the open yet non-commercial DC ethic. Eager to mate music and explicit radical politics, the band fostered a partnership with Positive Force, creating a potent musical-political fusion rarely if ever seen.

MacKaye sang the phrase "words are not enough" over and over at the climax of Embrace's Revolution Summer requiem "End of A Year." Reflecting that dictum, Fugazi spoke with its actions. While their songs conveyed powerful messages, delivered with utter conviction amidst a riveting mash-up of dub, Detroit rock, and post-hardcore, Fugazi's business stance was equally striking and uncompromised. Eschewing rock's most mundane commercial concession—a manager—as well as its most lucrative sideline—merchandise—Fugazi put out its own records via Dischord and toured relentlessly, playing low-cost all-ages shows, as well as dozens of benefits. It was a model few outside observers believed could be sustained, yet it was.

By 1989, Fugazi was drawing massive crowds not only in DC but across the country and in Europe as well, attaining a level of popularity sufficient to attract the hungry eyes of the rock industry. Tellingly, the band's success left them determined to do only benefits, protests, or free shows in the DC area, all done in collaboration with Positive Force. In September 1989, the band spurned an offer from CBS Records, the first of many major labels to court Fugazi. That same month, *The Washington City Paper* compared the Fugazi/Positive Force alliance with that of the MC5 and White Panther Party in the late 1960s (Andersen and Jenkins 2009, 293). The political visions of Fugazi and Positive Force stood starkly at odds with the "long-haired dope-smoking rock and roll street-fucking total assault on (middle American) culture" advocated by those predecessors (Hale 2001). It was nonetheless taken as a compliment.

While confused media outlets like *The Washington Post* alternatively described Positive Force as Fugazi's "street army" and the band as "the leading exponent of a musical movement called Positive Force," the pairing was fortuitous for both entities, helping each to more fully accomplish their separate—if connected—aims (Andersen and Jenkins 2009, 334). Surely The Clash might have been able to more convincingly and concretely express their political ideals if they had allied with such an organization, instead of being accused of simply dressing up the pursuit of rock stardom with revolutionary pretensions and rhetorical radicalism.

It might seem perhaps unfair to expect rigorous consistency from a rock band, but such were the expectations raised by the words and sound of "The Only Band That Matters." Now Fugazi carried much the same weight as The Clash, yet somehow seemed to carry it more gracefully. Regularly channeling fuel to frontline organizations through dozens of benefits and protests, they did not seek to exit the underground, but to bring it along with them, stepping nimbly around record company offers as if they were landmines. Surely it helped that Fugazi was also free of the drug and management dramas that dogged The Clash. While all four members played crucial roles in the band, they also had a secret weapon in MacKaye, who had proven himself to be an exceedingly rare bird: a gifted artist with not only deep radical political conviction but also a canny, detail-oriented business sense and diligent work ethic. As a result, the band dubbed "America's Clash" by no less an authority than Britain's *Sounds* magazine was able to sustain its unprecedented model for operation even as its popularity grew (Jenkins 1990, 21).

If anything, Fugazi became more steadfast in its approach, more willing to push the musical activism envelope. But while *The Washington City Paper* dubbed 1990 "the year of Fugazi," noting that the band had "taken the world by storm—and on their own terms" (Andersen and Jenkins 2009, 301), the limitations as well as the strengths of music as a weapon for change would become obvious as Positive Force and Fugazi grappled with the reality of war in the Middle East.

Punk Protest vs. the Persian Gulf War

The drama began when MacKaye came to me in summer 1990 with the idea for a mid-winter outdoor concert in front of the White House to draw attention to the plight of the homeless. While I quickly secured the necessary permits for this musical protest to be held on 12 January 1991, international events overtook our plans. Iraq, a country armed by the US for war against Iran, invaded Kuwait; the US began to mass troops in neighboring Saudi Arabia. While none of us had sympathies for the ruthless dictator Saddam Hussein, the danger of regional war and the deaths of tens of thousands of innocent civilians seemed frightening real. As fate would have it, our January date turned out to be the Saturday before the deadline President Bush had set for Iraqi withdrawal from Kuwait.

In response, the focus of our protest was expanded to make a direct anti-war statement, connecting extravagant military expenditures with inadequate domestic spending on programs to fight homelessness and poverty. Along with Fugazi's set, a rally and punk percussion protest were planned. An earlier Positive Force-organized drum-fest had helped to inspire a 24-hour-a-day anti-war percussion vigil, and we took great satisfaction when Bush complained to *The New York Times*, "those damned drums are keeping me up all night" (Andersen and Jenkins 2009, 301). The day before the event, a heavy snowstorm hit the city. The next day, temperatures nudged into the low 40s and the snow melted, but it was cold and rainy. With the country preparing for war, police blanketed the White House area. Despite the weather and the inhospitable police presence, thousands of people showed up, clustering across the street from the White House. A red, white, and blue banner proclaiming "There Will Be Two Wars"—meaning one in the Persian Gulf, and one at home in opposition to the other—fluttered from wooden poles on a makeshift stage, suggesting the seriousness of our intent.

The percussive protesters generated a thunderous cacophony, beating on oil barrels, drums, tin cans, and kettles amidst ongoing frigid drizzle. Meanwhile, Fugazi's concert hung in the balance, since playing on an unprotected stage in the rain could expose musicians and crew to potential electrocution. At one point the precipitation stopped, only to begin again just as the band was ready to go.

Frustrated, the band and I huddled on the stage, trying to decide what to do. Finally, feeling the immense gravity of the political moment, MacKaye said simply, "Let's fucking do it!" All available hands scrambled to uncover the gear and prepare for the chancy performance.

As the portion of the crowd now crunched tightly by the stage cheered, MacKaye spoke:

> Initially this was supposed to be a concert in the park, figuring that if people had to live out in the cold, we sure as fuck could come out and play for an hour and a half, do a little bit of a protest in support of the homeless groups who are working to give people shelter. In DC, there are thousands of people living on the streets. If you live here, you just start to walk by them after a while. It's inconceivable to me at least, that with the billions and billions of dollars that are being spent in the Middle East, that we can't spend more for the people who are dying in the streets here. (Fugazi 1991 live recording)

As the crowd applauded, MacKaye continued:

> In effect, there is a tie between the homeless problem and the healthcare problems and everything else. As this country begins to fold up on itself economically, we throw ourselves into yet another war to divert people's attention from the problems here in America. Everything ties together; there is a connection. We are Fugazi from Washington, DC, thank you very much for coming out. (ibid.)

As the band slammed into their opening song, the percussion protest faded and many of the drummers joined the crowd by the stage.

The stage quickly became a source of concern. It was sturdy, but rested on three layers of milk crates; park regulations barred affixing the stage to the ground. As the crowd surged, the pressure began to force the stage slowly southward, toward Pennsylvania Avenue. Stage-divers also began to mount the stage, further stressing the structure. MacKaye asked the crowd not to stage-dive, encouraging them to instead "give us some help with the words." The band played a confrontational new song, "Reclamation," built on a titanic, rolling riff. The lyrics had been inspired by anti-abortion extremists, but lines like "These are our demands/We want control of our bodies" took another meaning in the shadow of war.

It was so chilly and wet that MacKaye later said his hands "felt like blocks of wood," but the band was hot, feeding off the adrenaline of the situation. As the stage continued to shift, appearing to begin to split apart at one point, the musicians adjusted their songs to reflect the political situation. Picciotto added a line exhorting the crowd to "take it out into the streets" to "Two Beats Off." MacKaye stopped to note the presence of Park Police filming the assembly "for a new MTV special, I guess" (ibid.). Picciotto hit the air-raid siren two-note opening of "KYEO"—"keep your eyes open"—revamped specifically for this show. The newly streamlined song led into "Long Division," with a mournful evocation of fragmentation underscoring MacKaye's comment that "if George Bush wants one America, he better get out of the business of oil and war." By this point, the heat of the tightly packed audience had created a gigantic human smoke machine, sending thick clouds of steam over the stage (ibid.). Fugazi concluded with "Repeater" and "Burning Too." MacKaye prefaced the former by evoking DC's drug war, pleading that while "we seem to have become accustomed to the hundreds that have died here, I hope we can never become accustomed to the tens of thousands that might die in the Middle East." The crowd joined MacKaye in chanting the "1, 2, 3 ... repeater" chorus, as the song's desperate screech led to a lonely exhortation to "keep count." As MacKaye methodically recited "10,000 ... 20,000 ... 30,000 ... 40,000 ... 50,000 ... 60,000 ... 70,000 ... 80,000 ... 90,000 ..."—the potential body count in the conflagration about to erupt—the set rose to its heart-rending climax (ibid.).

Both Fugazi and Positive Force had sought to make their message clear, but without precipitating violent confrontation. Amazingly, in the end, nothing had gone wrong—with the police, the stage, or the rain. As armed agents watched from the top of the White House, Fugazi had played one of its greatest performances. Even though I was drenched to the bone, and so exhausted and ill that my voice was a hoarse whisper, I was exhilarated by the day, feeling a sense of immense power and determination. Some of this was illusory, to be sure; to echo one punk critique, we were offering protest songs in response to military aggression, a flimsy reed all-too-unlikely to stop the soldiers' guns. This was made painfully clear four days later when bombs began to rain on Baghdad, the most intense bombing in human history.

The American campaign moved quickly, smashing the Iraqi army in Kuwait and decimating large areas within Iraq itself. Despite the terrible cost in innocent Iraqi lives—158,000 by one US government estimate (Gellman 1992, A5)—Americans swiftly embraced the war. Known as "Desert Storm," the assault was viewed not only as a smashing success, but also as the harbinger of a new era in US foreign policy, opening the way for a return to American military adventurism. "Large Scale Victory Sweeps Away 'Vietnam Syndrome'," read a banner headline on the front page of *The Washington Post* as the campaign wound down (Dionne 1991, A1). In June 1991, hundreds of thousands joined in a massive, costly National Victory Celebration on the National Mall.

It was a crushing defeat for anti-imperialist advocates. Indeed, the war virus even infected local punk scenes. At a Fugazi show at a club in Richmond, Virginia, Positive Force activists handing out anti-war fliers were physically intimidated and nearly ejected from the premises; only the band's intervention stopped the confrontation. When Fugazi played a benefit concert in Philadelphia, MacKaye noted that "a lot of people" were not happy that the gig supported conscientious objectors (Andersen and Jenkins 2009, 304). At the same time, however, small victories could be savored. For example, Stephanie Atkinson, the first female soldier ever to become a war resister, credited Fugazi's music with giving her the courage to resist. Nor was Atkinson alone in this. Never before had music played such a role in keeping my own spirits up, helping me—and no doubt many others—to escape slipping into utter despair amidst the ugly outbreak of war fever.

Fugazi's "KYEO" ended with the fervent vow, "We will not be beaten down." This became Positive Force's credo, even after having been steamrollered by the American politico-military machine; and our rapid-fire series of benefits, concerts, and service work over the next months made it real. Even if, as MacKaye noted at a Washington Free Clinic benefit in June 1991, the $12 million reportedly spent on the Victory Celebration dwarfed the $5,000 raised that night to provide free medical care, we were still seeking to build the America of our dreams with our actions.

Fugazi: Revolution by Example

As Fugazi and Positive Force continued to accelerate, spreading some bits of light in the postwar darkness, DC's reputation as a "new youth Mecca" also blossomed, drawing crucial new recruits to the cause. In late spring 1991, Bikini Kill, an electrifying female-powered band from Olympia, Washington, joined the exodus, touring with local heroes The Nation of Ulysses and linking up with their friends Bratmobile in the capital city.

Bikini Kill's rousing arrival generated a hothouse of creativity and collaboration. The insurgent female punks labeled the moment "Revolution (Summer) Girl Style Now," echoing one of the band's anthems and DC's own fabled punk past. Energized by the ecstatic response they had received since landing in the other Washington, Bikini Kill's charismatic lead singer Kathleen Hanna suggested that girls and women begin to hold meetings at the Positive Force House to build networks of support for musical projects, consciousness raising, and political organizing. In the process, the feminist punk uprising Riot Grrrl was sparked.

Named after recent riots in the punk-infested neighborhood of Mount Pleasant, Riot Grrrl built upon—and in some ways surpassed—the foundation constructed by allies Fugazi and Positive Force, challenging punk to live its rhetoric of empowerment in a consistent and inclusive way. The catalytic vision of Bikini Kill and Bratmobile—and the power of their examples—pushed past what all-male bands like The Clash or Fugazi could accomplish alone. Sadly, the bands, the scene, and, above all, the Riot Grrrl movement itself was soon entangled in a poisonous punk civil war sparked by the explosion of the American underground into the rock mainstream via Nirvana's "Smells Like Teen Spirit." The anthem, released on the corporate label DGC and made ubiquitous by constant rotation of its "high school insurrection" video on MTV, simultaneously celebrated and critiqued the underground revolution. At the same time, punk—re-branded as "grunge"—became a popular yet often all-too-superficial consumer product.

Major strides had been made in developing an independent music network since The Clash signed to CBS in 1977; when major labels began to encroach on this territory, tremendous conflicts emerged within the scene about how to respond. Some saw this shift as victorious breakthrough, while many viewed it as impending sell-out and defeat. Few were neutral in the conflict, and the punk community splintered under the pressure. In the midst of the free fire zone that American punk had become, Fugazi was able to pull off something unimaginable with its 1993 album *In On The Kill Taker*: simultaneously receiving raves in both the most popular diehard underground zine, *Maximum RocknRoll (MRR)*, and the rock-establishment-Bible, *Rolling Stone*. Strikingly, both reviews proffered The Clash's weighty title upon Fugazi: "The Only Band That Matters" (Andersen and Jenkins 2009, 392).

Staying true to the punk emphasis on lowering boundaries between audience and performer, the band chafed under this onslaught of adulation, striving to preserve their creative focus and human scale as people and as a band. Dead set on avoiding the role of pop messiahs, the band sometimes turned defensive or uncooperative, frustrating politicized supporters like *MRR*'s Tim Yohannon or *Washington City Paper*'s Mark Jenkins with abstract lyrics or a reluctance to explain themselves.

For example, in a 1993 interview with *The Washington Post*, singer-guitarist Picciotto noted that people "want us to supply some sort of message, but if I had wanted to express a message in that way, I would have been a politician. I'm not. I'm a musician. It is in the songs, for people to use or not use" (Brace 1993, G5). This eminently unassuming statement coexisted uneasily with fiery Fugazi performances such as that at a Positive Force and Riot Grrrl-organized protest at the US Supreme Court only a few months before. On that day, Picciotto let loose with an impassioned soliloquy encouraging their massive crowd to commit acts of civil disobedience fighting unjust laws—then launched into a blistering rendition of "Dear Justice Letter," mourning the recent loss of the Supreme Court's liberal lion William Brennan.

Nor was this a lone aberration. If Fugazi's songs railed eloquently against evils like militarism ("KYEO"), inner-city violence ("Repeater"), racism ("And The Same"), Native American genocide ("Smallpox Champion"), sexism ("Suggestion"), consumerism ("Merchandise"), corporate rule ("Five Corporations") apathy ("Turnover"), and environmental devastation ("Burning Too"), the band backed up their words with a cascade of Positive Force benefits and protest shows, performances that exploded, one by one, like a string of firecrackers.

The reverberations resonated outside the concert halls—mostly church basements, union halls, community centers—where hundreds of audience members were inspired to assist with Positive Force's other projects, serving meals at soup kitchens, delivering food to inner-city seniors, passing out condoms and safe needle kits to street sex workers and intravenous drug users, organizing protests and book discussion groups ... or simply beginning to do their own activism with other groups, even starting their own projects.

Clearly, then, Fugazi were more than simply musicians. If not, their definition of the proper role of the musician was far broader than most. For the average band, a reluctance to speak out and articulate its message might be a convenient dodge. However, Fugazi's reticence seemed more a consistent application of its own radical anti-star principles, to demythologize themselves and thus hopefully empower their audience.

While clearly of the revolutionary Left, Fugazi was not eager to make broad rhetorical statements, or to assume a political leadership role, preferring their listeners to accept their own responsibility for self-directed action. MacKaye had once described this delicate balance as "revolution by example," and it accounted for the band's intense focus on hewing to its own path while often speaking primarily with its actions (Andersen 1991, 1). A quote from Spanish philosopher Jose Ortega Y Gassett was included in the cassette version of Fugazi's 1990 album *Repeater*, offering insight into this approach: "Revolution is not the uprising against preexisting order, but the setting up of a new order contradictory to the traditional one." In other words, if the lyrics of The Clash—indeed, the name of the band itself—called for confronting and overthrowing the old order, Fugazi's words sought to go deeper, to encourage the listener to begin building the new world right here, right now, in the shell of the old.

Of course, Strummer's critique of Crass could easily apply here. Fugazi's sales—while in the hundreds of thousands—were dwarfed by the millions attained by bands such as The Clash and Nirvana. Yet, perhaps even more than Crass, Fugazi blew past the narrow confines of the underground while refusing to give ground to rock "business as usual." In the process, they were helping raise hundreds of thousands of dollars for frontline organizations serving DC's hard-hit inner city, watering the grass roots of their home DC community, and nudging their audience towards concrete activism of their own. This achievement points toward a fundamental failing of The Clash in practical political terms. If the band was once described as "the Sound of the Westway"—a reference to a prominent highway that cut through their area of London—and became indelibly associated with the Notting Hill riots and the racially diverse (and often tense) district of Brixton, they rarely seemed to focus resources in a consistent way toward concrete projects. While the band certainly did benefits—including two at the Brixton Academy amidst the hard-fought British miners' strike of 1984–85, and an entire mini-tour in support of the Italian Communist Party—they never delivered on early promises to build a club or radio station to actualize their vision in a sustained, institutional way.

Influential American hardcore writer and activist Kent McClard scorched The Clash and Sex Pistols by name in his *No Answers* fanzine for failing to follow through on such commitments—just before going on to lionize Fugazi, Positive Force, and other DC artists as providing genuine follow-through (McClard 1990, 22). McClard was not alone in noticing these unpleasant gaps between rhetoric and reality. As Clash acolyte Billy Bragg noted in 2007 while publicizing his prisoner-support non-profit Jail Guitar Doors, this was "the failure" of The Clash: "You can talk, you can write, but do you actually do anything?" (Follos 2007).

Few could make the same critique of Fugazi, given its long, fruitful collaboration with Positive Force. The band's accomplishments brought grudging respect even from skeptics and erstwhile critics, generating responses both defensive and gracious. In MRR, members of popular Southern California punk band Bad Religion expressed the frustration of many bands about being held to Fugazi's exacting standards. Hyper-radical industrial outfit Consolidated constructed an entire track defending its business practices from fan complaints—many of them referencing a certain DC band—by repeatedly noting "We aren't Fugazi." Meanwhile, Dave Grohl—Revolution Summer veteran now world-famous as the drummer of Nirvana—remarked that, in his estimation, Fugazi's accomplishments dwarfed their own.[2]

The depth of Joe Strummer's own regard for the band first became clear in an interview he did in 1999. The recent use of "Should I Stay or Should I Go" for a Levi's commercial came up, leading to a discussion of the intra-band legal battle sparked when Dead Kennedys lead singer Jello Biafra turned down a request for use of their classic "Holiday In Cambodia" for a commercial. When one of the interviewers cynically suggested that Biafra didn't agree simply because the price wasn't high enough, Strummer wryly responded, "They always said that, didn't they? Everybody's got their price … But what about Fugazi?" (Johnson 1999, 74).

This was no idle query. Legendary punk/hip hop photographer Glen Friedman recounts a head-turning anecdote in his book *Keep Your Eyes Open*:

> I witnessed the legendary music mogul Ahmet Ertegun coming backstage to try to get this 'unsignable' band to sign with him. He offered them 'anything you want' and said 'the last time I did this was when I offered The Rolling Stones their own record label and $10 million'. Fugazi politely declined and Ian (MacKaye) then changed the subject and continued to talk about their shared love of Washington DC. (Friedman 2007, 47)

Such tales led Strummer to remark, "Ian's the only one who ever did the punk thing right from day one and followed through on it all the way" (Cogan 2008, 177). As if to underline this point, Fugazi continued on its own label, managing themselves, and working with community allies such as Positive Force until the band quietly went on an extended—and probably permanent—hiatus in 2003 to focus on family concerns and other artistic pursuits. Their steady, unbowed persistence in their political/artistic vision presents a stark contrast to the drug, ego, and industry-fueled tempests that destroyed The Clash.

---

[2]   Dave Grohl, interview by Mark Anderson, Arlington, Virginia, June 16, 1992.

From Music into Action

But did this achievement, however inspiring for its consistency and sheer punk anti-corporate defiance, necessarily mean that Fugazi was more successful in fostering political change than The Clash? Such matters are of course terribly hard to measure. Part of the answer probably rests in the simple fact that many readers will not know about Fugazi, but will be quite familiar with The Clash. In this sense, the band's Faustian bargain with CBS finds some support. Had The Clash not invaded the mainstream so successfully, made its imperfect but impassioned imprint on mass consciousness, few might care about their politics now, nearly three decades after the band's demise. As Strummer himself noted, "We didn't know *what* was going on (in signing with CBS), but ... our defense would be that it helped make punk a worldwide concern" (SPIN 2001).

Moreover, many listeners—including this writer—were jolted into political action by their encounter with the band's music, ideas, and performances, though they were spread by corporate channels. Lives were changed forever, and through those lives, the world itself was changed. In addition, the very imperfection of The Clash, their many blunders and contradictions can make them appealingly human, easier to identify with, whereas Fugazi might seem impossible to emulate.

On the other hand, The Clash's politics now often seem submerged under the growing adulation of them as rock icons, as if they were simple entertainers not so different than The Beatles, Stones, or Elvis. To Fugazi's credit, few would place them in such company. Indeed, their resolute opposition to the star-making machinery guaranteed them both more anonymity as well as the authenticity to step past rock stardom to humbly, stubbornly herald a radically different way to organize our lives and our world. Given their insistence on preserving this human scale interaction, it is very possible that while they reached fewer people, the inspiration was more direct, deep, and lasting.

This last point is critical, for it points past capitalist consumption to potentially revolutionary creation. Although the calculus of how music can best serve to advance revolution remains to be fully explored, we should consider that it can access something deep in the human spirit, thus opening doors of radical possibility and communal power. Music's magic resides in its ability to be a force that reaches past the surface to the substance, somehow accessing and activating the untapped power of humanity.

But note that the process can never stop with simple *transmission*. No, as Ian MacKaye has argued, *reception* is equally essential, and even more so what comes after: *action*. As a manifesto from the Crass-inspired anarcho-punk band Chumbawamba proclaimed in 1984, "The music's not a threat, but action that music inspires can be a threat" (Sprouse 1990, 28). This complicates matters considerably, for how to weigh success versus failure will depend much on one's expectations. Fifteen years after the collapse of The Clash, Strummer somewhat sadly confessed:

We never had any real power, other than in an abstract, poetic way. What I wrote on a piece of paper might influence someone somewhere down the line, and that's something I still take great care with. But it would've been nice to have the power to say, 'fifty thousand people down to the Houses of Parliament now!' … Ultimately, it's the big money men who have the power. (McKenna 2000)

In contrast, Tom Morello of Rage Against The Machine—who also attained mass popularity through a CBS affiliate—argued that "I was confident that, given the right dice throw of historical circumstance, a rock band could have started a social revolution in the United States of America that would have changed the country irrevocably. I put no limit on what the potential impact of cultural force like that could have, I thought the sky was absolutely the limit" (Lynskey 2011, 504).

This is an extraordinarily high standard for which to strive, and begs all sorts of practical questions about how this vision could be realized. It is hardly surprising that Morello considers his band to have failed on this score, as surely The Clash and Fugazi did as well. What band, indeed, could ever claim to have accomplished this mission? Moreover, this runs the risk of looking for revolution in the wrong place. As Jeff Goldthorpe argued in "Intoxicated Culture: Punk Symbolism and Punk Protest," "Post-Sixties youth subcultures (such as punk) have discovered the possibilities of solidarity and transformation in cultural arenas rather than political organizations." But, as Goldthrope notes, the resulting "ecstatic moments"—the sense of power I felt at the Fugazi White House protest, for example—inevitably pass, and the very real energy generated can easily dissipate if not channeled into concrete action and broader community building.

Goldthorpe then points toward one of the key lessons learned in my years in the punk rock wars:

Youth subcultures, defined by their marginality, do not offer any direct routes to the promised land. They will not, as in Sixties mythology, single-handedly lead a massive frontal assault against late capitalist order … The peaceful, egalitarian, decentralized society we seek can only emerge from widespread alliances, extending far beyond the field of radical cultural politics. (Goldthorpe 1992, 62)

My wrangling with the implications of this broader vision spawned *All The Power: Revolution Without Illusion*, a book whose title tips a hat to The Clash while also challenging some of the assumptions upon which their art was founded. This critique is not intended as a dismissal, however, for as Goldthorpe notes, that field of radical cultural politics is where so many of us get our start as activists. In that sense, Morello's vision gains some ballast, for bands such as Rage Against the Machine—like The Clash and Fugazi—can surely serve as catalysts for revolutionary education and action.

While no member of Fugazi would likely have echoed Morello's revolution-through-rock ambitions publicly, they surely lived with a similar sense of purpose, and played their songs with equivalent fire. Crucially, however, Fugazi's manner of operation—as suggested by MacKaye's *transmission/reception* theorem—quietly insisted that their audience must also find that fire, must take the lead as well, that revolution is something that has to be done *together*.

Perhaps this is a minor difference in emphasis, yet the nuance seems significant. Is our focus simply on the power of the band ... or of the audience as well? In the end, this turnabout in perspective was not far from Strummer's own deepest vision. During their 1984 miners' strike benefit, the singer paused before "We Are The Clash" to note that "when I say 'we,' I mean *we*," gesturing emphatically at the audience (Clash 1984 live recording). The song's own metaphor expands on this: while a band can strike a match, it is up to their listeners to provide the gasoline. Only through this communion can we hope to transcend mere commodity exchange to ignite an explosion of radical possibility, illuminating a path toward that holiest of Grails, the elusive yet entrancing and essential dream of revolution.

This was a punk insight, a challenge designed to awaken conscience, gently pushing both power and responsibility back toward those who otherwise so easily could be trapped in rock spectacle, becoming simple consumers rather than the active co-creators that both transcendent concerts and social transformation so urgently require.

While The Clash was unable to fully live out this insight, partly due to their enervating entanglement in corporate rock Babylon, the truth of that understanding is undeniable ... which means that now the challenge is ours. What will we make of the possibilities, this potential power, and what is the best way to proceed?

Many bands—and their fans—will not wish to tarry with this deep challenge, preferring unencumbered commercial exchange to the arduous work and inevitable risk implicit in our analysis. Moreover, there is no easy resolution to this conundrum, this struggle to ascertain ultimate value, to draw a revolutionary lesson. Perhaps this is just as it should be, for if The Clash and Fugazi were to agree on one thing it is that neither would wish to provide a substitute for that most punk action of all: the utter urgency to *do it yourself, and to do it together*.

For me, this imperative is expressed daily, not only through Positive Force DC, which remains vital and active, but through We Are Family, an outreach, advocacy, and organizing network that works for and with low-income seniors in inner-city DC.

We Are Family is built on a foundation of senior leadership, with its creative grass-roots approach to service and justice work carrying echoes of lessons learned from The Clash and Fugazi. Reclaiming the banner of "family values" for progressive ends, bringing together vastly diverse communities, We Are Family seeks to realize a punk vision for transformation in a small but significant way. The music of both bands remains an enduring, often daily presence in my life; in addition, Ian MacKaye's quieter yet equally uncompromising post-Fugazi unit, The Evens, is a current supporter of We Are Family and co-conspirator with Positive Force.

It is surely true that the power of music on its own is limited. Still, any time someone tells me that music changes nothing, I laugh, for it has profoundly changed me, and I—like any of us—can consequently help to change my world. As Joe Strummer said a few months before his death in December 2002:

> I will always believe in punk rock, because it's about creating something for yourself. Lift your head up and see what is really going on in the political, social, and religious situations, try and see through all the smoke screens … I'm always quite hopeful. I believe in human beings. Human beings won't let this happen. We won't all end up robots working for McGiant Corp or whatever. It can't happen.[3]

What this means is that, in the end, Strummer knew that it is not the "big money men" but *the people* who have the power. Bands can be companions; songs can be a spur to our rebel spirit, a reservoir of hope and determination. However, as the stories of The Clash and Fugazi suggest, in the end the power and the responsibility for transformation resides in our own hands, called to join together with those of many, many others.

Bibliography

Andersen, Mark. *All The Power: Revolution Without Illusion*. New York: Akashic/ Punk Planet Books, 2004.

Andersen, Mark and Mark Jenkins. *Dance of Days: Two Decades of Punk in the Nation's Capital*. New York: Akashic Books, 2003.

Andersen, Mark. *The Ideology of New Wave Rock Music*. Montana: Self-published booklet, 1981.

Andersen, Mark. "Fugazi: Revolution By Example." *Washington Peace Letter*, November 1991.

Brace, Eric. "Punk Lives!: Washington's Fugazi Claims It's Just a Band, So Why Do So Many Kids Think It's God?" *The Washington Post*, August 1, 1993.

Cogan, Brian. *The Encyclopedia of Punk*. New York: Sterling Publishers, 2008.

Coon, Caroline. *1988: The New Wave Punk Explosion*. London: Orbach & Chambers, 1977.

Dionne, E.J. "Kicking the 'Vietnam Syndrome'; Victory Sweeps Away US. Doomed-to-Failure Feeling." *Washington Post*, March 4, 1991.

Echenberg, Erica and Mark Perry. *And God Created Punk*. London: Virgin Books, 1996.

Eliot, Marc. *Death Of A Rebel: A Biography of Phil Ochs*. New York: Franklin Watts, 1989.

---

[3] Joe Strummer, uncredited interview, July 2002, http://en.wikiquote.org/wiki/ User:Pjoef.

Follos, Tim. "Johnny Clash: Billy Bragg," *The Washington Post Express*, October 22, 2007 http://www.expressnightout.com/2007/10/johnny_clash_billy_bragg/.

Friedman, Glen. *Keep Your Eyes Open: Fugazi*. New York: Burning Flags, 2007.

Gellman, Barton. "Census Worker Who Calculated '91 Iraqi Death Toll Is Told She Will Be Fired." *The Washington Post*, March 6, 1992.

Gilbert, Pat. *Passion is a Fashion: The Real Story Of The Clash*. Cambridge: Da Capo, 2005.

Goldthorpe, Jeff. "Intoxicated Culture: Punk Symbolism and Punk Protest." *Socialist Review*, April–June 1992.

Gray, Marcus. *Route 19 Revisited: The Clash and London Calling*. Berkeley, CA: Soft Skull Press, 2010.

Hale, Jeff A. "The White Panthers 'Total assault on the Culture'." In *Imagine Nation—The American Counter Culture of the 1960s and 70s*, edited by Peter Braunstein and Michael Doyle, 125–56. New York: Routledge/Taylor & Francis, 2001.

Jenkins, Mark. "So You Don't Want To Be A Rocknroll Star: Fugazi Sells Records But Doesn't Sell Out." *Washington City Paper*, July 20, 1990.

Johnson, Dave. "This Is Joe Strummer Speaking." *Hit List*, November/December 1999.

Jones, Allan. "We Never Came to Destroy!" *Melody Maker*, 25 November 1978.

Lacey, Liam. "After the clash, The Clash goes on." *The Globe & Mail*, April 28, 1984.

Lynskey, Dorian. *33 Revolutions Per Minute: A History of Protest Songs, From Billie Holiday To Green Day*. New York: HarperCollins, 2011.

McClard, Kent. "Positive Force DC: The Action Behind The Words." *No Answers*, Spring 1990.

McKay, George. *Senseless Acts Of Beauty: Cultures of Resistance Since the Sixties*. London: Verso, 1996.

McKenna, Kristine. "A Man That Mattered: Joe Strummer." *Arthur Magazine*, March 2003. http://www.arthurmag.com/2009/05/01/a-man-that-mattered-joe-strummer-remembered-by-kristine-mckenna-with-october-2001-interview/.

Mills, Fred. "Tune Into Your Own Spirit: Remembering Joe Strummer." *Blurt Magazine*, December 2011 http://blurt-online.com/features/view/1039.

Salewicz, Chris. *Redemption Song: The Ballad Of Joe Strummer*. New York: Faber & Faber, 2006.

SPIN Magazine, "The Word On Punk Past and Present From The Former Clash Frontman," 2001. http://en.wikiquote.org/wiki/User:Pjoef.

Sprouse, Martin, ed. *Threat By Example*. San Francisco: Pressure Drop Press, 1990.

Temple, Julian. *The Future Is Unwritten*. London: Vertigo Films, 2007.

Tucker, Robert, ed. *The Marx-Engels Reader*. New York, London: W.W. Norton, 1978.

Uncut. *The Clash: Ultimate Music Guide*. London: IPC Media, 2011.

Widgery, David. *Beating Time: Riot'n'Race'n'Rock'n'Roll*. London: Chatto & Windus, 1986.

Discography

Clash, The. Live concert recording, December 7, 1984, Brixton Academy, London, UK.
Crassical Collection, The. *Penis Envy*. Crass Records, CC03, 2010.
Fugazi, Live concert recording, January 12, 1991, White House, Washington DC, USA.

Videography

Haimes, Ted. Director. *The History of Rock'n'Roll: Punk*. Time-Life Film & Video, 1995.
Letts, Don. Director. *Westway To The World*. Sony Films, 2000.
Temple, Julian. Director. *The Future Is Unwritten*. Vertigo Films, 2007.

Chapter 2

Peter Gabriel: The Masked Activist

Mark Pedelty

Introduction

Peter Gabriel profoundly changed the politics of rock. Along with U2's Bono and Bob Geldof of the Boomtown Rats, Gabriel used his star status to organize fellow musicians into a coordinated and sustained effort. In the 1980s, Gabriel helped forge a link between popular music and human rights advocacy, changing the practice and public perception of musical activism. As a result, he was instrumental in launching the mega-event benefit phenomenon, which in turn fostered a more sustained global human rights movement. Upon awarding the Polar Music Prize to Gabriel in 2009, the Royal Swedish Academy of music noted that Gabriel had redefined popular music by combining entertainment and art in socially-relevant songwriting and performance.

Despite his reputation for political musicianship, however, Peter Gabriel has managed to avoid some of the greatest pitfalls of rock politics. Whereas Bono and Sting's stage-based advocacy often leads to critical ridicule, caricature, and dismissal (Negativland 1995, Grant 2009), Gabriel has been much more strategic. As an organizer and spokesperson, he tends to work backstage. When the activists' adulation becomes too strong, he recedes, rather than diverting attention away from the issue at hand. By maintaining fairly strict separation between creative stage performance, public persona, and backstage activism, Gabriel has remained an effective musical and political force. As will be explained later, Gabriel's "masked activism" has allowed him to impact the lives and life chances of several generations.

Popular music works on multiple scales. It is globally distributed, yet deeply personal. That is certainly true of Peter Gabriel's music. One goal of this book is to better understand the relationship between those two levels of experience: the personal and the social. Our knowledge of the musicians featured here is informed not just by reading about their lives, analyzing their music, or talking to other fans, it is also based on enjoying their music and watching them perform. As an additional entry into the musical and political impact of these artists, the goal is to start a conversation with fellow fans and activists. Therefore, after dedicating the bulk of this chapter to an historical retelling and analysis of Peter Gabriel's political musicianship, it will end with a story about how one of his earliest songs, "Biko" (1980), influenced a small group of anti-apartheid activists.

Peter Gabriel's Musical Political Life

Peter Gabriel founded his first band, Garden Wall, at the age of 15. Made up of students from the Charterhouse School of Goldaming in Surrey, Garden Wall eventually merged with another school band to create the international supergroup, Genesis. Gabriel left Genesis in 1975, an amicable divorce motivated, in part, by creative tensions between Gabriel's theatrical artistry and the band's interest in more conventional rock.

Gabriel turned out three albums in five years, all entitled *Peter Gabriel*. The first two yielded only one hit, "Solsbury Hill" (1977), an autobiographical piece referencing Gabriel's departure from Genesis. The song reached number 13 in the UK Singles chart and 68 on the USA Hot 100. The third album (1980) greatly increased Gabriel's following and yielded his most enduring political tune, "Biko," and his best-selling song up to that point, "Games Without Frontiers" (1980). "Games Without Frontiers" came close to breaking the Top 40 in the United States, stalling at number 48. It reached number four in the UK Singles chart.

A 1987 re-release of "Biko," recorded live, would make it to number 49 on the UK Singles chart. However, it failed to re-enter the USA charts. In the United States Peter Gabriel would become a famous pop artist, yet without the strong political reputation he carried forward in the UK.

"Biko" tells the story of murdered South African activist Stephen Bantu Biko, taking on the form of a news story to start:

> September '77
> Port Elizabeth, weather fine
> It was business as usual
> In police room 619
> Oh Biko, Biko, because Biko
> Oh Biko, Biko, because Biko
> Yihla Moja, Yihla Moja
> The man is dead, the man is dead.[1]

The song is about Stephen Bantu Biko, an anti-apartheid activist murdered while in custody of the South African police. "I'd been following the story of Biko's imprisonment," Gabriel explained to Robert Webb of *The Independent*, "I felt that he'd be protected because there was so much publicity about him. So when it was announced that he'd been killed, it came as a shock" (2003). The resulting song made Steve Biko's name known to millions who otherwise might have had no idea who he was, how he died, or why. Although Gabriel inserts the obligatory "I am not a political person" into the Webb interview, one cannot help but see political

---

[1]   Extract from Biko. Written by Peter Gabriel. Reprinted by permission. Published by Real World Music Ltd. International copyright secured. Courtesy of petergabriel.com.

intent in the song. Clearly one aim was to amplify knowledge of the subject and motivate redressive action. In other words: *politics*. The song continues:

> You can blow out a candle
> But you can't blow out a fire
> Once the flames begin to catch
> The wind will blow it higher
> "Biko" was an artistic attempt to fan the flames, and it did.[2]

Along with "Free Nelson Mandela" (1984), recorded by The Special A.K.A., and "Sun City" (1985), sung by Artists United Against Apartheid, "Biko" provided a soundtrack for the global divestment movement, calling for divestiture from companies doing business in South Africa. In fact, it was "Biko" that first set off the 1980s' wave of protest music against apartheid. The song informed Steve Van Zandt about apartheid and moved him to found Artists United Against Apartheid (Drewett 2007, 44–5). "Little Steven" Van Zandt, guitarist for the E Street Band, was sitting in a movie theater when he first heard "Biko." The song peaked his curiosity, led him to research the matter, and eventually led to Artists United Against Apartheid. Although never a big hit outside the UK, "Biko" had widespread effects nonetheless. The song effected political change through influencing other musicians to take action.

Gabriel also organized World of Music, Arts, and Dance (WOMAD) in 1980. WOMAD continues to sponsor a range of international festivals and is a central hub in the production of "world music," a genre that helped break down the Anglo-American stronghold on musical aesthetics. Yet, the world music movement has been criticized for ideologically reinforcing the West's editorial and distributive power over global music (Feld 2000). World music is largely selected, managed, and mediated by Western artists and companies. Nevertheless, because of organizations like WOMAD, more artists outside the anglophone world and Western Europe have received global distribution, diversifying the world's pop palate.

"The charge of cultural imperialism has frequently been thrown at Gabriel," states biographer Spencer Bright, "one he readily refutes" (2000, 177). At first glance, Gabriel seems to accept the charge: "Show me an artist who is pure and doesn't feed off other people" (ibid.). However, Gabriel goes on to defend Paul Simon and other musicians in Bright's biography, arguing that they are examples of Western artists who authentically collaborate, rather than appropriate, world music.

It would be several years into the 1980s before Gabriel would gain sufficient financial and musical capital to support WOMAD. His first step toward bankable fame came in 1982, when "Shock the Monkey" (1982) hit the USA's Top 40. Released on the album *Security*, the success of "Shock the Monkey" was enhanced by an exceptionally innovative music video featured on MTV's playlist. By 1982,

---

[2]   Extract from Biko. Written by Peter Gabriel. Reprinted by permission. Published by Real World Music Ltd. International copyright secured. Courtesy of petergabriel.com.

fledgling MTV had become the rock musicians' marketing tool of choice, and Gabriel's music videos were considered the finest examples of the emerging popular art form.

Gabriel's breakthrough to superstar status came in 1986 with the album *So*. *So* hit number two in the USA, and the song "Sledgehammer" (1986) made it to number one. "Big Time" (1986), another song from *So*, announced Gabriel's intentions to become a chart topper. "Big Time" made it into the Billboard Top 10. "In Your Eyes" (1986) achieved Top 30 status and lasting fame as the song John Cusack's character, Lloyd Dobler, used to woo his girlfriend in the film *Say Anything* (1989). Likewise, the video for "Sledgehammer" received critical acclaim, one of the first and best to use stop-animation. Such projects demonstrated Gabriel's skill in integrating the aural and visual arts. His concerts are no less elaborate, combining theatrical sound and vision into a thematic whole. *So* became Gabriel's first work to earn a Grammy. After several critical successes, but only moderate sales, *So*'s popular success made all of Gabriel's subsequent work possible.

Boosted by *So*, and following a personal invite from Bono, Gabriel headlined a benefit tour for Amnesty International in 1986. If "Biko" was the start of Gabriel's compositional politics, Amnesty marked the start of Gabriel's political performing and organizing. Then, as now, one reason for Gabriel's political success was selectivity. Rather than taking on a range of causes—and thus coming off as committed to none—Gabriel emphasizes human rights and, increasingly, healthy environment as a human right.

Gabriel has written and recorded only a few overtly political tunes, but each has had a profound impact. In addition to "Biko," his song "Wallflower" (1982) became an anthem for Amnesty International insiders. More recently, "Down to Earth" (2008) presented a hopeful call for sustainable lifestyles. Despite their topicality, Gabriel's political songs work on other levels as well. They are first and foremost good pop songs, catchy tunes with clever rhymes. For those willing to pay greater attention, these songs also manage to tell interesting stories. For those interested enough to listen even more carefully, these songs make political statements. Peter Gabriel's political songs are not what Bob Dylan calls "finger pointing songs" (Hentoff 1964, 2), but rather works that bring global problems down to a comprehensible, human scale. Gabriel uses music to humanize politics, making abstract issues more accessible and, therefore, amenable to democratic solutions.

Penning political lyrics was not enough for Gabriel. An avid watcher of "political programs" (Hilburn 1987), Gabriel's interest in politics goes beyond spectatorship, and even beyond music. After various smaller forays into humanitarian performance, Gabriel started working directly with Amnesty International to form the Conspiracy of Hope tour in 1986, which led to 1988's Human Rights Now! tour.

At the 2006 Technology, Entertainment, Design (TED) conference, Gabriel credited Bono, "the magnificent hustler," for first getting him involved in the

Conspiracy of Hope tour. At the same meeting, Gabriel explained how he felt "powerless" as a child when stripped and beaten by other kids, giving him a sense of empathy for those who have experienced much worse.

Perhaps even more impressive than Gabriel's ability to inspire audiences and support activists is his facility for organizing and motivating fellow musicians. He successfully recruited a diverse range of global superstars, including Bruce Springsteen, Tracy Chapman and Youssou N'Dour, for the Amnesty concerts. Furthermore, he has continually diversified their ranks with lesser-known musical contributors, insisting that benefit events include musicians from regions most heavily targeted by movements. Musicians know and trust Gabriel.

Continuing his human rights work, Gabriel helped organize the Nelson Mandela concerts in 1988 and 1990. In 1992, Gabriel co-founded WITNESS (witness.org), an organization that provides video cameras, computers, and other communication equipment to human rights activists.

While the 1990s were not as fertile musically, the albums *Us* (1992) and *Secret World Live* (1993) achieved critical success. Meanwhile, Gabriel's political work and innovative collaborations continued to gather steam. "Music is central to my existence," Gabriel explained in a Daily Telegraph interview, "I get excited by ideas, and I really enjoy collaborating with people who have more talent, smarts or skills than me, because I learn something every time" (McCormick 2003, 3).

In addition to continued political work and musical production, Gabriel has been a pioneer in working across media platforms. In 1993 Gabriel set up Real World Multimedia, an organization that continues to be ahead of its time in terms of integrating sight, sound, and the other senses into holistic art forms. Exploring novel ideas through new media technologies is central to Gabriel's musical process.

In 2002 Gabriel wrote the music for Phillip Noyce's *Rabbit-Proof Fence*, a film about the oppression of indigenous peoples in Australia, adding to his impressive soundtrack resume. In 2005, Gabriel co-produced the "Africa Calling" concert, a Live 8 event designed to call attention to global inequity, poverty, and the need for debt relief. Two years later, Gabriel and Sir Richard Branson provided the original funding and basic concept for the Group of Elders, a think tank comprised of world leaders such as Nelson Mandela, Jimmy Carter, Desmond Tutu, and former Irish President Mary Robinson. While there is little evidence this august body has changed the plight of people in Darfur, Zimbabwe, Turkey, Israel, or any of the other nations they have visited, they have received significant news coverage. The Group of Elders was founded on the premise of soft power, the idea that moral conscience might play a greater role in international politics. In an interview with Elisa Bray of *The Independent*, Gabriel explained that if he were a politician, he would attempt "to find ways of introducing wisdom into political decision-making" (ibid., 8).

Fittingly, Gabriel's foundational role in that group has largely been forgotten. Early press reports almost always noted Gabriel's primary role, whereas more recent coverage claims that the Elders were "brought together by Nelson Mandela" (Prusher 2009, 6). No doubt, Gabriel is pleased his catalytic role has been forgotten. As with past organizing efforts, Gabriel used his musical clout to form the Group of Elders but then retreated to let the primary players take over. Popular music has the ability to promote politics, but it also has the capacity to trivialize serious issues. Through this repeated cycle of creation, followed by strategic retreat, Gabriel seems to be critically aware of pop's political potential and limitations.

As a musical activist on a global scale, Gabriel helped create a new genre of coalitional star-politics, one that has become very familiar, if not taken-for-granted. Global rock stars are expected to leverage their star status to assist human rights and environmental causes, whereas once that marriage seemed forced and contradictory. For practical purposes, that trend began with Bono, Sting, Gabriel, and Geldof. Gabriel has been among the best at sustaining political commitment, and certainly the best at getting out of the way once things are rolling. There is an art to Gabriel's politics, mirrored and propelled by musical performance. In art and politics, Gabriel uses masks to advantage.

The Masked Activist

Whereas rock activists tend to promote singular public personas, seeking a sense of authentic, unshifting commitment, Gabriel plays with *masks*. Rather than make his political commitments seem superficial, creative shape-shifting onstage has helped Gabriel become more politically effective offstage. Among other things, Gabriel's play with masks has helped him to disarticulate himself, the human being, citizen, and activist, from his public pop persona and, in turn, his pop persona from the various stage characters he performs onstage. Conversely, we are made to believe that the "real" Bono is the same as the stage Bono. Choosing a different creative tact, Peter Gabriel signals us that he is playing characters onstage and in his music, whether that role is game show host Barry Williams, a psychopathic sniper, postmodern tribalist, or amnesiac. Peter Gabriel, the person, is able to support movements and organize fellow musicians without worrying that his staged character(s) will compete for public space. His shape-shifting performances have empowered and effectively integrated politics and art, allowing Peter Gabriel, the person, persona, and stage characters, to remain largely outside the political spotlight, at least in comparison to his pop star contemporaries. In an age when politics and popular art are viewed as antithetical, Peter Gabriel has created an effective marriage of musical artistry and political efficacy.

Perhaps the most remarkable thing about Peter Gabriel's musical activism is his ability to reach mass audiences with political messages. Whereas more traditional musician-organizers like Pete Seeger directly engage activists, Gabriel encourages relatively apolitical fans to consider the social dimensions of art. If only a small part of his fan base translates thought into action, Gabriel has done great service.

Few truly popular artists can get away with talking about human rights, torture, or environmental concerns without provoking a *Shut Up and Sing* reaction

(Ingraham 2003) from critics and fans alike. Especially in America, there are plenty of people policing the border between entertainment and politics. Both political activism and rock must be perceived as "authentic" in order to be effective, and mixing the two often erodes popular perceptions of a performer's authenticity.

Unlike more overtly political musicians, Gabriel tends to ensconce political messages within deep layers of the lyric, assisted by tone (for example, the funereal sound of bagpipes in "Biko") and performance context (for example, a quick shout out to Amnesty International before performing "Wallflower"). That keeps Gabriel from turning off his main mass audience. Internet fan sites, such as Alex Storer's "The Gabriel Room," make scant mention of the pop star's political orientations or political organizing, and even tend to downplay the political meanings of his songs. Gabriel has successfully disarticulated his musical and political personas in the minds of many fans, allowing both to succeed.

Yet, activists tend to take Gabriel seriously as well. He has established a level of political credibility that stars with less sustained commitment cannot match, keeping him from coming off as a movement dilettante. Relatively few critics have accused Gabriel of appropriating political fashion to boost his record sales or ego, whereas such criticisms are common for other rock stars with political proclivities. Internet fans like DolceVita laud Gabriel for not overly promoting the awards and adulation he has received. In a forum entitled "petergabriel.com," she explains, "Humility is one of the virtues of wonderful Gabriel." Indeed, when speaking to reporters Gabriel downplays his role in the organizations he supports. He is notoriously difficult to nail down for interviews, even for major press publications, perhaps fearing overexposure will threaten his behind-the-scenes work, not to mention diminish the mystery of his mask-work onstage. There is only one authorized biography of Peter Gabriel (Bright 2000). Bright's biography has never been published in the United States and has not been updated in this millennium.

Of course, there are limitations and even trade-offs to Gabriel's political artistry. For one, Gabriel's politics are not terribly controversial. Liberal and fairly consensual, Gabriel's political messages are a bit Mom-and-apple-pie compared to the labor messages in Billy Bragg's songs, for example, or Steve Earle's anti-war tunes. Instead, Gabriel calls for very basic proscriptions of the "don't do onto others" variety, rather than advocating for more equitable economic structures or policy-specific proposals. Gabriel encourages fan-activists to support the prohibition of torture, for example, putting him within the realm of social consensus. Little in Gabriel's music or politics would indicate serious opposition to the world's dominant political and economic powers.

This is not to denigrate Gabriel's political performance, but rather to locate the artist on a continuum of controversy. Regarding social critique and political ideology, Gabriel remains solidly in the Bono, Sting, and Bob Geldof camp. Yet, like Geldof, Gabriel's perceived levels of sincerity and authenticity remain high despite using pop's bully pulpit toward political ends. Unlike Geldof, however, Gabriel did not have to become a musical monk in order to gain legitimacy; he has kept recording and performing apace. He engages the contradictions of pop and politics by carefully melding social criticism and journalistic insight into songs that playfully mask underlying political elements, while working hard offstage to make it matter.

While each musician is distinct, political musicians perform on a continuum. At one pole are the committed activists for whom musicianship is secondary to political advocacy. Music is, for them, another means of political communication and expression. Such musicians work under no pretense that the "popular music" they perform will ever become truly "popular" in the vernacular sense (that is, sales and size of fan base). Musical marginalization is accepted by virtue of the serious time and commitment other forms of activism require as well as the recognition that overtly politicized music gains only niche audiences, at best. To borrow a phrase from Bob Geldof and the Boomtown Rats, protest music is a *Tonic for the Troops* (1979) rather than a means of placing political messages into the mainstream.

Moving further along the continuum, we reach those whose central social commitment is also political, but whose main means of political expression is musical. These are people like Joe Hill, Pete Seeger, Larry Long, and Utah Phillips, "movement musicians" who spend most of their time making music, but do so in movement contexts and for political purposes. Garnering the attention of larger audiences is secondary to political goals and tends to be facilitated by popular artists. For example, Joe Hill composed and performed for small groups of workers and union organizers during his bullet-shortened career. Hill's fame evolved posthumously, through invocations by popular artists like Paul Robeson, Woody Guthrie, Billy Bragg, Bruce Springsteen, and Rage Against the Machine's Tom Morello. Each generation of Left musicians pledges allegiance to the union labor movement by signing Alfred Hayes' (poem) and Earl Robinson's song, "I Dreamed I Saw Joe Hill Last Night" (Morello 2011). Movement musicians provide a useful stock of symbols through which popular artists can communicate with activist fans and include political elements in their broader repertories. In turn, popular musicians amplify the movement musicians' messages.

Which brings us to musicians like Woody Guthrie, Ani DiFranco, and Billy Bragg; artists who, in their own way, forgo the possibility of mega-stardom for sake of controversial political commitments. The time and effort required to become a professional musician means that such artists will be less directly engaged with activists and movements than the likes of a Joe Hill or Utah Phillips. However, professionalization also allows them to more fully develop their art and craft. Much more selective in their political engagements and performances than the singer-organizers listed above, such artists are nevertheless much more fully articulated within political activist networks and discourses than more popular peers.

Finally, we move across the continuum into the rarified air of global stars like Bono, Sting, and Peter Gabriel. They are still far removed from the apolitical end of the spectrum, as perhaps represented by Britney Spears, KISS, Ke$ha, or most pop and rock stars. Nevertheless, musicians like Bono and Sting recognize that their fan bases are both qualitatively and quantitatively different from those of Bragg or DiFranco. Their audiences will allow and even enjoy some layering of political artistry into their otherwise apolitical music. They might even join in for some direct activist applications of the music, such as signing postcards at mega-events or buying consumer products that benefit mainstream NGO's. However, too much politics is a turn-off for most pop audiences and critics.

I have set up this somewhat simplistic continuum in order to situate Gabriel within the subgenre of political rock. The goal is not to reduce his artistry to a categorical stereotype, but rather to indicate Gabriel's rare ability to reach across categories of performers and fans. There may be such a thing as an apolitical Billy Bragg fan or, conversely, a Britney Spears-loving activist, but both would occupy somewhat proportionately small niches within their favored artist's fan base. Yet, somehow, Gabriel has managed to appeal to committed activists as well as apolitical pop fans. His political polysemy is not so abstract as to seem socially irrelevant. On the other hand, his political messages and actions are not so overwhelming that they turn off the wider fan base. His unique segregation of stage persona(s), public outreach, and backstage organizing—facilitated by theatrical masking onstage and down-to-earth activism offstage—empower uniquely effective political art.

An Evening with Peter Gabriel

One of the important aspects of political pop, as opposed to other political music genres (for example, marching bands or political anthems) is the intimate relationship formed between listener and song. When that sense of intimacy is shared with larger groups—friends, concertgoers, protestors, and so on—amazing things happen. I will use the example of an anti-apartheid protest in the early 1980s to illustrate.

In the early 1980s I did not think of Gabriel as a political musician. Like many others, I found his music aesthetically compelling. I appreciated then, as I do now, how Gabriel presents the pedestrian realities of daily life in an exotic light. His music is anthropological, presenting what Marcus and Fischer call "defamiliarization by cross-cultural juxtaposition" (ibid., 138). In the album *Security*, for example, images like "fat men" playing with "garden hoses" are juxtaposed with sounds derived from African, Asian, and American First Nations, as well as sampled sounds from the natural environment. Gabriel helps us to see Western suburbia as the very odd and alien subculture it is. He does not let us rest comfortably in our cultural cocoons; his music and music videos represent our world through a new set of lenses.

While Gabriel's popular artistry may have political overtones, his lyrics' lack of articulation with any definable problem, policy, or personalities make it hard to label "political." Instead, that work is done through context, as in the case of the Amnesty International concerts as well as the anti-apartheid protest described below.

In 1980, my brother sent me a tape of the last of a series of three eponymous albums Gabriel made after exiting Genesis. I was a sophomore in a rural Iowa high school with no idea about apartheid. Nevertheless, the song "Biko" (1980) caught my ear. It stood out for its unusual instrumentation (bagpipes and synthesizer), haunting vocals, and funerary chant. In an age of punk and new wave experimentation, Gabriel's music still managed to stand out from the rest of rock.

After moving to Los Angeles in 1983, I attended Peter Gabriel's concert at the Greek Theater. It was impressive. He incorporated grand theatrics into the show, including dramatic lighting, costuming, and face paint. Gabriel sang "Lay Your Hands on Me" while being passed around the audience, creating an intimate bond with his audience. Even then, Gabriel's concerts drew in a remarkably diverse audience, not just in terms of race, but also age. Clearly, his appeal reached outside the typical rock demographic. Yet, there was little about the concert that would qualify it as a political performance. His songs were, and are, more about psychological catharsis than social transformation. If asked to write a chapter about a political rock star in 1983, I would certainly not have chosen Peter Gabriel.

"Oh, Biko." It finally hit me while sitting in a political science course later that year. I realized that Gabriel's song referenced a real person, in a real place, imprisoned and killed by a heinous political system. One of the great virtues of Peter Gabriel's political songs is that they work on many levels. They are first and foremost good songs, the sort that stand on their own musically and thus have some chance of delivering ideas as well. "Biko" is more than a political anthem set to music: protest music with little aesthetic appeal. It is the sort of song that attracts wider audiences, allowing its message to inform new audiences. "Biko" did not inform me about apartheid per se, I thank a college class for that. However, it led me to learn more about Stephen Biko and colored my understanding of apartheid, as it did for millions of others. While it may seem superficial to connect with distant horrors via rock, the song is very much about the connection, and disconnection, between a relatively privileged audience and what happens outside their bubble. Songs like "Biko" pop the rocktopian bubble. In the case of apartheid, intellectual and cultural disconnects were combined with fundamental material, political, and economic connections to form a global system of oppression. We did not know about apartheid, but we funded it and benefitted from its existence. Michael Drewett was dead on when describing "Biko" as a work of musical journalism (2007). As I discovered in a survey, political rock often serves as a headline service for young activists, encouraging them to learn more about under-covered news issues (Pedelty 2010).

More than anything else, I remember hearing "Biko" drifting down the halls of the Public Affairs building at the University of California, Los Angeles (UCLA), during an evening protest. A paid consultant to the apartheid regime, a UCLA professor was giving a lecture inside a large classroom. A small group gathered outside the door to protest. The protestors' chant fell silent in order to let Peter Gabriel's song communicate what they found difficult to articulate. The song helped congeal a fractured movement, gave voice to the dead, and played its own small role in ending a brutal political system.

In the 1970s there had been significant activist work against apartheid at UCLA, but by 1983 the movement had dwindled down to a small group of activists belonging mainly to the Progressive Students Alliance (PSA) and the Black Student Union (BSU). When a relatively small group started "demanding" that the UC divest its funds from companies investing in South Africa, the initial response was ridicule. It was the Reagan age. "Constructive engagement" with South Africa was official policy, and market *über alles* had re-established itself as the USA's dominant discourse. We were all told that the UC system had too much invested in companies doing business in South Africa to ever consider divesting. Surely a ragged coalition of college students would not shift them from that position. Most national anti-apartheid organizations seemed to be biding their time, waiting for better social conditions within which to reorganize divestment-organizing efforts, efforts that met with some success in the 1970s.

Only a handful of students showed up to the protests initially. Years later, after a take-over of an administration building, arrests, and disheartening setbacks, a growing number of protesters joined in. Eventually the UC system gave in to what had become widespread demands for divestiture: what may seem like historical inevitability now, at the time felt like the greatest of improbabilities. Of course, all of that activity paled in comparison to what South Africans experienced and did to overturn apartheid. However, the divestment activists played their own small, local role in a very global movement, work that received recognition from Archbishop Desmond Tutu, Nelson Mandela, and other leaders who described divestiture as an important part of the anti-apartheid movement.

It was not just conviction, however, that sustained the UCLA activists. Pleasure played its part: nourishing food supplied by local clergy, the good company of fellow activists, and an ability to laugh when things got too serious. One protest sign read, "We won't 'til they!" Two activists working together had accidently left out the words "rest" and "divest" ("I thought you were painting those in!") Similarly, music lightened the mood and motivated community building, keeping the group from falling into the deadly and stultifying seriousness to which the American Left so often falls prey.

Music was particularly important and location was an asset. Paul Simon presented an unannounced concert at the protestors' encampment, "Mandela City," as did Carole King. Singer-songwriter Holly Near described the anti-apartheid "tent city at UCLA" in her autobiography, *Fire in the Storm ... Singer in the Rain* (36). Jackson Browne and Daryl Hannah came by to sign the group's divestment petition, as did many other well-known, and not-so-well-known people. However, it was not that injection of live musical support I remember best. Instead, it was a recording of Peter Gabriel's "Biko" played at a small demonstration.

What sort of music does one play at a protest inside a classroom building? The group faced that problem in the winter of 1984. "Free Nelson Mandela" would not be released until later that year. "Sun City" (1985) was still gestating in Little

Steven's mind. The protestors owned very little South African music, despite the presence of several South African student exiles in the local movement. Even if they had, South African music was too controversial to play at a protest. The wrong song or singer, affiliated with the wrong anti-apartheid party, could offend members of one or the other faction of South Africans. So, somewhat by default, the group played "Biko."

UCLA's *The Daily Bruin* described how the protestors sat silently in the hall as Peter Gabriel's "Biko" played in the background. It was not designed as a silent protest. However, the juxtaposition of an academic setting with Gabriel's haunting bagpipes seemed to warrant the silent response. For once, none of the organizers used the moment to demonstrate self-aggrandizing "leadership." The level of discipline was remarkable for a group of young activists. It was one of those prime moments when self-indulgence seemed to completely give way to collective investment. In other words, the protestors' moods and actions matched the music, and the music helped facilitate a ritually warm response to the professor's cold contract. What could have been reported as anarchist disruption instead received favorable press.

There were internal debates concerning whether or not the group should protest a college instructor, especially during class time. Nevertheless, the protest led to a positive campus-wide discussion concerning the role of faculty and the ethical boundaries of protest. In our defense, the protest was short and to the point. After it was over, most of the group went over to UCLA's North Campus Commons for a bite to eat. They sat around one large table. Three exiled South Africans sat near the head. The rest knew that the South African students were risking a lot by attending the protest. Their presence made everyone much more willing to risk minor inconveniences like suspension and arrest.

One of the South African activists asked to borrow the portable stereo and Peter Gabriel's tape. They had not heard Gabriel's song before that evening. The song was banned in South Africa. The three listened to it over and over again throughout the meal. Clearly, the song meant even more to them than it did to everyone else in attendance. The song clearly spoke to the South African student protestors at a very deep level. It let them know someone much larger than a scruffy group of UCLA students was paying attention to their Nation's plight: "and the eyes of the world are watching you now ... watching you now." Multiplying this example by several thousands, we can imagine the impact "Biko" has had around the world.

Gabriel does a masterful job of creating catalytic imagery and getting out of the way. When we hear "Biko," we imagine Steve Biko, the subject, rather than Peter Gabriel, the artist. In other words, Peter Gabriel is an artist, evoking alternative social realities and provoking novel worldviews, but then getting out of the way. Perhaps more so than any other political rock musician, Peter Gabriel has strategically worked the "Big Time" (1986) in order to instigate meaningful change in the world.

Bibliography

Bray, Elisa. "The 5-Minute Interview with Peter Gabriel." *The Independent* (London). October 4, 2006: 8.

Bright, Spencer. *Peter Gabriel*. London: Pan Books, 2000.

Drewett, Michael. "The Eyes of the World are Watching Now: The Political Effectiveness of 'Biko' by Peter Gabriel." *Popular Music & Society* 30, 1 (2007): 39–51.

Feld, Steven. "A Sweet Lullaby for World Music." *Public Culture* 12, 1 (2000): 145–71.

Grant, Alistair. 2009. Have U2 Created a Monster? *Belfast Telegraph*, July 7, 2009, sec News: 2.

Hentoff, Nat. "The Crackin', Shakin', Breakin' Sounds." *New Yorker* 10, 24 (1964) Retrieved from http://www.newyorker.com/archive on August 10, 2009.

Hilburn, Robert. "Peter Gabriel: Headstrong Music Man." *St. Petersburg Times* (Florida). January 25, 1987: 2E.

Ingraham, Laura. *Shut Up & Sing: How Elites from Hollywood, Politics, and the UN are Subverting America*. Washington, DC: Regnery Publishing, 2003.

Marcus, George, and Michael Fischer. *Anthropology as Cultural Critique: An Experimental Moment in the Human Sciences*. Chicago: The University of Chicago Press, 1986.

McCormick, Neil. "Peter's principles" *National Post (Canada)*. November 10, 2003: AL3.

Near, Holly. *Fire in the Rain ... Singer in the Storm: An Autobiography*. New York: William Morrow and Company, 1990.

Negativland. 1995. *Fair Use: The Story of the Letter U and the Numeral 2*. Concord, CA: Seeland.

Pedelty, Mark. "Musical News: Popular Music in Social Movements." *The Anthropology of News and Journalism: Global Perspectives*. Elizabeth Bird. Bloomington, IN: Indiana University Press, 2009.

Prusher, Ilene R. "The 'Elders' Arrive in Israel to Boost Mideast Peace." *The Christian Science Monitor*. August 25, 2009: 6.

Technology, Entertainment, and Design. TED Conference. ted.com/talks/lang/eng/peter_gabriel_fights_injustice_with_video.html, 2006.

Storer, Alex. "The Gabriel Room." http://thegabrielroom.free.fr, retrieved September 23, 2009.

Webb, Robert. "Story of the Song Biko." *The Independent* (London). September 26, 2003: 15.

Discography

Artists United against Apartheid. *Sun City*. EMI, 1985. Re-released by Razor and Tie Music, CD RE2007, 1993.

Gabriel, Peter. "Solsbury Hill." *Peter Gabriel* (1st Album). Atco, Vinyl SD36-137, 1977.

Gabriel, Peter. "Biko." *Biko*. Charisma Records, 7-inch single CB370, 1980.

Gabriel, Peter. *Peter Gabriel* (3rd album). Charisma Records, CD PGCD3, 1980.

Gabriel, Peter. "Games Without Frontiers." *Peter Gabriel* (3rd album). Geffen, CD PGCD3, 1980.

Gabriel, Peter. "Shock the Monkey." *Security*. Geffen, Vinyl GHS2011, 1982.

Gabriel, Peter. "Wallflower." *Security*. Geffen, Vinyl GHS2011, 1982.

Gabriel, Peter. "Big Time." *So*. Virgin, Vinyl 207-587630, 1986.

Gabriel, Peter. "In Your Eyes." *So*. Virgin, Vinyl 207-587630, 1986.

Gabriel, Peter. "Sledgehammer." *So*. Virgin, Vinyl 207-587630, 1986.

Gabriel, Peter. 2002. *Long Walk Home, Music from The Rabbit-Proof Fence*. Real World, CD PGCD10, 2002.

Gabriel, Peter. "Down to Earth." *WALL-E*. Walt Disney Records/Pixar, 2008.

Geldof, Bob. *A Tonic for the Troops*. Columbia, Vinyl JC 35750, 1979.

Morello, Tom. "I Dreamed I Saw Joe Hill Last Night." *World Wide Rebel Songs*. New West Records, 2011.

Special A.K.A. "Free Nelson Mandela." *Nelson Mandela/Break Down The Door* 2 Tone, Vinyl 4V942793, 1984.

Filmography

Cusack, John, Ione Skye, and John Mahoney. *Say Anything*. New York: CBS/Fox Video. 1989.

Noyce, Phillip, Kenneth Branagh, John Winter, Christine Olsen, Gulpilil, Phil Noyce, Ningali Lawford, Everlyn Sampi, Tianna Sansbury, Laura Monaghan, and Doris Pilkington. *Rabbit-Proof Fence*. Magna Pacific, 2002.

Chapter 3
Bob Dylan: Someone Else's Stage

Keith Nainby

To be on the side of people who are struggling for something doesn't necessarily mean you're being political. (Bob Dylan, quoted in *No Direction Home* 2005)

You would have to make an impression on somebody. There was so many many singers who were good, but they couldn't focus their attention on anybody, they couldn't really get inside somebody's *head*. You've got to be able to pin somebody down. (ibid.)

This person had come onto someone else's stage, and while in some ways he seemed as ordinary as anyone in the audience, something in his demeanor dared you to pin him down, to sum him up or write him off, and you couldn't do it. From the way he sounded and the way he moved, you couldn't tell where he was from, where he'd been, or where he was going—though the way he moved and sang somehow made you want to know all of those things. (Marcus 2010, xiii)

More than 48 years after Greil Marcus' first sight of him as an unnamed, little-known onstage guest at a Joan Baez concert in the summer of 1963, Bob Dylan continues to dare all of us in the much more vast, mass-mediated audience to "pin him down, to sum him up or write him off." Dylan acknowledges, in the quote above, the vitality at the heart of live performance, the need to "pin down" a particular audience member and grasp that person's where and why. Yet he fiercely resists efforts to turn the relational tables by shifting personae rapidly, from song to song and album to album. He actively distances himself from specific parties, causes or movements that might "pin him down." He resists playing the songwriting and performing roles and the musical styles and interests that might "sum him up." He repeatedly freshens his relation to the popular music canon and the currents of critical evaluation that might "write him off."

Yet we can still seek to know more, despite Dylan's dare and despite his resistant stance, because "the way he moved," and still moves, has moved us. We have not only been changed in our relation to Dylan during the half century since Marcus first caught sight of him, but also in our relation to the broader public stages on which other rock artists have taken on the roles of musical and political avatars. During these five decades, artists from John Lennon to Thom Yorke have helped define the contours of popular music through innovations in how blues-based rock'n'roll might successfully integrate studio effects, nontraditional song structures, and tone colors that extend well beyond blues chord changes. Such artists have simultaneously framed political conversation by using their visibility to highlight unfolding issues that matter to them within song lyrics, interviews, and other mediated events. In these senses, important artists can be said to "take the stage" physically by making prominent their musical and political voices. They can also be said to move us, culturally, through "stages" in their successive efforts to transform their musical and political contexts.

Dylan's approach to these musical and political stages, however, is quite complex. His songs persistently treat both musical and political themes by showing how we are most defined not by our individual acts or aims but by our contingent, often ironic, relationships to one another and to our shared history and society. His work thus reveals that our grandest musical and political stages—physical and temporal—are as indeterminate and mysterious as an encounter with a single other human life. We are, in Dylan's implied political view, always already on "someone else's stage": we are at a place and in a time that we did not create and cannot fully conceptualize. For him, what we must "resist" are two related notions: first, that personal commitments (such as desires to "end racism" or "maintain racial separation") can reliably guide our political actions. Second, that an idealized vision of society (such as grass-roots democratic student groups or the election of progressive politicians) can reliably guide our efforts to organize. In this chapter I examine this view as Dylan's most enduring and overarching contribution to songwriting, performing, and taking action within rock music.

Given his struggle *against* "being political," it is difficult to produce a definitive biography of Dylan the political musician. This difficulty arises because struggle, in and through popular music, is most often staged through fans' developing identification with the causes, values, and personalities explicitly advocated by our favorite musicians. Indeed, Dylan himself was as strongly linked as any artist before or since to an emerging counterculture that defined itself largely by political dissent from the status quo. Those linkages were deliberate and ranged far beyond Dylan's protest-movement anthems like "Blowin' in the Wind," "Masters of War," and "The Times They Are A-Changin'." A number of acts mark Dylan's early articulation of popular music to politics: performances at major civil rights events in Mississippi and Washington DC in 1963, within months of Marcus' first sighting this "ordinary" appearing new artist; his early work on behalf of the Congress on Racial Equality, the Student Nonviolent Coordinating Committee, and Students for a Democratic Society; his edgy speech undercutting even the Left-wing status quo when given an award for his contributions by the Emergency Civil Liberties Committee; and the nascent Black Panther party's adoption of the language of "Ballad of a Thin Man" in its early publication efforts.[1] Yet Dylan himself, from the start, has been frequently and stridently critical of suggestions that his performances are authentic representations of his commitment to causes:

---

[1]   See Young 1998, 7; Marqusee 2005, 7–15, 93–6; Doggett 2007, 77–80 for evidence of this trend.

in a 1963 interview, interrupting Studs Terkel: "No, no, it wasn't atomic rain. Somebody else thought that too. It's not *atomic* rain, it's just a *hard* rain" (Terkel 2006, 7).[2] In a 1966 *Playboy* interview: "my older songs, to say the least, were about nothing. The newer ones are about the same nothing" (Hentoff 2006, 101). In a 1968 *Sing Out!* interview: "That doesn't really exist. It's not for or against the war" (Cohen and Traum 2006, 136). In a 1978 *Rolling Stone* interview: "I've heard it said that Dylan was never as truthful as when he wrote *Blood on the Tracks*, but that wasn't necessarily *truth*" (Cott 2006, 259). One of the defining touchstones for Vietnam-era radicals involved waiting, ever in vain, for Dylan to publicly declare his opposition to the war, part of his "repeatedly denying that he was motivated by political impulses" (Doggett 2007, 6, 80). Dylan's long-standing and ongoing disavowal of his work as either political statement or personal history presents challenges for those of us who try to articulate precisely how this body of work stands, now, as enduring model or resounding call for other popular musicians as political actors.

In what follows, I address this stance by treating Dylan's shifting performative personae as the most important contribution he offers other rock artists. Shifting performative stances, in response to evolving contexts, are a major example of vigorous resistance in Dylan's work. I hold that other artists may turn to this example for nourishment and for political resources. Dylan develops a rich and rewarding treatment of our contingent relationships to political contexts, and he does so through engaging a multiplicity of identities. I suggest five specific identities, five faces, that help us engage the daunting figure of Dylan the political performer:

1. *The Face of the Protest Singer*: perhaps the "simplest" face of Dylan the political musician, this Dylan energized the folk-based topical song resurgence of the early 1960s. He did so by emphasizing characters' distinctive perspectives, a change from the homogenizing approach of the "topical" song movement.

2. *The Face of the Expressive Youth*: this Dylan treated cultural questions as musical ones. He pushed old social boundaries that privileged rationality, adding a political thrust to the rock'n'roll infused passion of postwar baby boomers.

3. *The Face of the Pop Poet*: this Dylan offered songs influenced by folk and ballad traditions as well as by strong poetic devices. This allowed him to connect with a young, educated music audience.

4. *The Face of the Rock Star*: this Dylan created "Bob Dylan" as a mythic persona, an open text on which the desires and delirium of the listening audience could be (re)written. This Dylan established a new mode of critique, the possibility for larger-than-life rock artists to reach massive

---

[2]   Emphasis is mine based on aural evidence from a bootleg recording.

audiences with considerable economic power as well as governments, agencies, and diplomats with legitimate political power.

5. *The Face of the Radical Revisionary*: this Dylan has returned repeatedly to "roots" music of a wide variety of styles. From becoming a blues imitator on his first album and Americana scholar on *Basement Tapes* after his 1966 "retirement," to his current, extraordinarily catholic *Theme Time Radio Hour* program, he consistently returns to the roots of contemporary musical systems. This models for politically engaged musicians how innovations bridge future and past—and how musical innovations are "rooted" in history.

These five faces reflect several important aspects of Dylan's complexity as an artist whose work now spans five decades. His musical and lyrical approaches have evolved throughout this time span, in many cases at the vanguard of major cultural shifts connected to rock and related music. These shifts include the rekindled activism of the American New Left in the early 1960s, which was connected to topical, folk-style protest songs; the crystallization of the "counterculture" as resistance to dominant ways of life in the mid-1960s, which was connected to the widespread emergence of rock as the music of politically aware young people; the growing self-consciousness of rock as an art form documented by mainstream journalists in magazines such as *Rolling Stone* at the start of the 1970s, which was connected to the diversification of rock styles that included "roots rock" and country-rock; and the emergence of a generation of rock "establishment" figures whose work was canonized as "classic rock" beginning in the 1980s, which is still connected today to the fragmentation of rock into genres, subgenres and niches reflected in narrowly circumscribed, archival-style programming across FM, satellite and Internet radio.

Bob Dylan certainly did not begin as an establishment figure; indeed, he did not even begin as "Bob Dylan." Robert Allan Zimmerman was born in Hibbing, Minnesota on 24 May 1941, to middle-class parents in a mining town. He had a typical childhood, in contrast to the claims he would make as a very young celebrity in the early 1960s. He initially became a significant artist in New York City in 1963, through two means: playing clubs and coffee houses frequented by "bohemian" folk singers and poets in Greenwich Village, and recording two albums after being signed by John Hammond, a famous talent scout, to Columbia Records: *Bob Dylan* and *The Freewheelin' Bob Dylan*.

Dylan performed at two high-profile 1963 civil rights events, a rally in Greenwood, Mississippi, after the murder of Medgar Evers and the March on Washington later that year. These performances, coupled with his authoring of major protest movement songs like "Blowin' in the Wind," "A Hard Rains' A-Gonna Fall," and "The Times They Are A-Changin" were key factors in establishing his mainstream celebrity status and encouraging pundits to describe him as the "voice of a generation." Dylan actively challenged this label and refused to directly support, after 1964, any particular Left-wing position. His next several albums stretching through 1966, *Another Side of Bob Dylan*, *Bringing It All Back Home*, *Highway 61 Revisited*, and *Blonde on Blonde*, featured more oblique, surrealist lyrics than his earlier works; they also featured increasing use of electrified instruments and multi-piece backing bands. These developments spurred criticism from both artists and fans linked to the acoustic-folk-styled topical song community—most famously in the persistent heckling audience members directed at Dylan during his 1965–66 world tour. Dylan responded to the heckling by intensifying the rock qualities of his performances on this tour.

Dylan's period as a preeminent cultural icon came to an abrupt end in July 1966, when he was nearly killed in a motorcycle accident. His subsequent work in the 1960s consisted of country-tinged music and reflective, even pastoral lyrics on the albums *John Wesley Harding* and *Nashville Skyline*. His lack of touring and the comparatively sporadic studio output in this era ushered in the "bootlegging" industry; pirated recordings have been an important source of music for Dylan's fans ever since. His artistic styles sand personal stances continued to evolve at a rapid pace throughout the 1970s, even after his return to touring in 1974; these evolutions included using a large horn section on *Street Legal* and emphasizing evangelical concerns on several albums following his 1978 conversion to Christianity. Each evolution, like Dylan's early repudiation of the New Left connection, has to this day precipitated criticism from others and resistance to such criticism from Dylan.

Dylan's career as an influential artist appeared to be waning through most of the 1980s and 1990s, despite the critical acclaim afforded occasional albums like *Infidels* (1983) and *Oh Mercy* (1989). But 1997's *Time Out of Mind* ushered in yet another period of cultural relevance for the artist: this album and its follow-up, 2001's *Love and Theft*, were widely embraced by critics as well as old and new fans, and Dylan has continued to maintain his connection to this fan base through a demanding series of concerts (actually dating back to 1988) known to the Dylan community as "The Never-Ending Tour." Dylan's most significant recent impact, however, may be his lending, since 2006, of his name and DJ-ing voice to the archival program *Theme Time Radio Hour*, which offers a musical tour of a huge range of influential songs ranging from blues to country to folk to gospel to ballads.

I have learned much more than I can distinctly trace from Dylan through his original body of work and his deep knowledge of Anglo-American music. Nevertheless, I come belatedly to Dylan's work and to the mid-20th-century musical and cultural landscapes that define, and are defined by, this body of work. I was born in 1970, four years after the motorcycle crash that resulted in Dylan's withdrawal from the vanguard of 1960s' culture, by which time his place at the center of 20th-century popular music was already assured (Shumway 2009, 116–21). In about 1984, I became a serious listener of "classic rock" music as well as the contemporary music most directly influenced by "classic rock" radio's pantheon of deities, who included The Beatles, The Rolling Stones, Pink Floyd, and—if we mean only ever actually playing on the air "Like a Rolling Stone" or "Rainy Day Women #12 and 35"—Bob Dylan. By "serious listener," I mean one who could, from memory, quote lyrics, name songs and albums, and sprinkle in pithy statements from published interviews with my favorite artists. I understood, or at least thought I did, Bob Dylan's influence on what I considered serious rock music: I would confidently opine, throughout my teens, that he was "the most important songwriter in rock history other than Lennon and McCartney" as well as "the artist who made rock music politically significant." All this great knowledge I based on reading histories of the 1960s, which I did avidly, and synthesizing the occasional Dylan-centered statements of rock critics and documentarians. What I could not, and in some sense still cannot quite fully, understand is that simply being able to hear "Rainy Day Women" on mainstream radio aimed at a teenage audience signals cultural transformation and marks my own belatedness: Hunter S. Thompson, writing about the cultural landscape in 1967, recalls that the song was "banned by radio stations from coast to coast … mainly because of the chorus line" (Thompson 2004, 68). The "chorus line" in question encourages listeners, indeed everybody, to "get stoned." When I arrived at college, certain of Dylan's secure place in the canon of serious rock music, I still knew only those two songs, "Like a Rolling Stone" and "Rainy Day Women." I had heard the Peter, Paul and Mary version of "Blowin' in the Wind" and the Byrds' version of "Mr. Tambourine Man," but was unfamiliar with Dylan's performances of these songs or with his larger repertoire.

My passionate—all right, perhaps obsessive—interest in Dylan's work began later, kindled by two roommates who were hardcore Dylan lovers (and lifelong friends, it turned out). These friends urged me to enroll in a Shakespeare course taught by Christopher Ricks because Ricks was known to cite Dylan in his lectures; this course changed my life in several ways. I saw my first and, to this point, only Dylan concert in Santa Rosa in April 2006. This personal history puts me in an interesting position as an analyst of the artist's political impact: I was born, raised, and educated as listener/citizen in a society in which our rock musicians and our rock listening have not merely been *influenced* by Dylan, but in which our very conceptions of the possibilities of political work through rock performance have been defined by his impossible-to-supplant primacy. Even leaving aside his artistic impact, this primacy was permanently secured by Dylan's iconic presence at the dawn of modern rock and the 1960s' counterculture that paralleled it (Zinn 1984, 238, Doggett 2007, 6). The story of Bob Dylan's role in the politics of rock is very much an origin story; in wrestling with it, I wrestle with *mythos*. I surrender the impulse (doomed in advance) to get "underneath" the "Bob Dylan" myth, to "pin him down," and choose instead to turn to his songs and his legacy.

For this reason I embrace in this chapter my own belatedness, my own historicized relation to Dylan. This is appropriate because Dylan treats political themes by historicizing them, insisting on these themes' rootedness in unfolding narratives of particular people and places. To this end, I organize my discussion of the five "faces" of Dylan the political performer by thematically connecting each face to a different one of his songs, exploring tropes within each song as clues to one of the complex dimensions of his mythic persona. In choosing the five songs, I adopted the constraint of selecting from only those songs written and issued prior to mid-1964, by which point Dylan had certainly completed his ascent from exciting new singer/songwriter within the folk revival to major mainstream star (Hentoff 2006, 22–3). Through the use of this constraint, I explore how each of these five streams of Dylan's enduring influence on our music and our politics course throughout his total body of work, from 1961 to the present— acknowledging that by choosing these five songs, I am not directly "within" the contemporary rock genre, as these songs were not considered "rock music" when first performed. Thus, I show that the core impact of "Bob Dylan" the political figure has not been simply idiosyncratically "authored" by Robert Zimmerman, the individual, over his own rock career (extending since mid-1965). Instead, his impact on the politics of rock emerges from our engagement of Dylan's multiple texts as we encounter them in multiple contexts and in evolving forms, reaching back into the pasts we write and forward into the futures we imagine.

"The Lonesome Death of Hattie Carroll": The Face of the Protest Singer

In the courtroom of honor, the judge pounded his gavel [...]
Stared at the person who killed for no reason [...]
And he spoke through his cloak, most deep and distinguished
And handed out strongly, for penalty and repentance. (Dylan, *The Times They Are A-Changin'*, 1963)[3]

Here, in the final stanza of this great song about an African-American woman working as a servant who is killed by a wealthy young man in the party she serves, we have the judge in the case taking four separate acts that share a hint of relational violence in their meeting with the interlocutor: first pounded, then stared, then spoke, then handed out. Yet these four acts in this sequence gradually weaken in force, in their potential impact on the accused—the third act ("he spoke") further weakened by being softened through the judge's cloak, so that by the time the fourth act is described as "handed out strongly," we know that whatever is handed out will not be given strongly at all but, indeed, quite weakly, in a spirit of withdrawal from the other. The bitter irony of "handed out strongly" then coils back onto the preceding narrative, pulling down with it the phrase "most deep and distinguished," urging us to question whether there is any depth at all to this judge, and whether he is distinguished at all or is, rather, along with his cowardice, all too common.

The indictment of our pervasive cowardice in moments when we should stand strong, with outrage, is most compelling in this verse portion of the song's final stanza. When the refrain then follows for the final time, and the line "take the rag away from your face" becomes "bury the rag deep in your face," the poetic force

---

[3]   © 1964, 1966 by Warner Bros. Inc.; renewed 1992 by Special Rider Music.

is actually weakened in contrast to the power of the final verse; it is a kind of anticlimax paralleling, just as the weakening sequence of fours actions does, the sickening anticlimax of the courtroom resolution itself as well as the anticlimactic poetic tone of most verse lines' cadences, as Ricks observes (Ricks 2003, 226–33).

The song's power, then, lies not in the admonitions of the narrator to listeners, his advice to us about when and why to bring the rag to our face, but instead in the characters' unfolding relation to one another. Here the narrator is clearly on the side of somebody struggling, as he names Carroll's death as "lonesome"; yet even that naming is reserved only for the title and is not spoken within the song, which is "being political" most cogently not by taking sides but by dramatizing particular characters, side by side. The specific actions or values adopted by victim, defendant, or judge do not shape our understanding of sociopolitical forces in this song; what do so are the institutional structures that bring characters together and the possibilities for actions or values that are thereby created: "And emptied the ashtrays on a whole other level" from the third stanza chimes, again with bitter irony, with "To show that all's equal and that the courts are on the level" from the fourth (Dylan, *The Times They Are A-Changin'*, 1963). The third stanza centers on how Carroll and her family are distinguished from the song's other characters, and perhaps from us, by their social position, a position textured by histories of race, gender, and class and defined by constant work cleaning up others' leavings "on a whole other level" from the lives of defendant and judge. The courts may need to appear "on the level" for the sake of propriety, but on which level, exactly, are courts in the social hierarchy? For whose sake is this veneer of propriety maintained? Again, we are encouraged to reread the previous narrative, which began "At a Baltimore hotel society gath'rin'" (Dylan, *The Times They Are A-Changin'*, 1963). Which levels of "society" gather at this hotel and what are we to gather from the song's positioning of its characters in this historical and social context?

Dylan's early protest songs embed political questions, not answers, in dramatic narratives. Thus, I disagree with DeCurtis, who claims that Dylan's songs in the protest era are notable for "shifting the focus away from individuals to larger, but inevitably more abstract, social issues. If activists are often seeking to put a 'human face' on political issues that can seem difficult to personalize, Dylan often does the opposite" (DeCurtis 2009, 48–9). This is an odd claim given that the songs DeCurtis discusses each include sustained attention to individuals and are devoid of large-scale abstract references such as "justice" or "rights." I contend that one important narrative approach unites the characters in "The Lonesome Death of Hattie Carroll" with the unnamed assassin in "Only a Pawn in Their Game"; the broad-ranging group of participants associated with the boxing match in "Who Killed Davey Moore?"; the perplexed parent in "Oxford Town"; the nostalgic matriarch in ""North Country Blues"; the doomed Brown family in "The Ballad of Hollis Brown"; and the reflective narrator in "With God On Our Side": each is carefully positioned within a larger context of historicized social relations that spark the conflict at the dramatic heart of each song. These songs do not shift focus from people to issues. The songs do turn, as DeCurtis suggests, directly away from an investigation of individual intentions and actions. But I contend that this turn in Dylan's songs dramatizes how life and lifestyle are particular, in the sense that they meaningfully differ (politically and otherwise) from person to person and community to community. Yet life and lifestyle, in these same songs, are simultaneously contingent, in the sense that people and communities cannot be understood, nor serve as spurs to political action, apart from their dependence on a larger fabric of shared histories and shared resources. This is how Dylan bridges the personal and the political, rather than distinguishing them as DeCurtis claims.

Dylan's songs only occasionally, after 1964, feature specific individuals in overtly politicized settings; the most obvious examples would be "George Jackson," from 1974, and "Hurricane," from 1975. These songs' narratives reflect a dramatic approach to conflict similar to the approach I describe here, though with much less poetic force. But other songs of a different nature, with much, much greater poetic force than "Hurricane," followed immediately after Dylan's protest era: standouts include "Chimes of Freedom," "Mr. Tambourine Man," "It's Alright, Ma (I'm Only Bleeding)," "Desolation Row," "Visions of Johanna" and "(Stuck Inside of Mobile with the) Memphis Blues Again." This series of extraordinary pieces is often marked as a stylistic watershed, in conjunction with Dylan's notorious electrified performance at the traditionalist-dominated Newport Folk Festival in 1965. Typical of such claims, Wilentz describes this mid-1960s' period as an "innovation" within Dylan's career, while Tamarin claims that Dylan's songs are "more complicated" than those of the protest era.[4] I agree that stylistic development happens at this point in Dylan's work and is worth marking: in a later section of this chapter I trace the broader political implications of what Gray terms a "complexity of language" in Dylan's lyrics (Gray 2002, 122). Yet I contend that "discontinuity" would be too strong a way to characterize this stylistic development, because previous songs such as "The Lonesome Death of Hattie Carroll" and "Only a Pawn in Their Game" remain key to making sense of the subsequent mid-1960s' surrealistic work. They teach us how to read oblique, impressionistic narratives such as "Desolation Row" as political rather than idiosyncratically personal, because they teach us how modern socio-historical conditions—such as those we inherit from Greek mythology, the Catholic Church, Shakespeare, Einstein, Eliot, and Pound—form the only valid lenses through which we can make sense of personal experiences. They also teach us that particular, contingent personal perspectives like these, in turn, must anchor our political actions, if by "political" we mean transforming (even when we fail and remain in "desolation") this world we have inherited.

Wilentz demonstrates that the dramatization of contingent, historical situations of ordinary people was not simply "authored" by Dylan in popular American song, but is a legacy Dylan inherited, through Woody Guthrie at least and possibly through Aaron Copeland, Pete Seeger, and others. In that way, Dylan's work was

---

[4]   See Wilentz 2010, 103–4; Tamarin 2009, 131 for examples.

a legacy of the 1930s' and 1940s' Popular Front movement. The Popular Front sought to link everyday American life and art to Left-wing political organizing efforts (Wilentz 2010, 18–28). However, by the early 1960s the emphasis in the folk revival with which Dylan first associated was on authentic performance styles and song forms derived from traditional communities—an emphasis that helped secure the folk revival's artistic credibility and shield the movement from the polarizing connotations of McCarthyism's extremist characterizations of the Popular Front.[5] The boundaries of what was acceptable for Dylan and other performers were policed through reviews and other articles in both folk-centered and mainstream publications: Dylan's second album was criticized in a folk newsletter in Minneapolis by two of the folk scholars who helped introduce him to the music because it contained "hardly any traditional material, and most of the original material is not particularly folk-derived" (Nelson and Pankake 1998, 18); his third album in *HiFi-Stereo Review* by a music critic (who had previously celebrated him in *The Village Voice*) because of its "concern with [...] unexceptional causes" and its "self-conscious on-the-road poetry" (Goddard 1998, 24–5); and his fourth album by the editor of the "leading" folk magazine *Sing Out!* because his "new songs seem to be all inner-directed now" (Silber 1998, 26–8). These examples show how the loudest, most established political voices associated with the folk/protest movement considered Dylan's work inappropriately personal, even idiosyncratic. This is important because for Dylan, "idiosyncrasy" was itself a political position.

In writing about the 1965 performance that signaled Dylan's most obvious break from the norms of the folk/protest movement, Lee reminds us that "folk musicians [at Newport] were expected to wear 'work clothes'," something Dylan had stopped doing by that performance (Lee 2004, 58). However, each of the album-centered critiques cited above were published well before Newport 1965, indicating that challenges to what Marqusee, by way of Baudrillard, terms the "fake-authentic" impulses in the folk revival were already deeply intertwined with Dylan's existing, pre-Newport texts (Marqusee 2005, 42). "The Lonesome Death of Hattie Carroll" and parallel Dylan songs from 1962–64, such as those I name above, function as models of sustained questioning of received values and institutionalized associations. They function as models both in their dramatic structure, by staging particular personal struggles within contested social spaces, and in their cultural position, situated just before the dawn of modern rock music as youth-rallying political statement.

Gitlin notes the vital importance of such sustained questioning for the "New Left," the student-centered young activists emerging at the time of Dylan's new stardom to distinguish themselves from the "Old Left" of the 1930s and 1940s: "If all authority was suspect, why not the authority of the organizers themselves?" (Gitlin 1987, 42). MacDonald echoes this, describing "the revolt of youth against institutional authority" in the 1960s as "symbolized by Bob Dylan" (MacDonald

---

5   See Marqusee 2005, 40–42; Shumway 2009, 110; Wilentz 2010, 40–45 for examples.

1997, 26). In the following section, I examine the face of Dylan that reflects the politicized attitudes of young people from all generations, not merely his own.

"I Shall Be Free": The Face of the Expressive Youth

> Well, my telephone rang it would not stop
> It's President Kennedy callin' me up
> He said, "My friend, Bob, what do we need to make the country grow"?
> I said, "My friend, John, Brigitte Bardot,
> Anita Ekberg
> Sophia Loren." (Dylan, *The Freewheelin' Bob Dylan*, 1963)[6]

"I Shall Be Free" is a track on Dylan's second album that features a long list of now-outdated cultural touchstones and a few lyrics that refer to nothing other than an even more obscure, nuclear-fallout-centered song ("Talkin' World War III Blues") from earlier on the same album. Yet the song remains funny and, above all, fresh: though Dylan is now 72 years old and the most thoroughly established living star in popular music, the song still sounds irreverent, even bratty.

Elsewhere, I have explored in detail how this song stages its narrator's insistence on his place within the larger, established pantheon of cultural icons, from the president to athletes to activists to movie stars; his refusal to stand on received norms of hierarchy and protocol; and his grappling with the staleness of inherited language by, as Ricks and Bowden have also noted, enlivening previously dead clichés.[7] In tracing another of the narrator's resistant and youthful maneuvers, Ricks observes that in the opening stanza, the narrator matches his one-night-stand partner's subsequent exposure—"Til she started peeling off her onion gook" by exposing himself in turn, if not to her then at least to us—"I's high flyin, bare naked ... out the window" (Dylan, *The Freewheelin' Bob Dylan*, 1963, Ricks 2003, 150). In addition to speaking casually back to elders in quickened, slang-infused terms while boldly flashing through narrow openings, this narrator secures the freshness of the song by deliberately engaging the flow of time, especially the rapid currents of pop culture time, refusing to surrender to its calcifying force. He accomplishes this by speaking directly back into the pressing onrush of cultural relevance, reaching for more direct embraces than brief name-checks: in the song's final verse, for instance, Elizabeth Taylor and Richard Burton are not mere movie stars but potential interlocutors in the urgently felt discourse of tactile desire, a wished-for sexual partner and an angry cuckold, respectively, symbols to "make" and to "catch" rather than just to watch (Dylan, *The Freewheelin' Bob Dylan*, 1963).

---

[6] © 1963, 1967 by Warner Bros. Inc.; renewed 1991, 1995 by Special Rider Music.

[7] See Nainby 2011, 288–91; Ricks 1995, 366; Bowden 2001, 56–7 for further elaboration.

Similarly, Brigitte Bardot, Anita Ekberg and Sophia Loren are sex symbols, met as imagined immigrants (as future mothers?) with the witty, lascivious, phallic wink of "country'll grow." But they are also, when linked in the verse quoted above, symbols as immediately relevant and patriotically compelling as JFK himself. They are relevant and compelling symbols because all three are European stars connoting the world-leading-aspirations of a nation self-consciously called out as a still-young work in progress, a nation with much more open future than duty-bound past in the vision JFK sketched in his famous inauguration address to the "new generation" to whom "the torch has been passed" (Kennedy). As in "Hattie Carroll," for a much more light-hearted but still politically charged purpose, the narrative turns on the juxtaposition of historical situation and personal relation.

For the emerging youth counterculture of the 1960s, such a bold, confrontational stance was of singular importance. Several historians and sociologists credit Dylan's work with ushering in the confidence young people of the time needed to take political action: Zinn, discussing the cultural context that energized his own students and fellow protestors, recalls that "Bob Dylan [...] singing not only protest songs, but songs reflecting the new abandon, the new culture" was "a phenomenon unto himself [...] he offered a challenge to the old, hope for the new" (Zinn 1984, 238–9). Gitlin, then a student activist, explains the great need for youthful reinvigoration of Left-wing politics: "Because the Old Left had suffered political defeat and moral collapse in the Fifties, the New Left resolved to be a student movement and a left at the same time" (Gitlin 1987, 5). Gitlin adds that "whether he liked it or not, Dylan *sang for us*" (ibid., 197). Marshall finds that "the marker 'Bob Dylan' has often symbolized rock and the restless ideals of sixties youth" (Marshall 2007, 12–13). Lee uses the phrase that induces so much resistance from Dylan himself, "the spokesperson of a generation" (Lee 2004, 23); he then clarifies what such a hackneyed phrase specifically meant for young concertgoers in the UK in 1966:

> This is where Bob Dylan became supremely important to the lives of a whole generation, because he offered a cornucopia of influences that went way beyond anything experienced before. He became a guide, guru, and mentor for a whole generation of people [...] he introduced us to another world, and he enabled us to become part of this world without the need for a visa or passport. (ibid., 37)

In Lee's claim Dylan functions as a liminal servant introducing young listeners of the time to new knowledge. This resonates with Doggett's description of Dylan's function in a society marked by challenges to existing cultural and political foundations: "in a time of extreme turmoil, Dylan's words were regarded as having something approaching scriptural authority, as if they could be unraveled to reveal the secrets of the universe, or at least the state of contemporary America" (Doggett 2007, 7). Like the narrator of "I Shall Be Free," people reaching early adulthood in the 1960s used cultural markers—Dylan above all—to grasp and to signal their own immediate social relevance.

Rock music today continues to bear the legacy of its origins as a music of youthful impatience and impetuousness. This legacy predates Dylan: Gould maintains that "early rock n' roll songs accentuated this [Presley and blues derived] intense physicality" (Gould 2007, 103). Riley elaborates on the relevance of Presley in particular for the same counterculture generation spurred by Dylan: they were taught "not to settle for the security their parents had fought for but to take advantage of what the new world had to offer; [...] the richness they felt from their own experience—and heard in Presley's singing—demanded something more" (Riley 2002, 15–16). MacDonald locates the significance of rock'n'roll's visceral qualities in a humanizing rebellion against scientific rationalism: "science's analytical attitude and technological products came to be perceived as a threat to the realm of the imagination, provoking regular cultural revolts [and] stressing the authenticity of individual expression over dogma handed down from the past or the ruling class" (MacDonald 1997, 6). This thread of analysis shows that key 1960s' artists such as The Beatles reshaped rock'n'roll. Dylan did so as well by making rock not merely a music *for* the young, the vaguely not-yet-mature, but a music that is *of* youth, that channels the music's rhythmic push into a quite specific aesthetic marked by pushes back against expectations and pushes forward to create new ones. Marqusee maintains that in the wake of Dylan's work, "Youth must reject the categories of the past and define its own terms. Indeed, youth itself has become a touchstone of authenticity" (Marqusee 2005, 113). I discuss in a later section of this chapter how such energy is often subject to co-optation by consumer capitalism, and in another section how Dylan's body of work has always included a germ of attentiveness to the weight of history. The legacy of rock as a music of expressive youth is complicated in these ways, but rock remains an influential discourse for the reasons traced by Gould, Riley, MacDonald, and Marqusee.

Dylan's impact in particular, however, is more lasting than a "regular cultural revolt" because it permanently transforms the urgency of 1950s' rock'n'roll, giving it *gravitas* by broadening its complexity. This aesthetic is first evident in mid-1960s' albums such as *Highway 61 Revisited* and *Blonde on Blonde*. Both of these albums deploy aesthetic methods dependent on rock's "intense physicality" to sketch effective portraits of contemporary urban America from the perspective of a young, hip performer swept into the mainstream of the cultural currents he sparred with in "I Shall Be Free": Gitlin labels these portraits "nightmare surrealism" (Gitlin 1980, 202) and Gray calls Dylan's work here "a laser beam in surgery, descending from outside the sickness" and "a persona awash inside the chaos" (Gray 2002, 5). Dylan valorizes the sound of *Blonde on Blonde* as "the closest I ever got to the sound I hear in my mind [...] that thin, that wild mercury sound. It's metallic and bright gold" (Rosenbaum 2006, 208). These records are impossible to imagine without their anchoring in the physical power of rock music, a music with qualities like "wild" and "metallic." The same can certainly be said of other artists' later rock-based depictions of alienation and resistance on such records as *Never Mind the Bollocks*, *Darkness on the Edge of Town*, and *Nevermind*. Dylan's contemporary art continues this process, as Marcus names 1997's *Time Out of Mind* "a state-by-state, city-by-city guided tour of an America that has used itself up and a portrait of an American who has used up his country" (Marcus 2006, 43).

Roger McGuinn of The Byrds offers a telling shift in his terms when discussing Dylan's relationship to rock as young people's music:

> Dylan's lyrics changed the soul of pop music from undirected adolescent rebellion, to a more focused form of expression that captured the fears and dreams of youth, and led them into battle against established corruption and injustice. His music was at the forefront of a movement that made us believe we could change the world into a better place. (McGuinn 2000, 51)

McGuinn names "lyrics" in the first sentence and "music" in the second. In the following section I take up the question of the political significance of Dylan's lyrics; but I infer from McGuinn's shift in terms that he, too, feels the enduring political force of the music as distinct from the lyrics.

"One Too Many Mornings": The Face of the Pop Poet

> From the crossroads of my doorstep
> My eyes they start to fade
> As I turn my head back to the room
> Where my love and I have laid
> An' I gaze back to the street
> The sidewalk and the sign
> And I'm one too many mornings
> An' a thousand miles behind. (Dylan, *The Times They Are A-Changin'*, 1963)[8]

1964's *Another Side of Bob Dylan* is commonly cited as the album that signaled a focused, multi-year turn toward a poetics of individual expression in Dylan's work.[9] However, two songs on the previous album, *The Times They Are A-Changin'*, offered their own clues about this evolving focus. "Restless Farewell" is often read as Dylan's first public articulation of a break with the folk revival and movements (Marqusee 2005, 97–8). "One Too Many Mornings," too, marks a crossroads, apart from simply making reference to one. As I discuss above, songs like "The Lonesome Death of Hattie Carroll" and "Only a Pawn in Their Game" do strong poetic work, and evidence that Dylan's pre-1964 songwriting can be considered poetry comes from voices as authoritative as Allen Ginsberg, Maya Angelou, and

---

[8] © 1964, 1966 by Warner Bros. Inc.; renewed 1992, 1994 by Special Rider Music.

[9] See, for example, Marqusee 2005, 115–20; Shumway 2009, 112; Wilentz 2010, 77–81.

Christopher Ricks.[10] But "One Too Many Mornings" is significant because it is an early example of tightly concentrated poetic language. The hiss that persists across the stanza above ("crossroads," "doorstep," "eyes," "start," "as," "gaze," "street," "sidewalk," "sign") washes the scene in an urban—actually, quite specifically New York City—bath of intermittent nighttime steam. Only one line is free from this hiss, the moment when the narrator looks back into the room "where my love and I have laid," its liquid "l"s and vibrating "v"s and "m" humming through his memory of warmth and comfort. But memory, with its own two "m"s, is double-edged and turns again, in the refrain, into the poisoning, hiss-kissed regret of "many mornings" and "miles." The repeated "one too" beats like a march, like a two-step that the narrator longs to use to dance out of this dark place and into the metallic brightness implied by the ringing tone of "many mornings"; but, try and try again, he cannot, exhausted by the lengthening of "many mornings" each time they stretch out beyond the brief, hopeful "one too" and leave him once more "behind." The "one too" of the refrain also echoes the beckoning cry of its counterpart in "Hattie Carroll," in which we can hear "You who" as "yoo hoo," as a reaching out toward us for direct communication.

This song attests to the sharply tuned language that already laces Dylan texts, at least at times, prior to 1964. The song remains relevant in light of later themes of loss, alienation, and longing for individual freedom that become more central in the mid-1960s' work. An indication that the artist himself appreciated the song's ongoing relevance can be found in its place in the set list in his groundbreaking 1966 world tour (Dylan 1998). "One Too Many Mornings," like "Hattie Carroll" and "I Shall Be Free," frames its narrator's possibilities primarily in terms of the people and institutions that form his social environment—a past lover, a shared and now solitary bedroom, a city layered in concrete and signage. All of these become a kind of two-way mirror as they frame what the narrator can see (and cannot see) about the surrounding world and what he can see (and cannot see) about himself. In this case our attention to contingent social relations is engaged through poetic means rather than through the drama of characters in historicized contexts. "One Too Many Mornings" is persuasive because of what Gray calls, referring to the earlier poetry of "A Hard Rain's A-Gonna Fall," "the precision of the tone and the adequacy of the vision" (Gray 2002, 123).

Two rock critics (Christgau 2004, 63, Williams 1996, 16–21) and one literary critic (Bowden 2001, 1–4) each argue that Dylan songs cannot be usefully described as poetry; these authors contend that elements of musical performance are necessary components of the sense of the songs. While musical performance is indeed responsible for the force of many Dylan texts, the question of "poet" or "song and dance man" does not turn on some definitive list of mutually exclusive qualities of printed poetry or performed art, but on the way that the songs affect listeners and our sensibilities (KQED 2006, 62). Shumway acknowledges that the

---

[10]   Examples of this can be found in *No Direction Home* (interview with Ginsberg) 2005; Angelou 2000, 117; Ricks 2003.

poetry widely celebrated on Dylan's mid-1960s' records was also part of earlier texts, characterizing the value of Dylan's poetic aspirations as elevating the empty aesthetic of "pop" and the curator's aesthetic of "folk" to genuinely questing "art": "Seen in this light, Dylan declaring himself an artist was a less sweeping break with his past. But it was, nevertheless, a break, because to be an artist in the sense of Eliot or Picasso is to be something quite different than a folksinger" (Shumway 2009, 113). From another perspective, Rawlins credits Dylan with making culturally relevant the obscure aesthetic of 20th-century high art: "Bob Dylan is rescuing the art of poetry from oblivion in a way that neither Eliot nor Pound nor the American and jazz movement ever could" (Rawlins 1998, 73). Dylan's songs thus challenge us in ways that folk, pop, jazz and poetry cannot, separately, do— and the language of the lyrics is a part of this synthesizing challenge.

Listeners recognized distinct language in Dylan's songs early on: a 1962 *Sing Out!* article observed that "his method of writing places emphasis on the words, the tune almost always being borrowed or adapted from one he has heard somewhere, usually a traditional one" (Turner 1990, 25). Ginsberg claims to have wept upon hearing, for the first time, "Hard Rain" in late 1963 "with illuminated joy at what he sensed was a passing of the bohemian tradition [of the Beats] to a younger generation" (Wilentz 2010, 69). Young listeners, those who resisted mainstream values in the 1960s, shared Ginsberg's sense that Dylan's songs featured a politically significant challenge to contemporary norms that paralleled the Beats. A psychologist writing of his first encounter with Dylan's lyrics, at age 17 in 1963, remembers: "But I had a language now. [...] That morning, we had stood in the school assembly, the silence unbreakable, rigid and desperate for someone to take it all away. The same old hymns, the same old prayers [...] the clock ticking, the stages of nuclear alert, two minutes to midnight, all alone. But at least I had a language" (Miller 2000, 167–8). Another young man of the same generation recalls what stimulated his own pursuit of an education he had previously associated only with elites: "It was just Dylan. The lyrics, the whole thing of Dylan. What it did turn me on to, interestingly enough, was poetry. I mean, there I was, a working class kid, secondary modern school background, I wanted to find out more about Dylan [...] It was the poetry that I got into more ... He led me into literature, in a very intense way" (Metcalfe, quoted in Lee 2004, 96). Gitlin contends that Dylan's lyrics were themselves a kind of separate language of their own that constituted the countercultural community as such, especially in these lyrics' tone of personal and social freedom from previous norms (Gitlin 1987, 200–3). These reflections show that Dylan functioned poetically as a spark for the search for new language to explain new experiences when he began offering lyrics with concentrated imagery and tone. This parallels how he functioned musically as a flashpoint for generational aporias when he began using rock'n'roll, as discussed in the previous section. Both of these symbolic functions were highly significant in the development of 1960s' political critiques aimed at the status quo.

The influence of this face of Dylan, the "Pop Poet," is lasting in two ways. First, it has permanently raised the stakes for rock musicians who aspire to transformative work by showing that rock music can treat serious themes with serious linguistic resources. Marshall explains:

> The ideology of rock thus emerged as a way of stratifying popular music into a layer of serious music that represented individual sensibility and communal experience (rock) against lower strata subject to all the commercial manipulation and trivial meaning that the folkies so despised (pop). Rather than polemicizing *against* popular music, rock polemicizes *within* popular music [...] acknowledging the possibility of serious music within the mass media. (Marshall 2007, 11)

The second way that the "Pop Poet" endures is in the structures of rock songs themselves. Prior to rock becoming a viable commercial force for adults with buying power, mainstream popular song forms associated with radio and the recording industry were rigid in both structure and duration. This rigidity was due initially to the technological constraints of 78 rpm records and later, even after the development of microgroove technology that ushered in 33 and 45 rpm records, to the traditional marketing distinction between "pop singles" aimed at immature listeners perceived to have short attention spans and mature listeners perceived to have an interest in more established musical forms such as classical, jazz and folk (Gould 2007, 121, 198). Concomitantly, what was heard on radio was much more limited in terms of narrative force than traditional ballads, which could be molded to fit the communicative demands of the situation. Gould cites the advent of magnetic tape as an innovation that began to "decentralize the recording industry" and make recordings less formal, less driven by expensive rehearsal processes and therefore more able to capture the spirit of the moment from the performer's perspective (ibid., 19–20).

The song "Like a Rolling Stone" was a commercial landmark in this way, as it received extensive radio play despite being longer than six minutes, a duration quite rare on mainstream pop radio (Marcus 2005, 119–20). More importantly, however, Dylan's widespread use of traditional ballads resulted in songs that were more structurally complex than typical popular music (Yaffe 2009, 16–19, Marcus 2005, 119–20). In his wake, as Doggett notes, songs—with heavy radio play— followed those that were revolutionary not only in their lyrical pleas but in their structure and scope, such as "Eve of Destruction," "Ohio" and "Won't Get Fooled Again" (Doggett 2007, 7). Current trends such as internet radio and mp3 players may have fractured song delivery, making it permanently unlike the recording industry Dylan transformed; yet such trends will likely only amplify the change ushered in by expanded song forms and divergent uses of language.

Doggett connects imagistic songs in the mid-1960s to the entrenchment of the elevation of Dylan as an oracular figure who was charged with the impossible task of giving specific instructions to the counterculture (ibid., 7–8). This parallels Gitlin's claim that Dylan's lyrics were strongly linked with drug-stoked hunger for secret messages unavailable to those not in the know (Gitlin 1987, 203). In the following section, I explore how this face of Dylan, the "Rock Star," continues to shape rock politics.

"Eternal Circle": The Face of the Rock Star

> As the tune finally folded
> I laid down the guitar
> Then looked for the girl
> Who'd stayed for so long
> But her shadow was missin'
> For all of my searchin'
> So I picked up my guitar
> And began the next song. (Dylan 1991)[11]

Like many obsessive Dylan fans, I find it hard to choose a single favorite song of his; if pressed, I might choose "Visions of Johanna." But at times my favorite is "Eternal Circle" because it so gorgeously and imaginatively prefigures, from the vantage point of its 1963 authorship, Dylan's ensuing, dynamic career onstage.

Dylan is now quite famous as a songwriter and quite notorious as a songwriter who does not always cite his sources (Wilentz 2004, 265–7). Yet he considers himself primarily a performer (KQED 2006, 62). He grapples with this in the stanza quoted above: "As the tune finally folded" neatly notes that a "tune" has qualities that are not just aural but also physical. It reminds us that songs have an edge—they must end, and they sometimes cut—and that songs share qualities in common with objects that fold—like paper, on which we write, and like sheets, which cover and are covered. The placement of "guitar" and "girl" at the ends of two consecutive lines, not rhyming but triply chiming with alliteration, assonance and consonance, suggests that for the performer onstage the instrument functions as a surrogate, endowing the performer with greater power and authority while simultaneously standing in for another kind of object of desire. Two words that do rhyme are hidden, separated by a line in-between and appearing as the second word in a five-word line, the single place least likely to ring in our ears as a rhyme: "laid" and "stayed." These "wannabe" rhymes almost make the coupling work, especially given the cadence in which Dylan sings the song in its officially released version on *The Bootleg Series Volume 1*—just as the performer almost made "laid" and "stayed" parts of his connection with the "girl" (Dylan 1991).

Or was there a girl? She was not gone, exactly: "her shadow was missin'" (ibid.). The song leaves open two possibilities: first, that the performer's desire was never quite what he tells us it was, and second, that the "bullet" and "arrow" that seemed to call to him from the audience in earlier stanzas never showed him a genuinely straight path, even as his own responsive shapes "rolled" a "circle" and

---

an "echo," (ibid.). Resigned, he "picked up my guitar and began the next song," still traveling in an "eternal circle" of performative traditions—or a never-ending tour, perhaps (ibid.).

This wide-eyed young narrator stages his "eternal" relationship to a longed-for audience, and thereby defines the relationship by a performer's need for an audience member's sustained gaze. Yet the gaze a performer demands, despite the implicit interdependence, is never quite a reciprocal encounter—"circles" cannot meet "arrows" except tangentially and momentarily and never quite a permanent bond—so the audience member "was missin' for all of my seachin'" (ibid.). This relational structure at its apotheosis describes the rock star/mass audience relationship, one that Dylan could imagine in 1963, as he lived in a post-Elvis world. In the following year The Beatles would help sculpt the social role of rock star, earlier than Dylan would find himself in that role. However, Dylan opened for the role "rock star" a political meaning and not merely a socioeconomic one. He did so by self-consciously mythologizing, for the first time, the rock star's particular web of relationships to culture and to voice.

Robert Zimmerman's treatment of "Bob Dylan" as a text decoupled from his own personhood began early and extended beyond his adoption of this "stage" name: he created an entire imagined biography that he passed on to, among others, Nat Hentoff—who published it in *The New Yorker* in 1964 (Hentoff 2006, 20). This publication went forward despite the fact that nearly a year earlier, an article in *Newsweek* had provided evidence of the falsity of this same imagined biography: "In a niche of show business where 'authenticity' greatly mattered to the audience, Bob Dylan had been exposed as a mountebank," indicating not only that the "authenticity" of the folk movement was irrelevant in Dylan's deliberate construction of his public image, but that truth itself, as established in the journalistic record, was as well (Epstein 2011, 113).

Dylan actively helped the entertainment industry create the complex cultural text Marshall refers to as Dylan's "mythologized past" and his "star-image" (Marshall 2007, 152). Several members of the Greenwich Village scene early in his career independently chose Charlie Chaplin, one of the first movie stars, as a comparison for Dylan's persona even then (Nelson and Pankake 1998, 17, Epstein 2011, 91, *No Direction Home* 2005). Tamarin contends that "before our eyes, he fashioned himself into our first rock icon" (Tamarin 2009, 132). Tamarin's insight here is that, like Chaplin, Dylan was special in "fashioning himself" rather than being passively fashioned by an industry. Epstein notes Dylan's embrace of electrified arena rock: "Dylan tried to explain to interviewers—and there were many that year [1965]—that the band provided not only musical support for new songs, but moral support in the vulnerable posture one assumes in live performing" (Epstein 2011, 163–4). Marshall also emphasizes the performative and controlling dimensions of Dylan's iconic presence: "The great singers have 'authoritative voices', by which I mean that they demonstrate a total control over the song, to the point of domination or ownership. […] The great singers are those that can consistently 'take over' the song they are singing, their personality shines through the song rather than being subsumed within it" (Marshall 2007, 30–31). These gifts for authoritative command of his artistic and mediated presence enabled Dylan to forge, as with his use of rock and poetry, a place at the inception of rock stardom.

Dylan's stardom emerged in part from his staging of a particular relationship to his young audience. A remark from Lee epitomizes critics' frequent use of the term "cool" when describing Dylan's image: "In the mid-60s Dylan was the epitome of hip: he oozed cool from every pore in his body" (Lee 2004, 158). This relationship was codified by images of Dylan that situated him carefully within a cultural iconography distinctive for his hip audience, published on album covers and in magazines and filmed by a documentarian (Shumway 2009, 115–20). While earlier songwriting efforts like "Hattie Carroll" had dramatized relationships among characters in social hierarchies, now Dylan was authoring a new kind of relationship reflective of the new social hierarchy in which he lived: rock star to mass audience. Music publisher Artie Mogull holds that before Dylan, what mattered was the song itself, not the singer, and that after Dylan the industry shifted from being publisher-driven to being star-driven—an especially interesting claim given Dylan's strong association with songwriting (Mogull, quoted in *No Direction Home* 2005). The baby-boomer generation was the first to embrace rock music as an authoritative political text, as I discuss above, and "Bob Dylan" the rock star was, according to Thompson, "first and foremost" among its "heroes" (Thompson 2004, 70).

Apart from being "first," Dylan is a rock star who is unique in enduring *as* a rock star. Unlike Elvis, whose fade from cultural relevance was linear despite Vegas' efforts to narrate a series of "comebacks," and unlike The Beatles, whose reunion has been permanently deferred by the tragic early deaths of Lennon and Harrison, Dylan has managed to repeatedly reinvent himself as relevant "rock star." His 1974 "return from retirement," featuring a tour with The Band, was the first example, one paradigmatic of the rock star/mass audience relationship:

> The big difference between seeing Bob Dylan in 1963 and seeing him in 1974 is that now you could hardly see him. You could hear the band fifty yards away but as one of twenty thousand spectators in a sports arena you had no illusion of intimacy with the singer. You had the feeling he preferred it that way. (Epstein 2011, 189)

Alienating arena rock, complete with Jumbotrons in the venue itself, is one legacy—however disappointing—of Dylan the "rock star." But a concomitant legacy is signaled by another example of Dylan's reinvention of himself as politically relevant figure: the creation, and to this point continuation, of the Farm Aid concert series as a result of Dylan's onstage comment (*Farm Aid: Keep America Growing!*). This charity organization in the mainstream liberal tradition is what Doggett finds troubling about contemporary rock star activism: "Rock stars pose as radicals, and radicals as rock stars, compromising their idealism but feeding off each other's cultural power. Through it all, governments are forced to react to this unexpected coalition of forces" (Doggett 2007, 11). The notion of "governments forced to react" to the actions of popular musicians, unimaginable when Dylan first took that name, is a consequence of the modern, post-Dylan relationship between star and audience. Dylan has provided a foundation for cause-based mobilization for such later rock star activists as Peter Gabriel, Bruce Springsteen, Sting, Bono, and Thom Yorke by insisting on his personal role in constituting the star/audience relationship.

Marshall, however, argues that rock stars no longer connect with their mass audiences via the power of shared political beliefs: "Rock ceased to be something that people followed with passion and commitment and became a 'lifestyle choice' [...] rock ceased to be something one believed in but was, rather, something one consumed" (Marshall 2007, 160–1). Doggett echoes this critique of the co-optation of rock activism by consumer capitalism: "The lesson of revolutionary rock is that the music, and its idealistic ideology, was compromised and sold in the very instant that it was made" (Doggett 2007, 10). These scholars frame an important question connected to Dylan's political stance: what possibilities remain for political action through popular music? In the following section, I describe Dylan's implicit answer to this question through his latest reinvention of himself as roots music archivist.

"Song to Woody": The Face of the Radical Revisionary

> I'm out here a thousand miles from my home
> Walkin' a road other men have gone down
> I'm seein' your world of people and things
> Your paupers and peasants and princes and kings
> Hey, hey, Woody Guthrie, I wrote you a song
> 'Bout a funny ol' world that's a-comin' along
> Seems sick an' it's hungry, it's tired an' it's torn
> It looks like it's a-dyin' an' it's hardly been born. (Dylan 1962)[12]

This is the first song Dylan wrote; he claims that "I needed to write that song because I needed to sing that song, and … it hadn't been written yet" (*No Direction Home* 2005). The stanzas above reflect the song's profoundly relational stance, one in common with the stance I have traced throughout Dylan's work in this chapter. His very first song is, from start to finish, in the mode of direct address—in this case, direct address not to a general audience but to a specific individual, Woody Guthrie, an early musical obsession of his (ibid.). The narrator here narrows his perspective and acknowledges that his very own senses can perceive only what has been opened to him by Guthrie: "I'm seein' your world of people and things" (Dylan 1962). In this "world," hierarchies constraining the narrator's

---

[12]   © 1962, 1965 by Duchess Music Corporation; renewed 1990, 1993 by MCA.

choice among possibilities for response: "your paupers and peasants and princes and kings" are immediately followed by "Hey, hey, Woody Guthrie, I wrote you a song" (ibid.). Wilentz observes that in contrast to the more ambiguous later muse of "Mr. Tambourine Man," the muse this narrator addresses is a quite specific person, Guthrie himself (Wilentz 2010, 97). Thus, in his initial songwriting effort Dylan explores the contours of the unique vantage point we gain when we engage a single other person. This strategy offers us resources for listening to later songs of desperate citizens, lost loves, and surreal alienation, by encouraging us to consider our relational context prior to making claims about how we all ought to live.

Furthermore, the narrator of "Song to Woody" perceives a temporalized America in the song. Its possibilities are found in its relation to its own brief history—as this America, like Dylan in taking his first step into the vocation of songwriting inspired by Guthrie, is still a work in very early progress: it is "a-comin' along ... it's hardly been born" (Dylan 1962). Dylan attends to origins in his exploration of traditional music such as folk, blues, and gospel, as Leeder and Wells note (Leeder and Wells 2009, 211–27). He characterizes himself as distinct from other contemporary musicians because of his own historical relation to musical tradition: "My situation is peculiar. I didn't come out of the same environment. My tradition is older than all that. I came out of the environment of folk music" (Hillburn 2006, 401). He underscores the significance of this historical position for public musical performance: "Folk music is where it all starts and in many ways ends. If you don't have that foundation, or if you're not knowledgeable about it and you don't know how to control that, and you don't feel historically tied to it, then what you're doing is not going to be as strong as it could be" (Gilmore 2006, 423). Dylan's concern with origins and their weight thus pervades his approach to music.

Dylan, a notorious trickster in interviews, is not necessarily a reliable voice with respect to the political relevance of his work, and, again, he is ever wary of being linked to causes. But I find that the artist embodies his stated ideals in the specific case of exploring the enduring relevance of traditional music, and our relationship to it, as foundations for meaningful work. Marcus identifies the political implications of the engagement of traditional music on *The Basement Tapes* by Dylan and The Band, noting how personal responsibility is linked to history in ways that parallel Dylan's statements above: "[Dylan] saw a vanishing. He was present to witness an extinction, to see the last members of a species disappear. Thus it was left to him to say what went out of the world when the traditional people left the stage. [...] It's a possibility that instantly raises its own question. What will go out of the world with *you*." (Marcus 2001, 120).

The traditional music on *The Basement Tapes* is only one example of Dylan the "radical revisionary." The face is "radical" in its insistent search for its own roots and its repeated re-examination of the responsibilities that come with these roots. This face is clearly visible throughout Dylan's career: His earliest legacy as a songwriter includes developing traditional melodies and images into contemporary songs; as Harvey maintains that "through his influence, aspects of traditional music became a part of American popular music. His debt to traditional music, both in process and in repertoire, is clear, and at the same time his influence has permeated American popular culture" (Harvey 2001, xi). The "process" Harvey indexes is working with traditional songs as material, trusting in the resources of such music as a foundation for growth and change, as Marcus and Wilentz stress in discussing the traditional ballad "Barbara Allen" and its performance history as a pro-civil rights song: "Dylan's whole point [...] is that the song requires no such alterations to have this music speak of the contemporary world" (Marcus and Wilentz 2005, 15). Dylan insists: "songs to me are alive. [...] They're real songs and they're right now" (Gundersen 1998, 224).

And so, in what may turn out to be his final major persona—though of course, he may still surprise us—Dylan shows us how "right now" these songs are by sketching, in public performance via his role as "host" of *Theme Time Radio Hour*, a history of Anglo-American music. The format of the program, in which themes are introduced that unite songs from a very wide range of eras and genres, encourages listeners to consider fresh juxtapositions among artist, art, and context. The history of Anglo-American music—and, correlatively, the history of those of us who inherit this music—is thus treated as constantly in process, giving us another historicizing frame by yet another Dylan narrative voice. Though there may be some question as to who chooses the songs—in other words, who is the historian—a posting on the website *Expecting Rain* suggests how we might read Dylan's role: "Perhaps the strongest evidence of Dylan's commitment to *Theme Time Radio Hour* is the fact that he recorded the narrative for 100 episodes of the show from 2006 through 2008 during a period when he was touring, recording, and involved in numerous other projects" (Fred@Dreamtime). *Theme Time Radio Hour* re-envisions musical history because, like his songwriting, it situates particular characters and artists within historical textures. This process helps illuminate the significance of history for our current sense-making efforts. Weisbard describes these qualities in writing of Dylan eight years before the program began:

> He didn't exactly merge folk and rock: more a vast heritage of popular song with pure popcult iconography [...] Dylan has soul and blues feeling because he sang his own culture: bringing in rock, the movies, whatever was out there. [...] And that mixed up confusion of categories is a major part of his enduring originality. Within Dylan, many voices clamor for expression. (Weisbard 1998, 240)

For rock musicians looking to transform lives, the return to our shared musical legacy suggested by *Theme Time Radio Hour* is much like the model of Dylan's own "Never Ending Tour" of around 100 concerts per year, each year, since 1989: the "eternal circle" of questioning without end (*Expecting Rain*). Marcus and Wilentz claim that for Dylan, "the answer is that we will never find the answer, and never stop seeking it. And so we sing the song" (Marcus and Wilentz 2005, 16). This call to "never stop seeking" encompasses Dylan's ultimate impact on politics and rock music, his staging of the contingent relation between self and society.

Bibliography

Angelou, Maya. Quote in *Encounters with Bob Dylan: If You See Him, Say Hello*, edited by Tracy Johnson, 117. San Francisco: Humble Press, 2000.

Bowden, Betsy. *Performed Literature: Words and Music by Bob Dylan*. Lanham, MD: University Press of America, 2001.

Christgau, Robert. Excerpt from "Rock Lyrics are Poetry (Maybe)." In *Studio A: The Bob Dylan Reader*, edited by Benjamin Hedin, 62–63. New York: W.W. Norton & Company, 2004.

Cohen, John, and Happy Traum. "Interview, *Sing Out!*" In *Bob Dylan: The Essential Interviews*, edited by Jonathan Cott, 113–38. New York: Wenner Books, 2006.

Cott, Jonathan. "Interview, *Rolling Stone*." In *Bob Dylan: The Essential Interviews*, edited by Jonathan Cott, 251–70. New York: Wenner Books, 2006.

DeCurtis, Anthony. "Bob Dylan as Songwriter." In *The Cambridge Companion to Bob Dylan*, edited by Kevin J.H. Dettmar, 42–54. Cambridge: Cambridge University Press, 2009.

Doggett, Peter. *There's A Riot Going On: Revolutionaries, Rock Stars and the Rise and Fall of the 60s*. New York: Canongate, 2007.

Epstein, Daniel Mark. *The Ballad of Bob Dylan: A Portrait*. New York: HarperCollins, 2011.

Expecting Rain. "Main Page." http://www.expectingrain.com/. *Farm Aid: Keep America's Growing!*. "Past Concerts." http://www.farmaid.org/site/c. qlI5IhNVJsE/b.2723673/k.8C39/Past_Concerts.htm.

Fred@Dreamtime, *"Theme Time Radio Hour* F.A.Q." *Expecting Rain*. http://expectingrain.com/discussions/viewtopic.php?f=11&t=55690.

Gilmore, Mikal. "Interview, *Rolling Stone*." In *Bob Dylan: The Essential Interviews*, edited by Jonathan Cott, 411–28. New York: Wenner Books, 2006.

Gitlin, Todd. *The Sixties: Years of Hope, Days of Rage*. New York: Bantam, 1987.

Gitlin, Todd. *The Whole World is Watching: Mass Media in the Making and Unmaking of the New Left*. Berkeley, CA: University of California Press, 1980.

Goddard, J.R. "Times They Are A-Changin." In *The Bob Dylan Companion: Four Decades of Commentary*, edited by Carl Benson, 24–25. New York: Schirmer Books, 1998.

Gould, Jonathan. *Can't Buy Me Love: The Beatles, Britain, and America*. New York: Three Rivers Press, 2007.

Gray, Michael. *Song and Dance Man III: The Art of Bob Dylan*. London: Continuum, 2002.

Gundersen, Edna. "Dylan on Dylan: 'Unplugged' and the Birth of a Song." In *The Bob Dylan Companion: Four Decades of Commentary*, edited by Carl Benson, 223–25. New York: Schirmer Books, 1998.

Harvey, Todd. *The Formative Dylan: Transmission and Stylistic Influences, 1961–1963*. Lanham, MD: Scarecrow Press, 2001.

Hentoff, Nat. "The Crackin', Shakin', Breakin', Sounds." In *Bob Dylan: The Essential Interviews*, edited by Jonathan Cott, 13–28. New York: Wenner Books, 2006.

Hentoff, Nat. "Interview, *Playboy*." In *Bob Dylan: The Essential Interviews*, edited by Jonathan Cott, 93–112. New York: Wenner Books, 2006.

Hilburn, Robert. "Interview, *The Los Angeles Times*." In *Bob Dylan: The Essential Interviews*, edited by Jonathan Cott, 397–402. New York: Wenner Books, 2006.

Kennedy, John F. "Inaugural Address." http://www.bartleby.com/124/pres56.html.

KQED. "Television Press Conference, KQED" (San Francisco). In *Bob Dylan: The Essential Interviews*, edited by Jonathan Cott, 61–80. New York: Wenner Books, 2006.

Lee, C.P. *Like The Night (Revisited): Bob Dylan and the Road to Manchester Free Trade Hall*. London: Helter Skelter, 2004.

Leeder, Murray, and Ira Wells. "Dylan's Floods." *Popular Music and Society* 32, 2 (2009): 211–27.

MacDonald, Ian. *Revolution in the Head: The Beatles' Records and the Sixties*. New York: Henry Holt, 1997.

Marcus, Greil. *Bob Dylan: Writings 1968–2010*. New York: Public Affairs Press, 2010.

Marcus, Greil. *Like a Rolling Stone: Bob Dylan at the Crossroads: An Explosion of Vision and Humor that Forever Changed Pop Music*. New York: Public Affairs, 2005.

Marcus, Greil. *The Old, Weird America: The World of Bob Dylan's Basement Tapes*. New York: Picador, 2001.

Marcus, Greil. *The Shape of Things to Come: Prophecy and the American Voice*. London: Faber & Faber, 2006.

Marqusee, Mike. *Wicked Messenger: Bob Dylan and the 1960s; Chimes of Freedom, Revised and Expanded*. New York: Seven Stories Press, 2005.

Marshall, Lee. *Bob Dylan: The Never Ending Star*. Cambridge: Polity, 2007.

McGuinn, Roger. Quote in *Encounters with Bob Dylan: If You See Him, Say Hello*, edited by Tracy Johnson, 51. San Francisco: Humble Press, 2000.

Miller, Andy. "Series of Dreams." In *Encounters with Bob Dylan: If You See Him, Say Hello*, edited by Tracy Johnson, 166–73. San Francisco: Humble Press, 2000.

Nainby, Keith. "Free, Stuck, Tangled: Bob Dylan, the 'Self' and the Performer's Critical Perspective." *Contemporary Theatre Review* 21, no. 3 (2011): 286–301.

Nelson, Paul, and Jon Pankake. "Flat Tire." In *The Bob Dylan Companion: Four Decades of Commentary*, edited by Carl Benson, 20–23. New York: Schirmer Books, 1998.

Rawlins, Adrian. "What's Happening, Mr. Jones?" In *The Bob Dylan Companion: Four Decades of Commentary*, edited by Carl Benson, 72–75. New York: Schirmer Books, 1998.

Ricks, Christopher. *The Force of Poetry.* New York: Oxford University Press, 1995.

Ricks, Christopher. *Dylan's Visions of Sin.* New York: HarperCollins, 2003.

Riley, Tim. *Tell Me Why: The Beatles: Album by Album, Song by Song, the Sixties and After.* Cambridge, MA: Da Capo Press, 2002.

Rosenbaum, Ron. "Interview, *Playboy.*" In *Bob Dylan: The Essential Interviews*, edited by Jonathan Cott, 199–236. New York: Wenner Books, 2006.

Shumway, David R. "Bob Dylan as Cultural Icon." In *The Cambridge Companion to Bob Dylan*, edited by Kevin J.H. Dettmar, 110–121. Cambridge: Cambridge University Press, 2009.

Silber, Irwin. "An Open Letter to Bob Dylan." In *The Bob Dylan Companion: Four Decades of Commentary*, edited by Carl Benson, 26–28. New York: Schirmer Books, 1998.

Tamarin, Jean. *"Bringing It All Back Home."* In *The Cambridge Companion to Bob Dylan*, edited by Kevin J.H. Dettmar, 131–6. Cambridge: Cambridge University Press, 2009.

Terkel, Studs. "Radio Interview with Studs Terkel, WFMT" (Chicago). In *Bob Dylan: The Essential Interviews*, edited by Jonathan Cott, 5–12. New York: Wenner Books, 2006.

Thompson, Hunter S. Excerpt from "Owl Farm—Winter of '68." In *Studio A: The Bob Dylan Reader*, edited by Benjamin Hedin, 68–70. New York: W.W. Norton & Company, 2004.

Turner, Gil. "Bob Dylan—A New Voice Singing New Songs." In *Bob Dylan: The Early Years: A Retrospective*, edited by Craig McGregor, 22–27. New York: Da Capo Press, 1990.

Weisbard, Eric. "The Folk Slingers." In *The Bob Dylan Companion: Four Decades of Commentary*, edited by Carl Benson, 231–42. New York: Schirmer Books, 1998.

Wilentz, Sean. *Bob Dylan in America.* New York: Doubleday, 2010.

Wilentz, Sean. "American Recordings: On *Love and Theft* and the Minstrel Boy." In *Studio A: The Bob Dylan Reader*, edited by Benjamin Hedin, 263–73. New York: W. W. Norton & Company, 2004.

Wilentz, Sean, and Greil Marcus, eds. *Rose and the Briar: Death, Love and Liberty in the American Ballad.* New York: W.W. Norton & Company, 2005.

Williams, Paul. *Bob Dylan: Watching the River Flow: Observations on his Art-in-Progress 1966–1995.* London: Omnibus Press, 1996.

Yaffe, David. "Bob Dylan and the Anglo-American Tradition." In *The Cambridge Companion to Bob Dylan*, edited by Kevin J.H. Dettmar, 15–27. Cambridge: Cambridge University Press, 2009.

Young, Izzy. "The Missing Singer." In *The Bob Dylan Companion: Four Decades of Commentary*, edited by Carl Benson, 3–10. New York: Schirmer Books, 1998.

Zinn, Howard. *The Twentieth Century: A People's History.* New York: Harper & Row, 1984.

Discography

Dylan, Bob. "Eternal Circle." *The Bootleg Series, Vols. 1–3: Rare and Unreleased, 1961–1991*. New York: Columbia, 4680862, 1991.

Dylan, Bob. "I Shall Be Free." *The Freewheelin' Bob Dylan*. New York: Columbia, CS8786, 1963.

Dylan, Bob. "One Too Many Mornings." *The Bootleg Series, Volume 4: Bob Dylan Live, 1966: The "Royal Albert Hall Concert."* New York: Columbia, C2K 65759, 1998.

Dylan, Bob. "One Too Many Mornings." *The Times They Are A-Changin'*. New York: Columbia, CS 8905, 1963.

Dylan, Bob. "Song to Woody." *Bob Dylan*. New York: Columbia, CS 8579, 1962.

Dylan, Bob. "The Lonesome Death of Hattie Carroll." *The Times They Are A-Changin'*. New York: Columbia, CS 8905, 1963.

Earle, Steve. *Washington Square Serenade*. Los Angeles: CA, Near West Records, NW6128, 2007.

Videography

No Direction Home. Directed by Martin Scorsese. Hollywood: Paramount, 2005. DVD.

Chapter 4

Bruce Cockburn: Canadian, Christian, Conservationist

Aaron S. Allen

Since his first album was released in 1970, Canadian singer-songwriter Bruce Cockburn ("кон-bern") has produced 30 more, 20 of which have gone gold or platinum. His institutional honors includes 13 Juno awards, seven honorary doctorates, induction into both the Canadian Music Hall of Fame (2001) and the Canadian Broadcast Hall of Fame (2002), and many other honors. An official Canadian postage stamp was even issued in 2011 (see Figure 4.1). Such public recognition provides some insight into Cockburn's long, successful, and consistent career, but these facts only touch on the surface of the complex connections of identity, religion, and ethics that guide and define him.

Cockburn presents complex philosophical and aesthetic positions that go beyond typical pop-and-rock music messaging of sex, fun, and rebellion. Such a figure might not seem a likely candidate to produce so many gold or platinum albums. What is it that audiences find so compelling? Do audiences care primarily about his sound—that is, his voice, arrangements, virtuosic guitar techniques, and so on? Or is it the political messages in his poetry?

While tracing specific desires and reasons for aesthetic preferences of large groups is a slippery endeavor, there is a more specific question that interests me here: how does Cockburn engage with environmental issues and effect change? With regard to environmentally oriented popular music, David Ingram suggests that "Further research is needed in reception studies to investigate how particular pieces of music have actually affected listeners, and whether they have played a part in organizations or subcultures involved in environmental activism" (Ingram 2010, 236). While this short study cannot claim to make definitive pronouncements about either popular music in general or Bruce Cockburn in particular, I do hope to offer some insights into how we might understand him and how he engages with environmental issues.

Environmentalism is not an isolated issue for Cockburn; rather, it is part of a complex of concerns for nationality, personal religion, and humanitarianism. Cockburn's environmentalism is but one component of a broader expressive and activist agenda that links music and poetry with issues of identity, belief, and stewardship. And if we are to consider how Cockburn is a political musician—how he and his music have changed the world for the better—then we should consider his contributions in this ecological matrix.

There are no comprehensive book-length biographies about Cockburn, although he is reportedly at work on his own memoir. However, there is one master's thesis in theology that takes Cockburn as a topic (Olds 2002), and Canadian theologian Brian Walsh has written two books about Cockburn and religion (Walsh 1989, Walsh 2011). Cockburn has more often been the subject of websites, magazine articles, and book chapters. The collaborative "Cockburn Project" website (cockburnproject.net) lists all the albums, their credits and lyrics, and many of Cockburn's statements about each song from published songbooks and live interviews and concerts, as well as other primary sources, such as Cockburn's speeches and public writings. I have relied on many of the anonymous and credited submissions of fans to this website in order to flesh out my knowledge of Cockburn and his works. Further, I was fortunate to discuss him with various fans, including two that run popular websites on Cockburn and two Canadian musicians who grew up listening to him, and their reflections have also contributed to my understanding and appreciation of Cockburn.

Journalists, critics, and scholars have taken a variety of approaches to Cockburn's career. Regenstreif (2002) sees Cockburn as being a spiritual and political songwriter. Adria (1990) traces Cockburn through his "adopt[ing], in turn, the personas of happy hermit, travelling troubadour, Christian ecstatic and ... social critic." Wright (1994), in charting changes in nationalism among Canadian pop musicians in the 1960s through 1970s, locates Cockburn in the dynamic and often paradoxical relationship between musicians and Canada at this time. Rice and Gutnik (1995) seek to demonstrate that Cockburn is an artist, as opposed to an artisan, and an eclectic Canadian one at that. They categorize Cockburn's then career, from the late 1960s until the mid-1990s, into three phases: a first of bilingualism and national identity, a second of dance music and multiculturalism, and a third of world travel and north-south relations. Wright's and Rice and Gutnik's nuanced analyses are useful contributions to the following biographical overview, which situates his life and works in the context of Canadian identity, Christian belief, and conservation ethics. This last is of most interest to me, and so I also provide an ecocritical musicological analysis of Cockburn's songs in the pastoral mode.

Canadian Identity

Born on May 27th, 1945 in the Canadian capital of Ottawa and active since the late 1960s, Cockburn has come to be identified as quintessentially Canadian. After his string of successful albums in the 1970s, he was awarded in 1983 the Order of Canada, the second highest honor for Canadian civilians; in 2003 he was promoted to Officer of the Order. In 1984, one critic referred to Cockburn as "Canada's musical consciousness" (in Rice and Gutnik 1995, 249). In 2011, the Canada Post Corporation created a stamp of Cockburn to honor his lifetime of achievement: against a backdrop of ten of his song titles is a black and white image of his bespectacled visage next to the insignia of the Order of Canada. The stamp presents Cockburn as an icon of Canada.

Although he does self-identify in practice, if not always in word, as Canadian, Cockburn does not wrap himself in the maple leaf flag. Fans and critics regularly identify him as Canadian. Although a certain amount of contrast to American culture constitute his Canadian-ness, Cockburn goes beyond simple contrast to construct his national identity but does not become nationalistic. In 1971 he said:

> I'm a Canadian, true, but in a sense it's more or less by default. Canada is the country I dislike the least at the moment. But I'm not really into nationalism—I prefer to think of myself as being a member of the world ... The Canadian music scene is not yet as rotten as the US scene. But it's showing signs of catching up. (Quoted in Wright 1994, 287)

Cockburn's life in the intervening four decades has substantiated that claim. He has maintained his principal residence in Canada, moving from the outskirts of Ottawa to Toronto (1980) and then to Montreal (2001)—rather than moving, say, to New York, Nashville, London, or Paris. Furthermore, Cockburn has consistently published his English lyrics with French translations (and the occasional French language song, such as "Badlands Flashback," *Dancing in the Dragon's Jaws*, 1999); he has also written songs mixing English verses and French choruses, as with "Prenons La Mer" (*Further Adventures Of*, 1978). In doing so, Cockburn espouses the official bilingualism of Canada, which has been regulated by federal law since 1969, but which would not normally apply to poetic song lyrics. He has recorded exclusively with one Canadian label since his start, Bernie Finkelstein's True North, and has remained dedicated to the label despite changes in ownership.

Cockburn has traveled the world extensively for tours and social causes, particularly through the Unitarian Service Committee (USC) of Canada. In addition to travel to promote his albums, receive accolades, and make appearances at prestigious venues (for example, Saturday Night Live, Madison Square Gardens, and so on), he has also made numerous international tours: Central America (1983), Australia and New Zealand (1983), Europe (1986), US Solo (1988), and so on. Furthermore, he has traveled extensively for humanitarian work: Nepal (1987 and 2007), Mozambique (1988 and 1995), Cambodia and Vietnam (1999), Baghdad (2004), and so on.

In the latter half of the 20th century, the idea of a Canadian nationalist artist was a contested category, particularly in the realm of rock, pop, and/or folk music and particularly in the period after the Canadian Centennial of 1967. Robert Wright (1994) has explored the nationalist dilemma English-Canadian musicians faced ca. 1968–72, particularly regarding tensions with the mainstream American pop music industry. This period saw a flourishing of accessible Canadian popular music, but it "had less to do with homage to Canadian geographical and historical landmarks than with the extent to which it had co-opted and preserved an earlier American folk-protest tradition" (Wright 1994, 284). Many, including Cockburn and Gordon Lightfoot, Neil Young, Joni Mitchell, et al., both protested against and participated in that American system.

In addition to the multicultural policies of the federal government of Canada, led by Prime Minister Pierre Trudeau, one common element for Canadian musicians of this period was a rule promulgated by the Canadian Radio-Television and Telecommunications Commission (CRTC). Starting in January of 1970, 30 percent of all programming had to be written, performed, or produced by Canadians. Also beginning in 1970 were the Juno Awards, named for CRTC president Pierre Juneau and based on Canadian content criteria. According to Wright, "Paradoxically, however, the CRTC ruling was problematic for Canadian performers. Perhaps unexpectedly, it fostered a keen and what would become an enduring awareness in the Canadian pop music industry of the limitations of nationalism." Canadian musicians wanted to avoid appearing nationalist or sanctioned by their government, and many felt "constrained rather than liberated" (Wright 1994, 286–8).

The American folk music scene burgeoned in the 1960s and 1970s, which is just the time when Cockburn developed his style and approach to composition and performance. Between 1964 and 1966, he studied at the Berklee School of Music in Boston; he did not graduate but did receive three honors from this institution: their Songwriter's Award (1988), Distinguished Alumni Award (1994), and an Honorary Doctorate (1997). Cockburn's time in the United States studying and traveling influenced his musical style and ideology. The mainstream American music industry of the 1950s strove to be apolitical. By the time of the Vietnam War and the folk music movements of the 1960s and 1970s, however, music took on greater political resonance, particularly in the hands and voices of Pete Seeger and Bob Dylan, who were particularly influential for many Canadians, including Cockburn (Wright 1994). Canadians drew on American music industry, styles, and artists in a manner resembling Bloom's (1997) "anxiety of influence": it is neither simple copying nor complete avoidance, but rather a sophisticated style of learning that builds on and changes the model. In this case a Canadian might either succumb willingly or try to avoid completely the American model; more likely, he might want to avoid it but be helpless to do so.

Cockburn avoided mainstream American styles and the strictures of the pop market, but he nevertheless learned stylistic and political lessons from American folk music. As Cockburn explained in 1972:

> I think a lot of the songs that are being written are distinctively, if not obviously, Canadian. Playing something close to American music but not of it. I think it has something to do with the space that isn't in American music. Buffalo Springfield had it. Space may be a misleading word because it is so vague in relation to music, but maybe it has to do with Canadians being more involved with the space around them rather than trying to fill it up as Americans do. I mean physical space and how it makes you feel about yourself. Media clutter may follow. All of it a kind of greed. The more Canadians fill up their space the

more they will be like Americans. Perhaps because our urban landscapes are not yet deadly, and because they seem accidental to the whole expanse of the land. (Quoted in Wright 1994, 292)

In this statement we can see the complex relationships here: American music, or "something close to" it, is okay but Canadians should emulate Americans less. Furthermore, the urban-rural contrast is important for Cockburn's reception as Canadian and for his conservationist ideals.

Cockburn's year in Boston and other travels in the US led to his distrust of America. He felt uncomfortable being there, believed the politics and bellicose positions of the government to be reprehensible, and found the urban decay and violence disturbing. At the same time, however, he knew Canada did not have all the right answers; it was just different. Cockburn and other Canadian musicians who had similarly conflicting impulses did not express a simple anti-Americanism; rather, as Wright concludes, "they were able to judge life in America from the vantage point of the outsider and the insider simultaneously, blending toughness and sympathy in a way that was unique to the American music scene" (294). Canadian musicians like Cockburn combined numerous factors—a distaste for American society and a deep understanding of Canada, an engagement with policies such as the CRTC's nationalism and Trudeau's multiculturalism, and an appreciation of America's musical styles and protest singers—to create the Canadian national folk style of the 1960s and 1970s.

Simultaneously despite and because of his relationship with the United States, Cockburn's style was influenced by American folk styles of the 1970s: Appalachian music, white gospel, blues, jazz, and so on. Cockburn picked up some elements of his early acoustic guitar picking style from the American bluegrass musician David "Fox" Watson; such influence can be heard on *Bruce Cockburn* (1970) and *High Winds, White Sky* (1971). The title track of *Sunwheel Dance* (1971) is an instrumental piece that reflects Cockburn's learning from Watson. Cockburn's albums *Night Vision* (1973) and *Salt, Sun and Time* (1974) are infused with jazz chords, jazz instruments (for example, clarinet), and extended jazz solos. He first recorded using electric guitar, electric bass, and synthesizer in "It's Going Down Slow" (*Sunwheel Dance*), in which his distorted blues guitar style reflects the war protest of the text (Rice and Gutnik 1995).

If there are distinctive so-called "Canadian" elements in Cockburn's music, they might be traced to some general aspects of English folk songs or, more specifically, native Canadians themselves. Cockburn references First Nations peoples in text, as in his lament for their being imprisoned ("Gavin's Woodpile," *In the Falling Dark*, 1976), and in music, as with a refrain using the non-lexical vocables common to many First Nations' songs in "Red Brother, Red Sister" (*Circles in the Stream*, 1977) (Rice and Gutnik 1995). The texts of two songs included on the 2011 Canada Post stamp also resonate with Canada. "Coldest Night of the Year" (on *Resume* and *Mummy Dust*, both from 1981) cites "the Scarborough horizon" and "Yonge Street," both well-known features of Toronto. Paradoxically, "Tokyo" (*Humans*, 1980), which was written after Cockburn's tours in Japan, also resonates with Canadian-ness: the lines in the verse, "Tonight I'm flying headlong/To meet the dark red edge of dawn," and in the chorus, "Oh Tokyo—I never can sleep in your arms," both indicate going home, eastward to Canada.

Beyond American and Canadian styles and references, Cockburn draws on many national and international influences, including those he experienced close to home in Toronto. His father was a doctor and went to Europe after the war, but that perspective was not the only thing that influenced young Bruce. The Trudeau government (1968–79 and 1980–84) promoted a multiculturalism that impacted the cultural fabric of major urban centers. This multiculturalism is reflected in Cockburn's music, and it is perhaps this international musical language that most identifies Cockburn as Canadian.

Cockburn included Caribbean calypso in "Burn" (*Joy Will Find a Way*, 1975) and reggae in "Wondering Where the Lions Are" (*Dancing in the Dragon's Jaws*, 1979), "Rumours of Glory" (*Humans*, 1980), and four of the nine songs on *Stealing Fire* (1984). *Stealing Fire* includes at least two songs—both on the 2011 Canada Post stamp—that were inspired by Central American crises: "If I Had a Rocket Launcher" is stifled anger at the fate of Guatemalans along the Rio Lacantún (bordering the state of Chiapas in Mexico), while "Lovers in a Dangerous Time" is about finding beauty despite the tenuousness of life. Songs on *Stealing Fire* use various Latin American instruments and devices picked up on Cockburn's 1983 tour. Cockburn continued the use of Latin American instruments on *World of Wonders* (1986), about which he admitted: "It's true that the new songs have a more consciously internationalist sound, but that has less to do with those particular styles than with the fact that I come from a country with no musical tradition at all" (in Rice and Gutnik 1995, 250).

This sentiment is one Cockburn also expressed some ten years earlier, when he stated that, "With a few minor changes, I ripped off an Ethiopian thumb harp piece to make the guitar part" for the title track of *Joy Will Find a Way* (1975) (in Rice and Gutnik 1995, 248). On that same album are two pieces, "A Life Story" and "Arrows of Light," that reference North Indian classical music. An earlier song, "Shining Mountain" (*High Winds, White Sky*, 1971), evokes a Persian *avaz* and Turkish and Balkan meters: the unmetered introduction is played on a hammered dulcimer, a cousin of the Persian *santur*, while the metrical groupings of the song shift between two and three, referencing Turkish and Balkan traditions. Middle Eastern music is also cited in "Sahara Gold" (*Stealing Fire*, 1984), and Klezmer gets a nod in "Anything Can Happen" (*Big Circumstance*, 1988) (Rice and Gutnik 1995).

In more recent works, such widespread interests continue together with Canadian references. "Each One Lost" (*Small Source of Comfort*, 2011) is about Canadian soldiers killed in the Middle East; together with appropriate solemnity there is anger in the verse: "… all these inventions/arise from fear of love/and open-hearted tolerance and trust" which is followed by "Well screw the rule of law/we want the rule of love/enough to fight and die to keep it coming." Death and potential death (by suicide, perhaps) is explored in "Anything Can Happen" (*Big

Circumstance, 1988), in which the opening verse references the Bloor Street viaduct in Toronto. Numerous albums and live performances include guest appearances by Americans Bonnie Raitt, Ani DiFranco, and many other accomplished musicians. *Breakfast in New Orleans, Dinner in Timbuktu* (1999) references its two cities verbally and sonically: lyrics refer to Chartres Street and Kaldi's Coffee House in "When You Give It Away," and jazz and blues inspired "Down to the Delta." Various songs on *Breakfast* also use non-Western instruments: "Deep Lake" uses a dilrubā, a fretted string instrument resembling an Indian sitar but played with a bow; and "Mango," "Let The Bad Air Out," and "Use Me While You Can" all include a kora, a 21-stringed bridge harp of the Mande people of West Africa and, specifically, of Mali, in the center of which is the city of Timbuktu. In "Tibetan Side of Town" (*Big Circumstance*, 1988), various scenes from Kathmandu are described. On the instrumental "The End of All Rivers" (*Speechless*, 2005), Cockburn plays Tibetan bowl and Navajo flute. *You've Never Seen Everything* (2003) uses recordings of frogs from northern Zambia. And Cockburn goes beyond just non-Western instruments to demonstrate a broad aesthetic palate: *Life Short, Call Now* (2006) incorporates a string orchestra, and an instrumental on that album, "Nude Descending a Staircase," begins with random radio static.

By synthesizing an entire world of sound, Cockburn was being distinctly Canadian. His multicultural musical references reflect the politics of Canada from the 1970s to the 1990s, particularly under the internationalizing Trudeau government and particularly in Toronto. Rather than settle into a comfortable career writing love songs or Christian music in a system that could guarantee airplay for a Canadian musician, Cockburn expanded his horizons for artistic and political reasons, all the while not losing site of his home and native land. Fans report a certain kind of nostalgia with Cockburn's music. In part, this stems from his long career of making music and from many fans that have followed him for decades; but it also may relate to a broadening of cultural horizons that came with being a Canadian. While Cockburn could have rested on his domestic laurels and reputation as a nationalist artist, his broader outlook made him more a citizen of the world.

Christian Spirituality

Cockburn wears his religion on his sleeve, which may seem unusual for a musician not in the "Christian Rock" category. He is neither a fundamentalist, nor an evangelical, nor a mystic; rather, he is an open and committed Christian, one who does not easily fit into simple categories. Cockburn's beliefs have been the subject of intense study and interpretation (Olds 2002, Regenstreif 2002, Walsh 1989, Walsh 2011), and I do not intend to expend much further energy on the matter. My goal is, rather, to situate his spirituality as one element of the complex positions he espouses and presents to audiences; moreover, as many fans attest, there are various ways to interpret and categorize the issues in his songs, and Christianity is but one. Cockburn's spirituality mutually reinforces and is reinforced by both his global perspective as a Canadian and his conservation ethics. Together, these forces fuel Cockburn's politically informed music.

An important question here is: what, and who, defines the "Christian Rock" category? The standard musicological source for an answer, the venerable *Grove* encyclopedia, does not provide a subject entry on that or related categories, nor does it provide an entry on Cockburn. One popular website (www.drindustrial.com) that bills itself as "the ultimate online Christian rock CD database" makes no mention of Cockburn. The leading music industry trade magazine in the USA, *Billboard*, does include two charts, "Christian albums" and "Christian songs," which use data from Nielsen SoundScan and Nielsen BDS, respectively, to provide rankings. But Cockburn has never appeared on these charts, although he has appeared on other *Billboard* charts (see Table 4.1). Apple's iTunes has one relevant category, "Christian & Gospel," but it includes only one song by Cockburn: "Strong Hand of Love" on the compilation album *Strong Hand of Love: A Tribute to Mark Herd* (1994), which includes 16 other artists or groups. Twenty-seven of Cockburn's albums instead appear in the iTunes "Singer/Songwriter" category.

Cockburn may not be presented as a "Christian musician," yet he self-identifies and is recognized as a Christian and as a musician. This is itself the most telling aspect of his religious worldview: open and committed, yet not easily categorized. A variety of experiences led to Cockburn's eventual realization of his faith, and both biographical context and poetic texts contribute to understanding how he presents his ideas.

To please his Presbyterian grandmother, the Cockburn family, of Scottish descent, he attended the United Church (Adria 1990, 86). But he had no moment of conversion; rather, his realization was gradual. As he explained in 2002:

> I didn't grow up in a religious household. We were exposed to the imagery of Christianity. We went to Sunday school when we were little, that sort of thing. But it was purely for social reasons and not out of a deep faith on my parents' part. I first became aware of the need to pay attention to the spiritual aspect of life in high school when I was reading beat literature. I got introduced to Buddhism through that. It seemed to make sense to me. Later on, I flirted with a few different things. I went through a period of being interested in the occult in its various aspects and gradually evolved through all that into becoming more and more like a Christian. I became so much like a Christian that I started calling myself one. (In Regenstreif 2002, 36)

His songwriting relies on his faith as much as other experiences of his life:

> I think it's sort of the job of an artist to translate what we can understand of life into whatever form you're working in and that includes all aspects of life: the political, the romantic, the sexual and the spiritual are all fair game for subject matter for songs. Spirituality is central to everything in existence. It's central to

my understanding of the world and therefore affects what goes into the songs a lot. (ibid.)

Cockburn's musical education did not emphasize religion; rather, as a teenager he supplemented his formal studies in clarinet, trumpet, piano, guitar, and composition with his own studies of jazz guitarists (Herb Ellis, Gabor Szabo), jazz pianists (Oscar Peterson), and pop and rock music (Les Paul, Buddy Holly, Richie Valens, Elvis Presley). Late in his teen years, before and amidst his semesters at Berklee, he got into folk, particularly the music and poetry of John Lennon and Bob Dylan (Adria 1990, 86–7). Moreover, blues guitarist Mississippi John Hurt was a great source of inspiration for Cockburn, and he contributed two pieces to the compilation album *Avalon Blues: A Tribute To Mississippi John Hurt* (2005).

Cockburn says that solitude is a necessary element for his creativity. Reading Beat works, such as Kerouac's *On the Road*, and traveling in Europe and the USA encouraged Cockburn's introspectiveness. The young Bruce sought out solitude as a way of coping with his sensitivity to what he termed "another side of life." Myrna Kostash, an early chronicler of Cockburn, described him in the early 1970s as "still playing the part of the wilderness poet." That desire for solitude was personal, spiritual, and musical: his reliance on an ever-changing group of "mercenaries" as bandmates fits into that trait. Cockburn prefers to not work with the same musicians too much; his four decades of albums and tours demonstrate that, but he also says that he does not want to "settle in to certain musical habits" because he needs "to be shaken up every now and then" (in Adria 1990, 85–7). After studying at Berklee and returning to Ottawa, Cockburn was involved in a number of bands, including The Esquires, The Children, and Threes a Crowd. But by 1969, he went solo full-time and played at the Mariposa Folk Festival and in popular clubs in Toronto, Ottawa, and Montreal. During this period Cockburn connected with Bernie Finklestein, who is still his manager today (Regenstreif 2002).

Cockburn expressed his ideas of being solitary in the love song "Loner" from *Inner City Front* (1981):

> I'm a loner
> With a loner's point of view
> I'm a loner
> And now I'm in love with you[1]

He even switched into Spanish for part of a verse to establish a bit of distance from his otherwise mostly French-Canadian or English audiences (or, perhaps, the language shift was intended as some intimate message). In "Use Me While You Can" (1999), Cockburn reflects:

---

[1]   Written by Bruce Cockburn. Used by permission of Rotten Kiddies Music, LLC c/o Carlin America, Inc.

I've had breakfast in New Orleans
Dinner in Timbuktu
I've lived as a stranger in my own house, too
Dark hand waves in lamplight
Cowrie shell patterns change
And nothing will be the same again[2]

This verse also provides the line for the album as a whole, and it illustrates his loner status, distance, introspection, and role as a citizen of the world.

Adria interprets Cockburn's early career (up to the late 1980s) as going from first being a "happy hermit" then to a "travelling troubadour" and finally to a "Christian ecstatic." Such teleology, however, displays more about the interpretation and opinions of the author than it does about his subject. Nevertheless, there is no doubt that Cockburn changed, and in the early 1970s he began to shift from the poetic introspective images of the rural to more explicitly Christian references in his songs. Since then, he has regularly identified as a Christian.

Cockburn first publicly proclaimed his Christian belief in "All the Diamonds" (*Salt, Sun and Time*, 1974), a song he wrote in 1973 "the day after I actually took a look at myself and realized that I was a Christian" (in Regestreif 2002, 36). Adria observes (1990, 85) that the popular culture acceptance of religion was not unusual in this period and cites the success of the Broadway musicals *Godspell* (1971) and *Jesus Christ Superstar* (1969/1971). While Cockburn's confession is clear, it is subtler than these contemporaneous popular manifestations of Christian belief. Even before "All the Diamonds," the chorus of "My Lady and My Lord" (*Sunwheel Dance*, 1971) makes a veiled reference to religion: "Come on, come on, wind and rain/I know the sun will shine again/Till then my lady and my Lord will keep me sane." In "The Bicycle Trip" (*Bruce Cockburn*, 1970), he sang of "Shades of the eternal dancer/God has buttered the land with sunlight." However, the lyrics for "All the Diamonds" are more explicitly Christian:

All the diamonds in this world
That mean anything to me
Are conjured up by wind and sunlight
Sparkling on the sea
I ran aground in a harbour town
Lost the taste for being free
Thank God He sent some gull-chased ship
To carry me to sea
Two thousand years and half a world away
Dying trees still grow greener when you pray
Silver scales flash bright and fade

---

    [2]   Written by Bruce Cockburn. Used by permission of Rotten Kiddies Music, LLC c/o Carlin America, Inc.

In reeds along the shore
Like a pearl in sea of liquid jade
His ship comes shining
Like a crystal swan in a sky of suns
His ship comes shining[3]

Here, as with "My Lady and My Lord," nature frames spiritual belief. The clear reference to God is complemented with the subtle imagery of fish scales. The fish connects with the biblical stories of Jesus feeding the multitude and of several of Jesus' Apostles being fishermen, both literally and figuratively. Furthermore, the fish is a Christian symbol, based on the Greek acronym for Jesus: "Ichthys" ("fish").

This subtlety is a hallmark of Cockburn's poetic style. Explicit statements are common on the album *Christmas* (1993), as would be expected with covers of carols, but his own poetry is usually more obscure. As such, Cockburn's poetry is likely to be interpreted as Christian by those who want to find it, whereas those who may not express or share such faith may not be put off by it. A few examples of the many Christian references in his songs will have to suffice here.

A number of songs on *Dancing in the Dragon's Jaws* (1979) continue the mix of natural and religious imagery. Consider "Creation Dream":

Centred on silence
Counting on nothing
I saw you standing on the sea
And everything was
Dark except for
Sparks the wind struck from your hair
Sparks that turned to
Wings around you
Angel voices mixed with seabird cries
Fields of motion
Surging outward
Questions that contain their own replies[4]

On the one hand, this could be a love song. The opening track of the album, the first lines are accompanied by marimba (along with guitars and drums) and might conjure the image of a surge of love from the poet seeing his beloved, framed by some tropical ocean, hair touched by the breeze, with angelic seabirds nearby. The second verse becomes more ecstatic with references to dancing, shooting stars, power, mercury waves, and "Shots of silver in the shell-pink dawn." But the

---

[3] Written by Bruce Cockburn. Used by permission of Rotten Kiddies Music, LLC c/o Carlin America, Inc.

[4] Ibid.

title, together with various comments Cockburn made at concerts, point also to potential Christian interpretations.

Also on *Dancing*, "Northern Lights" has more explicit references, but the set-up in the song shies away from being preachy and thus allows for other interpretations. Three statements of "Sunday night and it's half past nine" are followed by "I'm leaving one more town behind"; the pattern repeats with the three-fold statements of subsequent verses, describing what seems to be a nighttime drive during which the "Stars are pinned on a shimmering curtain of light." But then: "I've been cut by the beauty of jagged mountains/And cut by the love that flows like a fountain from God." The nature imagery and reference to a relatively common experience (the grandeur of a night sky) soften the explicit Christian reference to "God" late in the song (preceded elsewhere with "heaven"), but the poignancy of belief still comes through.

"Wondering Where the Lions Are" (also from *Dancing*) is another song from the 2011 stamp. It mixes nature, ethics, and the spiritual:

> Walls windows trees, waves coming through
> You be in me and I'll be in you
> Together in eternity
> Some kind of ecstasy got a hold on me
> …
> Young men marching, helmets shining in the sun,
> Polished as precise like the brain behind the gun
> (Should be!) they got me thinking about eternity
> Some kind of ecstasy got a hold on me[5]

Cockburn reports that the song, which went on to be featured on an episode of the television program *ER* in 1999, was inspired by a conversation that he had with a relative who worked for the government and feared an impending Sino-Russian nuclear war (Ladouceur 2003). The liner notes to the album also indicate the importance of British novelist Charles Williams, perhaps his *The Place of the Lion*, which deals with spiritual strength.

Big Circumstance (1988) includes at least three songs with Christian references, one of which caused a bit of a stir. In "Shipwrecked at the Stable Door," Cockburn says the album title twice, which functions as a sort of fate (or deity) amidst vague references to the crèche (nativity scene). The fourth and final verse of "Shipwrecked" contains clear references to the Sermon on the Mount from the Gospel of Matthew:

> Blessed are the poor in spirit
> Blessed are the meek

---

[5]   Written by Bruce Cockburn. Used by permission of Rotten Kiddies Music, LLC c/o Carlin America, Inc.

For theirs shall be the kingdom
That the power mongers seek
Blessed are the dead for love
And those who cry for peace
And those who love the gift of earth
May their gene pool increase[6]

In the liner notes to the album, Cockburn acknowledged Brennan Manning's book *Lion & Lamb: The Relentless Tenderness of Jesus*, which includes a chapter "The Shipwrecked at the Stable." In "Where the Death Squad Lives," Cockburn ends with a positive outlook—"This world can be better than it is today/You can say I'm a dreamer but that's okay"—but the previous five verses are bleaker. The song begins:

Goons in blackface creeping in the road
Farm family waiting for the night to explode
Working the land in an age of terror
You come to see the moon as the bad news bearer
Down where the death squad lives[7]

He acknowledges that "It'll never be a perfect world till God declares it that way/ But that don't mean there's nothing we can do or say." Other Christian references in the song include a mention of a "never-ending Easter passion" and a reassurance that "Bombs aren't the only things that fall from above."

A third song from *Big Circumstance*, "Gospel of Bondage," caused a bit of a stir due to its explicit critique of the so-called "Religious Right":

We're so afraid of disorder we make it into a god
We can only placate with state security laws
Whose church consists of secret courts and wiretaps and shocks
Whose priests hold smoking guns, and whose sign is the double cross
But God must be on the side of the side that's right
And not the right that justifies itself in terms of might
Least of all a bunch of neo-Nazis running hooded through the night
Which may be why He's so conspicuously out of sight
Of the gospel of bondage …[8]

Cockburn told his audiences that this song was his "way of saying 'fuck you' to them," that is, Pat Robertson (the "grinning skull") and his ilk ("scum-bags") (in Richardson 1988). He may be a Christian, but Cockburn is particular about the kind

---

[6]   Written by Bruce Cockburn. Used by permission of Rotten Kiddies Music, LLC c/o Carlin America, Inc.

[7]   Ibid.

[8]   Ibid.

of Christians with whom he is associated. He also recognizes multiple Christian perspectives—perhaps on a spectrum from progressive (him) to fundamentalist (them).

On *Breakfast in New Orleans, Dinner in Timbuktu* (1999), a number of songs continued Cockburn's typical less confrontational, more subtle, but no less sincere religious infusions. In "When You Give It Away," Cockburn's lyrics allow for sacred and secular interpretations simultaneously:

> Deep in the city of the saints and fools
> Pearls before pigs and dung become jewels
> I sit down with tigers, I sit down with lambs
> None of them know who exactly I am[9]

Here the loner is talking about New Orleans and alters the biblical verse from the Sermon on the Mount (Gospel of Matthew) that is usually translated as "pearls before swine." Yet for those unfamiliar with the Bible, the verse might also reference the comic strip by Stephan Pastis called *Pearls Before Swine*, or even the quip by American poet and writer Dorothy Parker: after being told "age before beauty" when a door was held open for her, she replied "pearls before swine" and walked through. Another song on *Breakfast*, "Look How Far," is ostensibly about an encounter with Ani DiFranco, but many of its words and phrases—"Glasses of wine on a crate between us/Catch the light—seem to glow from within," "Like you're lit up from within," "And this is simple/And this is grace," and the refrain in the chorus "Look how far the light came"—could be interpreted in a generically religious way. The song "Embers of Eden" also mixes the title's explicit Christian references with a love song ("Your lips were hot and my shocked heart screamed") together with a view of planet earth from space:

> And the embers of Eden burn
> You can even see it from space
> And the great and winding wall between us
> Seem to copy the lines of your face[10]

That refrain, sung twice, hints at those well-known sights visible from so far away: the Great Wall of China and burning forests.

Written after a trip to Iraq, *Life Short, Call Now* (2006) includes songs, such as "This is Bagdad" and "Mystery." In the latter, Cockburn exhorts his listener to "Grab that last bottle full of gasoline"; such a line might resonate more with the theme of the war in the Middle East, but the only repeated verse includes "You can't tell me there is no mystery" and "And don't tell me there is no mystery/

---

[9]   Written by Bruce Cockburn. Used by permission of Rotten Kiddies Music, LLC c/o Carlin America, Inc.

[10]   Ibid.

It overflows my cup." Together with references to a "Shaman" and "Star-strewn space," he again opens up the text for interpretations from multiple perspectives. Another song continues this trend: "To Fit in My Heart" mentions "Wave forms" and observes that "Seas come, seas go/Where they stood deserts flow" in the first two verses, while the third verse reads "Spacetime strings bend/World without end/God's too big to fit in a book." The refrain for all three verses is "Nothing's too big to fit in my heart." Here the biblical reference is from "Saecula saeculorum" ("Age of ages" or "World without end"), the ending words of many Christian doxologies; amidst the nature imagery, Cockburn also references secular science and love, and the idea of love could be either sacred or secular.

Of Cockburn's over 300 songs and more than 30 albums, the selections here are but a small and selective sampling. One could have, perhaps, chosen other songs to represent the more devout or more secular sides of Cockburn, but I find that his ability to appeal to both sides in explicit and subtle ways is part of the successful messaging in his music.

Despite the clear Christian elements of his poetry and in his life, Cockburn's spirituality has continually evolved and drawn on non-Christian religious practices. In his late teens and early 20s, Cockburn explored Buddhism and the occult, and he has read widely in fiction and non-fiction Christian writings by modern writers. But he has also returned to Buddhism and Sufism. Cockburn summarizes his openness and respect for multiple perspectives:

> In the end, I think it comes down to language, culture and modes of thinking. We're all heading for the same place and we're all after the same thing. We have, for many different reasons, different ways of expressing or getting at it, but the crux of the matter is do we, or do we not, have a relationship with the divine. If we do have one, what is it? It's the attempt to try and understand what it is that is the journey. (In Regenstreif 2002, 37)

And journeys have been a significant part of Bruce's experiences to understand the world and spirituality and to express himself as an artist. In addition to his worldwide touring, he has traveled extensively for humanitarian purposes to be a witness and voice of conscience. In 1983, he visited Central America for the international relief agency Oxfam; the experiences of refugees that he conveyed in his songs on *Stealing Fire* (1984), especially "If I Had a Rocket Launcher," were so powerful that it shocked those who thought he was a gentle Christian troubadour (Regenstreif 2002, 37). He has also worked with the International Campaign to Ban Landmines, which organization was a co-laureate of the 1997 Nobel Peace Prize. The song "Mines of Mozambique" (*The Charity of Night*, 1996) reflects his involvement with that organization and a trip he made to that country in 1995. The second verse illustrates the problem as understood through his compassionate lens:

> There's a wealth of amputation
> Waiting in the ground

> But no one can remember
> Where they put it down
> If you're the child that finds it there
> You will rise upon the sound
> Of the mines of Mozambique[11]

One further example, included on the 2011 stamp, is the title track from *Waiting for a Miracle* (1987). The strained voice seems to express the impatience of searching for peace, for shelter from the "hot sun":

> Somewhere out there is a place that's cool
> Where peace and balance are the rule
> Working toward a future like some kind of mystic jewel
> And waiting for a miracle[12]

Cockburn wrote this song after his second trip to Nicaragua—as if he knew they too were waiting for a stop to the bloodshed.

One of Cockburn's long-standing affiliations has been with the international development and aid agency the Unitarian Service Committee (USC) of Canada; that involvement reflects both his commitment to a religious organization and his ethical desire to help. He says that, "their overhead was low and that the money you gave actually went where it was supposed to go, and so I donated money, and I kept on doing it" (in Young 2007, 40). He traveled to Nepal twice with the USC, in 1987 and 2007; he worked with them on the landmine issue; and they collaborated on a film regarding desertification in Mali. His open and committed Christianity connects to his global perspective as a Canadian and his ethics of conservation.

Conservationist Ideals

In addition to publicly proclaiming his spirituality to the public, Cockburn's "All the Diamonds" also indicated his conservationist ethics when he sang, "Two thousand years and half a world away/Dying trees still grow greener when you pray." These two lines encapsulate the fundamentally optimistic perspective that Cockburn brings to his music, message, and activism. They also touch on each of the three elements on which I have focused. First, Cockburn's global Canadian perspective is indicated by his orienting himself "half a world away"; I interpret this as his being in Canada yet referring to Jerusalem (or perhaps the Holy Land in general of the eastern Mediterranean). Second, his spirituality comes through

---

[11]   Written by Bruce Cockburn. Used by permission of Rotten Kiddies Music, LLC c/o Carlin America, Inc.

[12]   Ibid.

clearly with the exhortation to "pray." And third, Cockburn's environmentalism is expressed in his lament for "Dying trees" and hope for them to "grow greener."

In 2010, Cockburn received Earth Day Canada's Outstanding Commitment to the Environment Award. This recognition acknowledges his decades of working for and singing about the natural world. Since the 1980s he has participated in and donated time and money to environmental causes, such as the Haida Nation's land claims, as referenced in the song "Stolen Land" (*Waiting for a Miracle*, 1987), and the anti-logging fights in the Stein River Valley, both in British Columbia. In the mid-1990s, he was honorary chairperson of Friends of the Earth Canada. In his album *Dart to the Heart* (1994), he includes the following appeal in the liner notes:

> The ozone layer is being depleted. UV-B radiation is on the increase. The threat to our food supply, to animals, to our health, becomes more ominous by the minute. If this scares you as much as it does me, you might consider contacting: Friends of the Earth, we are an international organization working hard on ozone protection, as well as other environmental issues.

In his 1997 acceptance speech for the honorary doctorate Berklee College of Music awarded him, Cockburn cited a litany of issues that he wanted the students to address: "Land mines, the quality of life for inner city folks, loss of the ozone layer, the treatment of migrant workers, the depletion of the earth's resources, social atrocities like the School of the Americas—it's an endless list. Endless but not overwhelming. Just pick one you relate to and kick ass."

In a 1999 collaboration with the USC, Cockburn was the subject of the hour-long television documentary *River of Sand*, which chronicled desertification in Mali and featured him interacting with local musicians. Some musical upshots from the event were included in the album *Breakfast in New Orleans, Dinner in Timbuktu* (1999). More recently, he has signed on to public protests against oil pipelines in Canada, and in 2005 at the United Nations Summit for Climate Control in Montreal he performed his anthem "If a Tree Falls" (*Big Circumstance*, 1988).

That song was featured on the David Suzuki sponsored album, *Playlist for the Planet* (2011), which was a celebration of the Canadian environmentalist and educator's 75th birthday, a fundraiser for his foundation, and an attempt to develop environmental anthems. Over 600 musicians and ensembles submitted songs on which the public voted. The final "Playlist" represented 12 winners. The album on iTunes included 18 bonus tracks, the first of which was Cockburn's. Suzuki and Cockburn worked together a number of times in the past decade, including fundraiser events for the USC; Suzuki even participated (with Gordon Lightfoot) in Cockburn's 2001 induction into the Canadian Music Hall of Fame.

While Cockburn is certainly known for his celebrity involvement in conservationist causes, his environmentally themed music has reached an even larger audience. His most popular environmental song is "If a Tree Falls," one of the dozen or so titles that Cockburn made into music videos. The video, which begins with a "whole earth" shot of the planet and zooms in to the upper Amazon, presents scenes of the pristine forest and native peoples contrasted with logging and deforestation while Cockburn renders the verses in spoken word:

> Rain forest
> Mist and mystery
> Teeming green
> Green brain facing lobotomy
> Climate control centre for the world
> Ancient cord of coexistence
> Hacked by parasitic greedhead scam
> From Sarawak to Amazonas
> Costa Rica to mangy B.C. hills
> Cortege rhythm of falling timber.
> What kind of currency grows in these new deserts,
> These brand new flood plains?[13]

Cockburn invokes his internationalist perspective (Sarawak in Malaysia, Amazonas in South America, Costa Rica in Central America, and the "mangy B.C. hills" in Canada), spiritual side ("mist and mystery"), and conservationist ethic and desire to protest against the "parasitic greedhead scam" of corporations. He even adds a touch of punning on the musical "chord" and the wood measurement "cord." But then the philosopher comes through when he sings the chorus, at which point in the video he is finally visible, in stark contrast to the proceeding images, with his electric guitar and in black leather:

> If a tree falls in the forest does anybody hear?
> Anybody hear the forest fall?[14]

Returning to spoken word, he injects just a little appropriate pedanticness, reinforced with associated images in the video, for the next verse:

> Cut and move on, Cut and move on
> Take out trees
> Take out wildlife at a rate of species every single day
> Take out people who've lived with this for 100,000 years
> Inject a billion burgers worth of beef
> Grain eaters—methane dispensers.[15]

---

[13]   Written by Bruce Cockburn. Used by permission of Rotten Kiddies Music, LLC c/o Carlin America, Inc.

[14]   Ibid.

[15]   Ibid.

Without an intermediate chorus, the final verse jumps to emphasize the poetic message that music can convey so well:

> Through thinning ozone,
> Waves fall on wrinkled earth
> Gravity, light, ancient refuse of stars,
> Speak of a drowning
> But this, this is something other.
> Busy monster eats dark holes in the spirit world
> Where wild things have to go
> To disappear
> Forever[16]

A final repetition of the chorus sends the message home. In this song, Cockburn mixes seamlessly the many aspects of his poetic career: the nature images flow between and among spiritual reverence for the mysteries of the word and real world problems. "If a Tree Falls" did not spring *ex nihilo*; it is a logical culmination of Cockburn's Canadian perspective on nature, his spirituality, and his desire to leave the world a better place.

Nor is "If a Tree Falls" an isolated venture. He used the contrast of spoken and sung in other songs (for example "Look How Far," "Use Me While You Can," "When You Give It Away"), and many other songs express his environmentalist perspective. "The Embers of Eden" make reference to burning rainforests. "Down where the Death Squad Lives" compared deforestation to senseless killing of people. Cockburn associated the instrumental "The End of All Rivers" with the sea, but at a 2006 concert wondered "is a river still a river if there is nothing to swim in it?" Cockburn wrote "Radium Rain" (*Big Circumstance*, 1988) after his visit to Germany just after the Chernobyl disaster; in the song, the refrain laments "Ain't it a shame/Ain't it a shame/About the radium rain," while the second verse warn us: "don't eat anything that grows and don't breathe when the cars go by." The anger comes out in the third verse, with "I walk stiff, with teeth clenched tight, filled with nostalgia for a clean wind's kiss," while the final verse concludes:

> A flock of birds writes something on the sky in a language I can't understand
> God's graffiti—but it don't say why so much evil seems to land on man
> When everyone I meet just wants to live and love, and get along as best they can
> Ain't it a shame[17]

And in "Gavin's Woodpile" (*In the Falling Dark*, 1976), Cockburn muses while splitting firewood; the third verse references a local Ontario environmental issue:

---

[16]   Written by Bruce Cockburn. Used by permission of Rotten Kiddies Music, LLC c/o Carlin America, Inc.

[17]   Ibid.

I remember crackling embers
Coloured windows shining through the rain
Like the coloured slicks on the English River
Death in the marrow and death in the liver
And some government gambler with his mouth full of steak
Saying, "If you can't eat the fish, fish in some other lake.
To watch a people die—it is no new thing."[18]

The liner notes report that the Reid Paper Company polluted the English River. The song concludes with optimism: "The earth is bread, the sun is wine/It's a sign of a hope that's ours for all time."

The *Playlist for the Planet* project was preceded by another socially and environmentally oriented project, the compilation album *Honor: Benefit for the Honor Earth Campaign* (1996). Cockburn's contribution was "Wise Users," a critique of the anti-government "wise use movement," which is less an organized movement and more an anti-environmentalist position advocating stewardship of nature purely for human benefits. The five verses are separated with the repeated chorus:

Use it wisely ... go on
Reap your harvest, Wise Users
'Til everything is gone[19]

Cockburn's anger is evident in the verses that might evoke the same kind of surprise as "If I Had a Rocket Launcher." He begins "Wise Users" by calling out his opposition:

Hear me you business blackmailers
When I see what you've done to the wild
I feel like a man standing over
The corpse of his murdered child[20]

The environmentalist concerns come out in the second verse:

Haul the last fish from the ocean
Poison the beds where they spawn
Drag the last tiger to market
So some prick can stand tall in Taiwan[21]

---

[18]   Written by Bruce Cockburn. Used by permission of Rotten Kiddies Music, LLC c/o Carlin America, Inc.

[19]   Ibid.

[20]   Ibid.

[21]   Ibid.

The third and fourth verses express his anger, "I'd take your wallet and spit right in your eye," and even go so far as to suggest the wise users commit suicide: "If I gave you a gun with one bullet." Unusual for Cockburn, the optimist does not win out; rather, resolute anger continues in the final verse:

> And yes, I believe there is beauty
> And yes, I believe in truth
> And in the seemingly infinite hunger
> Of humans for destroying them both[22]

In addition to Cockburn's conservationist perspective—his desire to point out environmental problems and the need to address them—he also is a keen observer of nature. Many of his early songs render this perspective; the text of "When the Sun Falls" (*Sunwheel Dance*, 1971) is a particularly concentrated example:

> When the sun falls
> The bird of paradise
> Spreads his wings wide
> When the rain shines
> The earth sighs gratitude
> And spreads her hues bright
> You come to me
> Bringing the sun and rain
> Bringing my song[23]

And it is Cockburn's interest in nature—in documenting it, poetically conveying emotions about it, and exhorting engagement with the problems that both it and humans face—that brings us to a broader examination of his work as a pastoral poet and musician.

Ecomusicology is the study of the dynamic relationships between music, culture, and nature; it often draws on the field of literary ecocriticism, which considers the human-environment relations imagined and portrayed in cultural products such as literature and poetry (Allen 2013). Ecocritics have been particularly interested in environmental ideologies, such as the pastoral, a perspective common in environmentally themed literature and music (Ingram 2010, Allen 2011). Cockburn's pastoral texts are thus ripe for ecomusicological analysis. What kind of pastoral worlds do Cockburn's songs imagine? Do they tell us about his conceptions of nature? And do such perspectives help us understand how he may have changed or imagined changing the world?

---

[22] Written by Bruce Cockburn. Used by permission of Rotten Kiddies Music, LLC c/o Carlin America, Inc.

[23] Ibid.

Lawrence Buell defines the "[t]raditional pastoral, dating from the poetry of Theocritus, [as] a stylized representation of rusticity in contrast to and often in satire of urbanism, focusing in the first instance on the life of shepherds" (Buell 2005, 144). Cockburn's music, life, and reputation fit into this idea of the pastoral. His song texts and musical materials often provide urban-rural contrasts. Cockburn initially fled from the city to the country, but later moved from his rural home to urban environs; once in the city (Toronto, Montreal), he continued to visit the country—in person and via his songs. Considering not only his personal and musical confessions of faith, students of Cockburn can find a place for understanding their bard in a different pastoral sense: Theocritus' Greek sheep herder in pastoral poetry becomes instead God's messenger in the Bible. The metaphor of the shepherd, or "pastor," tending his flock, or congregation, can be extended to the singer-songwriter offering spiritually uplifting messages for his audiences—be those messages about multiculturalism, spirituality, or the environment.

Such reflection on worldly and spiritual life relates to another aspect of the pastoral that Buell identifies: the genre of the pastoral "may direct us toward the realm of physical nature, or it may abstract us from it" (Buell 1995, 31). As with many musical experiences, there is contradiction in Cockburn's pastoral music: it is usually experienced in large social situations (concerts) or via technological mediation (stereos) often indoors.

The tradition of the pastoral is millennia long, and there are various archetypes of Arcadian pastoral (for example those presented by Gifford 1999). Buell and Leo Marx, however, have elaborated on four types of pastoral relevant for understanding Cockburn. First, pastoral nationalism is a way of understanding the hinterlands of one's own country, in contrast (or even similar) to how European colonial lands were understood in pastoral terms (Buell 2005, 144). Second, pastoral outrage relates to concerns of landscape degradation in the context of environmental justice advocacy (Buell 2005, 15). The third and fourth types of pastoral relevant for considering Cockburn come from an often cited (and critiqued) theory of the pastoral: Leo Marx's *Machine in the Garden* (Marx 1964), which David Ingram's *Jukebox in the Garden* (Ingram 2010) expanded with regard to music. Marx outlined two types of pastoral: the simple or "popular and sentimental" pastoral, and the "imaginative and complex" pastoral (ibid., 5). The simple pastoral reflects feeling: "the felicity represented by an image of a natural landscape, a terrain either unspoiled or, if cultivated, rural" (ibid., 9); and/or a movement "away from the city and toward the country" (ibid., 10). That simple pastoral is essentially the "garden" of Marx's title; the complex pastoral, however, introduces the machine into that space: "What begins as a conventional tribute to the pleasures of withdrawal from the world—a simple pleasure fantasy—is transformed by the interruption of the machine into a far more complex state of mind" (ibid., 15). The complex pastoral presents "the illusion of peace and harmony in a green pasture" (ibid., 24). Although Ingram does not make his critique of Marx explicit, the former's *Jukebox in the Garden* is a corrective to Marx's notion that the simple and complex pastoral were indicated by low and high culture, respectively (Ingram

2010, 11–12ff, 54ff). Ingram's work shows that popular music can express the complex pastoral, and Cockburn's music illustrates that point well.

The four categories of the pastoral—simple, national, outrage, and complex—find resonance in Cockburn's works. Simple pastorals are most evident in the nature imagery of songs like "When the Sun Falls," but they crop up in small moments of other songs as a fleeting image, as in "All the Diamonds." The national pastorals are his homage to the Canadian landscapes and other locales (New Orleans, Timbuktu, Tokyo) on albums such as *Breakfast* and songs such as "Gavin's Woodpile" and "Red Brother, Red Sister." Pastoral outrage finds a place in "If a Tree Falls," "Wise Users," and "Radium Rain." The complex pastoral describes Cockburn's work and career as a whole: beautiful, spiritual music, tinged with anger and outrage at the injustices of the world.

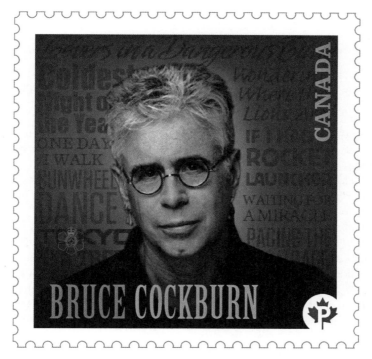

Figure 4.1   Canadian Stamp Honoring Bruce Cockburn
Source: © Canada Post, 2011.

Cockburn's Complexity

Cockburn's passions go beyond conservation, he believes in more than just Christianity, and he is more than a Canadian artist. His words and deeds plead

Table 4.1   Cockburn on *Billboard* Charts (from www.billboard.com, accessed 27 December 2011)

Album/"Song"	Chart Name	Peak on Chart	Time on Chart
Small Source of Comfort (2011)	Folk Albums (2011)	7	3 weeks
Speechless (2005)	Jazz Albums (2005)	14	17 weeks
"If a Tree Falls" (1988)	Alternative Songs (1989)	20	8 weeks
"Wondering Where the Lions Are" (1979)	Hot 100 (1980)/Adult Contemporary (1980)	21/22	17 weeks/13 weeks
"A Dream Like Mine" (1990)	Alternative Songs (1991)	22	—
Stealing Fire (1984)	Billboard 200 (1985)	74	15 weeks
"If I Had a Rocket Launcher" (1983)	Hot 100 (1985)	88	3 weeks
World of Wonders (1986)	Billboard 200 (1986)	143	7 weeks
Dart to the Heart (1994)	Billboard 200 (1994)	176	2 weeks
The Charity of Night (1996)	Billboard 200 (1997)	178	1 week
Big Circumstance (1988)	Billboard 200 (1989)	182	7 weeks

for love and human rights and against militarism and corporate greed around the world. Neither spiritual nor environmental music are new, but Cockburn brings his global audiences a complexity of positions that goes beyond simplistic pop-music messaging.

Cockburn's music itself—sounds, texts, performances—is sometimes complex. The *New York Times* has hailed his "quiet virtuosity" on the acoustic guitar, and guitar aficionados regularly extol his talents. One fan I interviewed said, "It was as a guitarist first and humanist second" that he was drawn to Cockburn; his unique approach to the guitar was greater than his influence as "a citizen," particularly in the "use of my right thumb," which is treated "as a separate instrument" in order to "cultivate its independence from the rest of the hand." This kind of complex virtuosity—as a composer, poet, and performer—goes against the grain of typical pop folk music, just as his complex positions are not easy to simplify or fit into neat categories such as "Canadian," "Christian," or "environmentalist," or in genres such as "folk," "rock," or "political."

Can such complexity lead to change, particularly regarding pressing environmental issues, or is it just a form of (post)modern art? Regenstreif (2002, 38) observed that, "As a listener, I've often found that political songs, by Bruce and by others, have sparked an interest in an issue or helped to clarify my feelings." He asked Cockburn about making a difference through writing and performing, and Cockburn replied:

> I don't know how much I've been able to contribute in terms of ideas for improving things, but it's certainly easy enough to react strongly to the things

that are around us and it's that kind of strong emotional reaction that tends to produce songs for me. For me, it takes some kind of personal contact with an issue for a song to be born and the song is really just how I feel about it. I hope in exposing that to people, and in sharing my feelings with people, that they might be inspired to look around and see and wonder if that's right. Sometimes it works, sometimes it doesn't, but the original motive for writing those songs is exactly the same as writing a love song or a song about spiritual things or anything else. It's just what's happening.

Cockburn's witnessing and telling stories indeed impacts his listeners. In my conversations with fans, all agreed that, while he may have been an "incidental activist" (according to one) or communicating with people who "shared similar beliefs anyway" (according to another), Cockburn was someone who increased awareness of emotional, identity, political, environmental, and humanitarian issues. While such awareness-raising may not be the same as changing behaviors, it is an important precursor. Cockburn does not preach about the problems and insist we do something, but nor does he ignore entirely the issues that concern him. Rather, through his complex positions—his personal identity, the problems to which he has dedicated himself, and his poetry and music—he affects and opens us to believe in a better world, to raise our voices individually and collectively, and to ask for change.[24]

Bibliography

Adria, Marco. *Music of Our Times: Eight Canadian Singer-Songwriters*. Toronto, Ontario: Lorimer, 1990.

Allen, Aaron S. "Ecomusicology." *The Grove Dictionary of American Music*. 2nd ed. New York: Oxford University Press, 2013.

Allen, Aaron S. "Symphonic Pastorals." *Green Letters* 15 (2011): 22–42.

Bloom, Harold. *The Anxiety of Influence: A Theory of Poetry*. 2nd ed. New York: Oxford University Press, 1997.

Buell, Lawrence. *The Environmental Imagination: Thoreau, Nature Writing, and the Formation of American Culture*. Cambridge, MA: Harvard University Press, 1995.

Buell, Lawrence. *The Future of Environmental Criticism: Environmental Crisis and Literary Imagination*. Malden, MA: Blackwell Publishers, 2005.

Gifford, Terry. *Pastoral*. London and New York: Routledge, 1999.

Ingram, David. *The Jukebox in the Garden: Ecocriticism and American Popular Music Since 1960*. Amsterdam, New York: Rodopi, 2010.

---

24   My thanks to Gavin Douglas, Bernie Finkelstein, Daniel Keebler, David Newton, Mark Pedelty, Jennifer C. Post, Kailan Rubinoff, Arminda Trevino, and Kristine Weglarz.

Ladouceur, Liisa, "Songs That Stick with Us: 'Wondering Where the Lions Are'," *Words & Music 10*, no. 4 (2003).

Marx, Leo. *The Machine in the Garden: Technology and the Pastoral Ideal in America*. New York: Oxford University Press, 1964.

Olds, Peter. "Questions That Need Answers: An Examination of the Roles of Context and Art in Theology with Specific Reference to the Music of Bruce Cockburn." *MTheol*, University of Auckland, 2002.

Regenstreif, Mike. "Bruce Cockburn: On Spirituality, Activism & Music." *Sing Out! The Folk Song Magazine*, Summer 2002.

Rice, Timothy, and Tammy Gutnik. "What's Canadian About Canadian Popular Music? The Case of Bruce Cockburn." In *Taking a Stand: Essays in Honour of John Beckwith*, edited by Timothy J. McGee, 238–56. Toronto, Ontario: University of Toronto Press, 1995.

Richardson, Derek. "Pop Proselytizing: Bruce Cockburn. At Zellerbach Hall, U.C. at Berkeley, Friday, Feb. 27th." *San Francisco Bay Guardian,* March 9, 1988.

Walsh, Brian J. *Kicking at the Darkness: Bruce Cockburn and the Christian Imagination*. Grand Rapids, MI: Brazos Press, 2011.

Walsh, Brian J. *The Christian Worldview of Bruce Cockburn: Prophetic Art in a Dangerous Time*. Toronto: Institute for Christian Studies, 1989.

Wright, Robert A. "'Dream, Comfort, Memory, Despair': Canadian Popular Musicians and the Dilemma of Nationalism, 1968–1972." In *Canadian Music: Issues of Hegemony and Identity*, edited by Beverley Diamond and Robert Witmer, 283–301. Toronto, Ontario: Canadian Scholars Press, 1994.

Chapter 5
Billy Bragg: Mixing Pop and Politics

Douglas M. McLeod

Never one to bury his viewpoints in the vagaries and vicissitudes of evasive word play, Billy Bragg has always worn his politics on his sleeve. Whether through the medium of political song lyrics or through more direct forms of political expression, Billy Bragg is a consummate activist, who not only provides a voice for the British working class, but also has been visible as a political advocate on behalf of a variety of Leftist causes. Bragg's musical compositions, which are, by his own admission, a healthy mix of political rousers and forlorn love ballads (as reflected in the title of his 2008 album, *Mr Love & Justice*), comprise a unique blend of punk rock and standard folk music. They reiterate the two common Bragg themes of social protest and unrequited love. His 30-year foray "mixing pop and politics" has established Bragg as a leading voice in decrying the excesses of modern capitalism and extolling the virtues of socialist alternatives. Bragg's unabashed commitment to various political causes has uniquely positioned him as a leading figure in the arena of political rock.

Musical Career

Stephen William Bragg was born on 20 December 1957 in Barking (which later led to Bragg's moniker as "The Bard of Barking"), a working-class suburb on the East Side of London. Going by the name of Billy Bragg, he began his career as a punk rocker in a London pub band called Riff Raff. After modest success, he joined the British Army for a time in 1981 until he paid a fee to get out of his commitment. In 1983, he returned to his music career as a solo guitar player under the name Spy vs. Spy, recording the now legendary EP, *Life's a Riot with Spy vs. Spy*. This 7-song, 15-minute 45 rpm recording was rereleased on G0! Discs later that year and included the song *A New England*, which ultimately became a Top 10 hit on the British charts in 1985. He followed this recording with *Brewing Up with Billy Bragg* in 1984. Another EP, *Between the Wars*, was released in 1985, which featured several distinctly pro-labor songs and cemented Bragg's standing as a prominent spokesperson for the politics of the British working class. And with that, Billy Bragg had arrived on the British pop stage.

By 1986, Bragg had produced a top ten album on the British charts, *Talking with the Taxman about Poetry*. Building on this success, his early EPs were released in 1987 under the title, *Back to Basics*. Up to this point, Bragg had established himself through the distorted, echo-laden sound of his solo guitar and the distinct Cockney accent through which he delivered his politically charged and romantically themed music. During the late 1980s and early 1990s, Bragg altered his distinct sound by adding backup musicians on two of his most commercially successful albums, *Workers Playtime* and *Don't Try This at Home*, though he clearly retained his two dominant musical themes. The latter album included a single, "Sexuality," which earned him minor acclaim in the United States as a video in rotation on MTV. During this period, Bragg doggedly toured throughout Europe (including the Soviet Union) and the US, developing a loyal cult following.

His 1990 EP release *The Internationale* included, not only the eponymous socialist anthem, but also a version of the folk classic "I Dreamed I Saw Joe Hill Last Night", which Bragg adapted to pay tribute to legendary folk singer, Phil Ochs. This song is significant as it foreshadowed Bragg's subsequent folk tributes to the great Woody Guthrie that were prompted by Guthrie's daughter Nora, who commissioned Bragg to write music to accompany some of a vast trove of song lyrics that Guthrie left behind. In collaboration with the band Wilco, Bragg produced two highly acclaimed albums of songs with Guthrie lyrics, 1998's *Mermaid Avenue* (named in honor of Guthrie's house in Brooklyn) and 2000's *Mermaid Avenue Volume II*.

During the past decade, Bragg has continued to perform his political and love songs on tour and at rallies for various political causes. He has also recorded songs and albums that range from the style of his punk-inspired folk rock (that is, *England, Half-English*) to modern versions of traditional English folk songs (see the *Imagined Village Project*). In 2008, Bragg released the album *Mr Love & Justice*, with a unique twist—a two-disc set with one disc featuring Bragg as a solo act and the other containing the identical 12 tracks recorded with his backup band, The Blokes. For the latest entry in his music catalogue, Bragg has adopted his own advice to "cut out the middleman" and marketed his own CD, *Pressure Drop*, recorded for his theatrical performance project of the same name.

In sum, Billy Bragg has engaged in a prolific career in music (and related performing arts) that continues to expand its boundaries in terms of form and content. He has also toured extensively to share his music and politics with diverse audiences throughout the world, all the while maintaining his commitment to social activism and political causes.

The Musical Politics of Billy Bragg

Billy Bragg's political commitment and causes are readily apparent in his lyrics, album art, and choice of cover songs. His lyrics span a diverse set of political issues and concerns. What emerges most prominently is that Bragg is an advocate for socialism, peace, and compassion. The messages that he delivers represent the perspectives of the oppressed, including workers, soldiers, and minorities.

First and foremost, Billy Bragg recognizes the forces of class warfare and class struggle with a depth that exceeds even the most politically active musicians on the current political scene. Many of his songs are infused with lyrics designed to pull up the veil on class domination. For example, in "Ideology" (*Brewing Up with Billy Bragg*), he indicts mainstream politicians for representing the interests of privileged classes and failing to respond to the needs of common people. Bragg's sharpest criticism is reserved for the Conservative Party as expressed through his song "Thatcherites" (*William Bloke Reissue*), lambasting the Tories for privatizing collective resources.

Through many of his musical compositions, Bragg questions the forces of capitalism, corporations and consumption. For example, he challenges an American society that is oblivious to inequity in "Help Save the Youth of America" (*Brewing Up with Billy Bragg*). Another common theme in Bragg's critique of capitalism can be found in "The Marching Song of the Covert Battalions" (*The Internationale*) and in "North Sea Bubble" (*Don't Try This At Home*) in which he indicts consumption as a weapon in the process of imperialistic exploitation. As reflected in "It Says Here" (*Brewing Up with Billy Bragg*), Bragg sees mainstream media as a complicit partner in capitalism.

Bragg's lyrics identify an alternative working-class perspective to counter this ideology, as found in the lyrics of "Between the Wars" (*Back to Basics*). Bragg calls on governments to recognize working-class contributions to social welfare by providing the conditions for peace and prosperity.[1] Bragg even brings a deep historical perspective to this class struggle through his cover of Leon Rosselon's salute to The Diggers, "The World Turned Upside Down" (*Must I Paint You A Picture? The Essential Billy Bragg*), an agrarian collective of 17th-century Britain that espoused an egalitarian philosophy rejecting private ownership of property and emphasizing the primacy of the collective good. Although powerful landowners eventually crushed the Diggers Movement, its ideas have stood the test of time and have lived on through the music of Billy Bragg. Though clearly well versed in the philosophical underpinnings and historical roots of class struggle, Bragg also spreads an awareness of the practical, day-to-day struggles of the working class. In "To Have and To Have Not" (*Life's a Riot with Spy vs. Spy*), he points out the radically different life chances for the upper versus working classes:

As part of his initiative to spread class consciousness, Billy Bragg follows the folk music tradition of championing the cause of unions in his song "Never Cross a Picket Line" (The Internationale/Live and Dubious) and through his recordings of classic union rousers such as: "There is Power in a Union" (Talking with the Taxman About Poetry), "Which Side Are You On?" (Life's a Riot/Between the Wars), and "A Miner's Life." (The Internationale/Live and Dubious)

In many of Bragg's political songs, Bragg adopts the perspective of the powerless, the disenfranchised, and the suffering. In addition to being a champion

---

[1]   For a more thorough discussion of "Between the Wars," see Trammer 2001, 125–42.

of the worker, Bragg also laments the plight of the soldier sent into combat, the shunned homosexual, the harassed immigrant, and the abused spouse.

For example, Bragg's forays into the anti-war tradition of folk music dedicates many songs to the soldier sent off to war including "Everywhere" (*Don't Try This At Home*), "Island of No Return" (*Brewing Up with Billy Bragg*), "Like Soldiers Do" (*Brewing Up with Billy Bragg*), "Rumours of War" (*Don't Try This at Home*), and "Tender Comrade" (*Workers Playtime*). In "Island of No Return," "Everywhere," and "Tender Comrade," Bragg adopts the first person perspective of a soldier at war and references the indelible impact left by the war experience.

Bragg adopts another voice of the downtrodden in "Rotting on Remand" (*Workers Playtime*) when he exposes the injustice of the British penal system. Again, Bragg adopts a first-person narrative to tell the story of an innocent man shipped from prison to prison, suffering from the overcrowded and inhumane conditions in outdated facilities.

Bragg frequently promotes tolerance through his music. For instance, in "England, Half English" (*England, Half English*), Bragg attacks the racism of anti-immigrant hostility in Britain by pointing out that many of the icons of British culture, such as St. George and the three the lions on the Royal Arms of England, have origins outside the UK. He stands up for tolerance of sexual differences in "Sexuality" (*Don't Try This At Home*).

Bragg consistently opposes violence, whether on the battlefield or in the home. In "The Homefront" (*Brewing Up with Billy Bragg*), Bragg decries the violence that saturates modern culture. He notes the irony in how the media's violence obsession induces generalized anxiety about the scary world outside that obfuscates the violence that takes place close to home. In "Levi Stubb's Tears" (*Talking with the Taxman About Poetry*), Bragg exposes the horror of domestic violence and the tension that exists for the victim torn between love and abuse. In "Valentine's Day is Over" (*Workers Playtime*), Bragg adopts the voice of the victim taking a stand against domestic violence:

> Don't come round reminding me again how brittle bone is.[2]

Beyond the lyrics of Billy Bragg's songs there are several other indicators of his political sympathies and commitment—the cover songs that he selects to record and the cover art on his albums. In addition to the aforementioned Mermaid Avenue project albums (that set Woody Guthrie's lyrics to music) and traditional union rousers, Billy Bragg has covered Sam Cooke's "A Change is Gonna Come" (*The Internationale/Live and Dubious*), which declares steadfast optimism about inevitable progressive social change. Bragg has also covered Woody Guthrie's "This Land is Your Land" (*The Internationale/Live and Dubious*) in celebration of the collective spirit of socialism. Bragg's sympathies with common people are

---

echoed in "A Pict Song" (*William Bloke*) in which he set to music the words of Rudyard Kipling. And in another classic example, Bragg adapted "I Dreamed I saw Joe Hill Last Night" to "I Dreamed I Saw Phil Ochs Last Night" (*The Internationale*), as a tribute to fellow musical activist, Phil Ochs (who earlier penned a tribute to Joe Hill).

Another window into the unabashed socialist politics of Billy Bragg is the political imagery found on his album covers. For example, the cover of *Talking with the Taxman About Poetry* presents a cartoon image of a capitalist machine feasting on dollar bills. *The Internationale* features a large bolt cutter that symbolizes the spirit of the popular phrase that has been loosely adapted from Karl Marx's *Communist Manifesto*, "Workers of the World, Unite. You have nothing to lose but your chains!" The iconography on many of Bragg's album covers reflects traditions in the art of socialism. *Brewing Up with Billy Bragg* adopts the style of the socialists of the 1930s. The cover of *Workers Playtime* is adorned by a painting from the communist movement in China and features a quote from socialist theorist Antonio Gramsci in the liner notes.

The brilliance of Billy Bragg's mix of pop, politics, and humor is exemplified by his facility for adapting his most popular songs to fit changing times and the venues where he is playing. For example, Bragg updated the lyrics from his widely popular song "The Great Leap Forward" (*Workers Playtime*) from the original:

> In the Soviet Union a scientist is blinded
> By the resumption of nuclear testing
> … To a post-Cold War version:
> In the former Soviet Union, the citizens demand
> To know why they're still the target of strategic air command.[3]

Though the focus of this book is politics, a chapter on Billy Bragg would be incomplete without at least a nod to the romantic poetry of Billy Bragg love songs, which are often melancholy reflections on lost or unrequited love. "St. Swithin's Day" (*Brewing Up with Billy Bragg*) is a poignant example in which Bragg ruminates about the false optimism of the notion of ever-lasting love.

By integrating the traditions of folk music with many of the standard conventions of rock'n'roll (for example, heavy distortion guitar riffs, catchy pop melodies, and themes of unrequited love), Bragg has brought folk music to the masses (in Britain especially). Moreover, he has conveyed the ideals of socialist politics to new generations. But most importantly, as we shall see in the section below, he has put these ideas into political practice.

---

[3]   Waiting for the great leap forward. Lyrics by Billy Bragg. © Sony/ATV Music Publishing. All rights reserved. Used by permission

Political Causes, Contributions, and Controversies

As variegated as his musical endeavors have been, this diversity pales in relation to the variety of political causes that Billy Bragg has championed. Bragg has been on the frontlines for the peace and justice movement, labor strikes, leftist political parties, the environment, media democratization, and socialist principles. He has been a strong voice against violence, the arms race, nuclear proliferation, fascism, sexism, homophobia, and racism. He has been an advocate for the rights of workers, peasants, prisoners, and recording artists. He has played benefit concerts to support strikers and laid-off workers, among others.

Unlike Bob Dylan, who has been steadfastly resistant to extending the politics of his music into real world practice, Bragg has taken causes to heart and engaged actively in political causes. Indeed, the vast number of causes and the scope of Billy Bragg's efforts are too voluminous to catalogue exhaustively in this chapter. Instead, some examples of the forms that Bragg's activism has taken will be identified, and some of the different causes that Bragg has supported are highlighted along the way. In the process, we see Bragg playing many political roles such as: a voice for the oppressed, union representative, global ambassador, celebrity spokesperson, protester, confidant, political organizer, reformer, impresario, and scholar.

First and foremost, Billy Bragg has been a *voice for the oppressed*, including workers, the poor, and, in one case, even defending foxes being hunted for sport! (Bragg 2001). As noted in the above discussion of Billy Bragg's lyrics, he has often identified with the plight of the common person in the struggle against powerful interests. He frequently lends this voice to support their causes. For example, Billy Bragg supported British coal miners during their tumultuous conflict with the British Coal Board in 1984/85. The conflict was initiated when the Coal Board announced its intention to close up to 20 coalmines, an action that would result in 20,000 jobs lost. British miners, under the leadership of the National Union of Mineworkers' President Arthur Scargill, organized a series of work stoppages in protest that lasted up to a full year. The duration of the strikes, and the fact that they were so widespread throughout Britain, imposed a financial hardship on the union strike funds and the families of union workers. To assist them, Bragg played a series of benefits to support the miners:

> He played at the Docks United Social Club in Newport (raising £223.20 for the Gwent and Rhymney NUM food fund), and Corby Civic Centre, but it was the third miners' gig at The Bunker in Sunderland on 28 September that truly galvanized him… By the end of this short tour, Billy Bragg considered himself totally politicized: "It had gone beyond being a punk rocker and playing lip service to a set of ideals." (Collins 2007, 145–6)

While on the subject of unions, it is interesting to note that, in a sense, Bragg serves as a *union representative* for his own trade. He is on the Board Directors of the Featured Artists Coalition since its founding in 2009. This organization represents the rights of British musicians and performers, seeking to secure greater control over the products and revenues that they produce. In 2008, Bragg published an Op-Ed piece in *The New York Times* in which he lays out his viewpoints on protecting the royalty rights of "fledgling" musicians (Bragg 2008, A13).

Throughout his career, Bragg has been a *global ambassador*, traveling extensively to forge common bonds of people across state and ideological boundaries. He has visited such political hotspots as Bolivia, Chile, and China. He has visited Nicaragua in support of the Sandinista movement. During the Cold War, he visited Moscow and East Germany to foster East/West relations and to encourage the Mikhail Gorbachev's reform policies of perestroika and glasnost. He considered his early visits to Moscow and East Berlin (in 1986) a diplomatic success; however, his 1989 visit was more difficult. Bragg's comment that the Berlin Wall was an impediment to the success of reform policies put him in conflict with East German authorities and he was told he was no longer welcome there (Collins 2007).

Over the years, Billy Bragg has frequently lent his role as *celebrity spokesperson*, as well as his musical talents, to various causes by appearing at rallies and concerts. During the 1980s, for example, Bragg played at many events sponsored by the Greater London Council (GLC), a governing body for the greater London area that, until it was disbanded in 1986, frequently stood in opposition to Thatcherism. As part of these GLC events, Bragg played in a series of shows in 1984 with the London Against Racism campaign. These shows followed in the tradition of Rock Against Racism concerts (see Frith and Street 1992, Roberts and Moore 2009), which Bragg credits as playing a major role in his personal political awakening in 1978 (Collins 2007), making him a living testament to the potential of music to foster political engagement.

In another example of his role as a celebrity spokesperson, Bragg was the headline performer, along with Tom Morello of Rage Against the Machine and Steve Earle, at the inaugural meeting of the National Conference for Media Reform (NCMR) in Madison, WI, in 2003. The NCMR is an organization dedicated to addressing issues of media conglomeration. Other notable participants in the Madison conference included Russ Feingold, Al Franken, Amy Goodman, Jesse Jackson, Naomi Klein, Bill Moyers, Ralph Nader, and Bernie Sanders (Hagengruber 2003, C1). More recently, Bragg has played on behalf of the Hope Not Hate campaign (Standford 2010).

Billy Bragg himself has been a *protester*, engaging in acts of civil disobedience. In one 1985 anti-apartheid protest outside London's South African embassy, "After a peaceful 30,000-strong picket was barred by the Metropolitan police, preventing those taking part from decorating the building with flowers and tokens as an anti-apartheid action, they opted for a sit-in. Billy was there. He was also among the 322 who were arrested and carted away in vans" (Collins 2007, 175). He was arrested again shortly thereafter (in 1986) as part of a protest sponsored by the Campaign for Nuclear Disarmament, an anti-nuclear group that was engaged in civil disobedience outside the Bawburgh nuclear bunker near Norwich (Collins 2007).

During the 1980s, Billy Bragg served as a *confidant* of Labour Party candidate
Neil Kinnock. The two had frequent meetings to discuss political strategy related
to youth mobilization. In fact, "The image of Billy Bragg and the Labour leader
became ubiquitous in the years running up to the 1987 general election: usually the
shot of the pair of them sipping tea and laughing" (ibid., 160).

Billy Bragg's career has also included ventures into mainstream politics as a
political organizer. For example, in 1985 Bragg helped form The Red Wedge, a
group of musicians who sought to mobilize young adults in political causes such
as defeating Margaret Thatcher's Conservative government. As part of Red Wedge
activities, concert tours (including such bands as Madness, The Smiths, The Style
Council, and The The) and comedy tours were organized to support the Labour Party
in the 1987 election.[4] While the group ran out of steam after the Conservative Party
was re-elected, the Red Wedge initiative served as a model for how musicians and
other celebrities could engage in the political process (Collins 2007).

Bragg's involvement in political elections didn't subside with the demise of the
Red Wedge. The fact that Bragg had a falling out with the Labour Party has allowed
him to become more creative in his political strategizing against the Conservative
Party. Bragg has become a supporter of "tactical voting," a pragmatic approach in
a multiparty, parliamentary system in which Left-leaning voters in key districts are
encouraged to vote the party best positioned to defeat the Tory candidate rather than
their preferred party. In addition, Bragg has endorsed a voter swapping website (an
activity once referred to in the US as "Nader trading") in which voters from the
Liberal Democratic Party in one district swap their votes with Labour Party voters
in another district in order to block the election of Conservative Party candidates
(Bragg 2001, Matthews 2005). In a radio interview with the BBC, Bragg explained
that being free of party affiliations allowed for "the sort of mischief I do down in
West Dorset with vote swapping and tactical voting, you know, in my constituency
I'm encouraging people to vote Liberal Democrat. I'd get chucked out the party if
I was doing that sort of thing" (BBC News 2006).

In the aftermath of the Conservative Party victory in 1987, many supporters
of the Left-wing of the Labour Party became disenchanted both with the nature
of the British political system and, indeed, with the Labour Party itself. As the
Red Wedge faded, Bragg threw his support behind Charter88, an organization
that advocates for Constitutional and election reform. In the process, Bragg, who
once proposed that the capital of England be moved to York (*Local Government
Chronicle* 2000), launched himself into a new role as a political *reformer*.

Since this time, Bragg has been a visible advocate for reforming the British
House of Lords. In 1999, he testified before Lord Wakeham's Royal Commission
on the Reform of the House of Lords that was set up by then Prime Minister Tony
Blair. Bragg is listed as an expert witness in the Wakeham Commission Report,
lending his voice to the movement to make the House of Lords more democratic

---

    [4]   For a more thorough discussion of The Red Wedge, see Frith and Street 1992, 67–
80; and Tranmer 2001, 125–42.

and to control the patronage and influence peddling that compromise its legitimacy (Royal Commission on the Reform of the House of Lords 2000). While there has been consensus that the system needs reform, no consensus has emerged on how to achieve it. As such, the issue of reforming Parliament's second chamber has remained on the political agenda, and Bragg has continued his role as an advocate for reform, declaring his support for the proportional distribution of seats in the House of Lords in proportion to general election voting (*The Economist* 2004, *The Guardian* 2004, Bragg 1999).

Bragg has even dabbled as a theater *impresario*. In conjunction with Artistic Director Mick Gordon, Bragg developed what was billed as "part play, part gig, part installation." It dealt with "three generations of the same white working-class family as they struggle to deal with change around them." Bragg songs were featured throughout the performance that explored issues related to national identity (Standford 2010). In a similar vein of exploring issues of national identity, Bragg contributed music to a Royal Shakespeare Company production of Henry V (Austin 2001, 6).

Bragg is an accomplished working-man's *scholar* taking up the mantle of anthropologist, historian, and author. Enraged by the appropriation of political symbols like the Union Jack by the far right British National Party (BNP) and reactionary anti-immigration forces in Britain, Bragg has taken a stand for racial and ethnic tolerance and against xenophobic hate crimes. His viewpoints on these issues are thoroughly articulated in his book, *The Progressive Patriot: A Search for Belonging* (Bragg 2006). Bragg notes that his opposition to racism—in the form of the neo-Nazi National Front Party that preceded the BNP in the early 1970s—was his initial call to political activism. Issues of racism, immigration, and identity came to the fore when BNP politicians won city council seats, including seats in Barking where Bragg grew up.

In his book, Bragg confronts racism and xenophobia masquerading in the forms of patriotism and British nationalism. Ultimately, he seeks to reclaim the meaning and symbols of British patriotism, reclaiming patriotism for the Left (Aitkenhead 2006). In chapter two of *The Progressive Patriot*, Bragg provides a concise anthropological history of the evolution of the "English people," demonstrating that the people who are conventionally considered to be English are in actuality a diverse mix of different cultures resulting from numerous successive waves of immigration. Toward that conclusion, he notes that the term "Anglo-Saxon" itself is hyphenated. Bragg concludes his book with the statement: "In staying true to my inheritance, I hope to repay the debt I owe them by continuing to play my part in the creation of a fairer society, which we in turn can pass on to our children" (Bragg 2006, 351).

Personal Recollections

The uninitiated fan is in for a pleasant surprise when seeing Bragg perform live for the first time. Bragg's quick-witted sense of humor and stage presence rivals that of a professional comedian. His comic monologues are laced with political critique, self-deprecatory humor and heavy doses of charisma. For the fan, the experience of a live Bragg concert quickly becomes a mental tug of war. You can't wait to hear his next song, but you don't want him to stop talking.

My first exposure to Billy Bragg was when I stayed in England with Luke Blumler, a fellow musician and boyhood friend from the time during which I lived in England. Luke played lots of different tracks of new music that night, including tracks from Bragg's *Life's a Riot with Spy vs. Spy*. I vividly remember being captivated by the unfamiliar sound of Bragg's powerful, yet stark, music. The combination of his thick Cockney accent and distorted solo guitar defied classification. Power chords made his music sound like rock'n'roll, but it was not. The hard-edged spirit sounded like punk, but it was not. The lyric poetry sounded like folk, but it was not. While I couldn't say what type of music this was, it was clear that it had something to say. Of all the bands we listened to, it was Billy Bragg that stuck with me and I bought all of his CDs before leaving the country.

Shortly thereafter, the Billy Bragg tour stopped in Minneapolis where I was living at the time. Bragg was playing at First Avenue, a cutting-edge club frequented by pop legend Prince. A young and soon-to-be-famous Tracy Chapman opened the show, exemplifying Bragg's penchant for showcasing politically conscious, up-and-coming talent. The brilliance of this show hooked me as a Bragg fan for life.

I wasn't disappointed by Bragg's return engagement to First Avenue the following year. The opening act was a band from San Francisco called the Beatnigs. Fronted by Michael Franti, this band had an industrial punk funk sound with a political edge. Several members of the band used power tools and car parts as instruments. They were followed by a set by folk rocker Michelle Shocked. After Bragg's set, all three acts joined together in a rousing encore homage to Prince's "Purple Rain," changing the lyrics to Acid Rain as sparks from the Beatnig's circular saw on a metal gas tank rained out across the audience. It was quite the spectacle.

When I moved to the East Coast, I was able to catch Bragg twice at Philadelphia's Chestnut Cabaret. One of these occasions was marked by the return of Michael Franti, who was then fronting the Disposable Heroes of Hiphoprisy as the opening act. This show was highlighted by a sendup of Deee-Lite's "Groove is in the Heart" as the encore. I saw Bragg one more time in Philadelphia at a free show on Penn's Landing. The last time I saw Billy Bragg was at the Madison, WI, event mentioned above. Along with Rage Against the Machine's Tom Morello, Bragg provided music infused with astute political commentary, a thrilling capstone to the weekend conference.

The Impact of Billy Bragg

It is hard to imagine a more politically engaged musician than Billy Bragg. His dedication and commitment are as deep as his political causes are wide. He has been a dogged social critic and passionate advocate for change. He has been equally adept at pushing governments to be more compassionate and individuals to be more understanding. For those whose lives he has touched, Bragg has made it cool to believe in socialism again.

But first and foremost, Billy Bragg is a great and prolific songwriter. It just so happens that his songs often carry powerful messages and have the ability to mobilize people. With his musical roots that trace back to the protest songs of Woody Guthrie to his current websites, Billy Bragg is a link between our political past and future. On that point, Bragg comments, "When I started to make music, there weren't many ways for someone from my background to articulate ideas. There was no Internet; I didn't have access to the mainstream media. The best way was to pick up a guitar, write songs and do gigs. The internet and social networking sites have replaced that urge" (Saner 2011).

The arc of Billy Bragg's career has seen him evolve from a musician who sings about politics into an active figure in British politics. During that time, he has also seen the demise of the Cold War that was so influential in shaping his early political ideas. And with that, Bragg's political agenda has shifted somewhat. As he told to *New Internationalist*'s Silja J.A. Talvi, "We haven't abandoned what we believe in, but we must find a way to articulate it to the majority of people ... In the end, we have to make people understand that they can either live in a society based on a compassionate idea, or a society based purely on exploitation. From that we will build our new ideals" (Talvi 1998).

Ideologically, it would seem that Billy Bragg has had to manage his personal struggle between the political pragmatism of supporting the Labour Party in its struggles against the Tories, and his socialist ideals that often put him to the Left of Labour. This tension was manifest in his involvement with the Red Wedge, which presented a contrast between the socialist inspiration behind its name and its espoused goal of mobilizing political support for the Labour Party.

His frequent contacts with Members of Parliament (for example, Neil Kinnock, the Wakeham Commission, and so on) and appearances on the BBC underscore that Billy Bragg is a player in British politics. At the same time, his songs have periodically graced the British pop charts. Thus, in Britain, he is arguably unparalleled in his stature and influence as a political musician. But he has also taken his message off the island and spread it to peoples around the world.

As impressive as his political impact has been, it is interesting to speculate on why he hasn't been more visible in the United States, both musically and politically. From a musical standpoint, his style doesn't really fit commercially viable genres pushed by the mainstream American music industry; it doesn't fit with commercial radio formats; or with record store categories; or with the conventional sounds promoted through music television. Certainly, many Americans may not warm up readily to Bragg's thick Cockney accent. Moreover, there are not many commercially successful examples of vocalists backed by solo guitar; and, it is interesting to note that the songs that have garnered Bragg his greatest notoriety in the American market (for example, "Sexuality") have been on the pop side and backed by a full band.

But the impediments to Bragg's US visibility no doubt have a political component as well. Not since the 1930s has the US working class exhibited the kind of politicized spirit and class-consciousness that are found in Britain. Whereas Britain's working class tends to be more politically active than its middle class (it is called the *Labour* Party after all), that is not the case in the US where class and socialism are considered dirty words. In the US, strikes have been relatively fewer, farther between, and far less visible; and anti-Union sentiment runs strong. Moreover, American culture is permeated by the ideology of rugged individualism, which is not as conducive to notions of collective interests. Structurally, there is no equivalent of the BBC, a medium free of overt commercial interests; instead, American media tend to be run by corporations, who may not appreciate radical critique. As such, the American market is less conducive to Bragg's music and his proletarian viewpoints.

That is not to say that Bragg's influence has not been felt in the US. Though exposure to his music and views have not been delivered through mainstream media channels, and they certainly haven't achieved anything close to mass persuasion, Bragg has been a darling of the indie music scene. He has also received widespread critical acclaim. Initially, his music reached a loyal audience through college and community radio, and through word of mouth that was driven by his unique sound and messages. However, when it comes to the American audience, Bragg has been (in his words) "reaching to the converted."

But, as the Internet (with its various forms such as websites, file-sharing programs, iTunes, Pandora, and so on) has begun to eliminate dependence on large corporations as an intermediary to bridge the gap between musical artists and audiences, the future may be brighter for politically charged musicians like Billy Bragg and young artists he has inspired (that is, future Tracy Chapmans, Michelle Shockeds and Michael Frantis).

There is no question that Billy Bragg has had a major political impact in Britain, and indeed around the world. This is true largely because of his vision and dedication as a performer, but even more so as someone who wants to make a difference. The life and philosophy of Billy Bragg can be captured no better than by his own words from "Don't Need This Pressure Ron" (*Reaching to the Converted*):

> I see no shame in putting my name
> To socialism's cause.[5]

---

[5]   Don't Need This Pressure Ron. Lyrics by Billy Bragg. © Sony/ATV Music Publishing. All rights reserved.

Bibliography

Aitkenhead, Decca. "A New England: Billy Bragg's Use of Personal Details in The Progressive Patriot Elbows Out the Argument for a Leftist Patriotism." *The Guardian*, November 11, 2006. http://books.guardian.co.uk/print.

Austin, Jeremy. "Bard of Barking: Billy Bragg, Anti-establishment Activist of the Eighties, Is Now Working with the RSC. But the Issues of Nationalism and Racism in Henry V Put Him on Familiar Ground, Says Jeremy Austin." *The Stage*, 29 March 2001.

BBC News. "Radical Performer: On Sunday 18 June 2006, Andrew Marr Interviewed Billy Bragg, Singer Songwriter." *BBC News,* June 18, 2006. http:// www.bbc.co.uk/news/.

Local Government Chronicle. "Billy Bragg Proposes York as Capital of A New England." 18 January 2000. http://www.lgcplus.com/lgc-news/billy-bragg-proposes-york-as-capital-of-a-new-england/1393278.article.

The Guardian. "Billy Bragg Presents Lords Reform Plans." 9 Feb 2004. TheGuardian.co.uk.

The Economist. "Billy Bragg's Modest Proposal." 13 March 2004.

Bragg, Billy. "Don't let the fox-hunting lobby drive a wedge between town and country." *The Independent*, 3 June 2001. http://www.billybragg.co.uk/press/story.php?ID=21.

Bragg, Billy. "I Have Designed My Own Website for Tactical Voting. It is the Only Way to Punish the Tories." *New Statesman*, 23 April 2001. http://www.newstatesman.com/200104230004.

Bragg, Billy. *The Progressive Patriot: A Search for Belonging.* London: Black Swan, 2006.

Bragg, Billy. "UK Politics: Ensuring the Will of the People." *BBC Online Network*, 22 July 1999. http://www.bbc.co.uk/news/.

Collins, Andrew. *Still Suitable for Miners: Billy Bragg.* London: Virgin, 2007.

Frith, Simon, and John Street. "Rock Against Racism and Red Wedge: From Music to Politics, from Politics to Music," *Rockin' the Boat: Mass Music & Mass Movements*, edited by Reebee Garofalo, 67–80. Cambridge, MA: South End Press, 1992.

Hagengruber, Matt. "Rally for Media Reform: Conference and Rally is in Opposition to Media Conglomeration." *Wisconsin State Journal*, 27 October 2003: C1.

Matthews, Jenny. "The Tactics of Tactical Voting." *BBC News*, 8 April 005. http://www.bbc.co.uk/news/.

Roberts, Mike, and Ryan Moore. "Peace Punks and Punks Against Racism: Resources Mobilization and Frame Construction in the Punk Movement." *Music and Arts in Action 2* (2009): 21–36.

Royal Commission on the Reform of the House of Lords. "A House for the Future." *Royal Commission on the Reform of the House of Lords*, 2000. http://www.archive.official-documents.co.uk/document/cm45/4534/report.pdf.

Saner, Emine. "Billy Bragg and Johnny Flynn: Where Have All the Protest Songs gone?" *The Guardian*, 4 November 2011. http://www.guardian.co.uk/commentisfree/2011/nov/04/young-people-politics-protest-songs.

Standford, Peter. "Free Radical: Why It's Showtime for Billy Bragg." *The Independent*, 4 April 2010. http://www.independent.co.uk.

Talvi, Salji J.A. "Billy Bragg: The British Singer-songwriter Talks About His Career, His Politics and a Series of New Recordings that Breathe Life into Old Woody Guthrie Songs." *New Internationalist*, December 1988. http://findarticles.com/p/articles/mi_m0JQP/is_308/ai_30188339/.

Tranmer, Jeremy. "'Wearing Badges Isn't Enough in Days Like These': Billy Bragg and His Opposition to Thatcher Governments." *Cercles* 3 (2001): 125–42.

Discography

Bragg, Billy. *Back to Basics*. London: Cooking Vinyl, 8366782AGOCD8, 1987.

Bragg, Billy. *Bill's Bargains/Going To A Party Way Down South*. London: No Label, BB5109, 2002.

Bragg, Billy. *Billy Bragg Volume 1*. Chapel Hill, NC: Yep Roc Records, YEP2600, 2006.

Bragg, Billy. *Billy Bragg Volume 2*. Chapel Hill, NC: Yep Roc Records, YEP2605, 2006.

Bragg, Billy. *Bloke on Bloke*. London: Cooking Vinyl, COOK CD 127, 1997.

Bragg, Billy. *Brewing Up with Billy Bragg*. London: Go! Discs, AGOLP 4, 1984.

Bragg, Billy. *Don't Try This at Home*. New York: Elektra Records, 9 61121-2, 1991.

Bragg, Billy. *Fight Songs: A Decade of Downloads*. London: Bragg Central Ltd., BB5112, 2011.

Bragg, Billy. *Life's a Riot with Spy vs. Spy*. Newark, NJ: Utility, ZUTIL 1, 1983.

Bragg, Billy. *Life's a Riot/Between the Wars*. London: Go! Discs, AGOEP1, 1985

Bragg, Billy. *Live and Dubious: Help Save the Youth of America*. New York: Elektra Records, 9607872, 1988.

Bragg, Billy. *Live at the Barbican*. London: Cooking Vinyl, BB5110, 2006.

Bragg, Billy. *Live Solo Bootleg Recorded in Australia October 2001*. London: Billy Bragg, BB5109, 2001.

Bragg, Billy. *Mr Love & Justice*. London: Cooking Vinyl, COOKCD452, 2008.

Bragg, Billy. *Must I Paint You a Picture? The Essential Billy Bragg*. Burbank, CA: Rhino Records, R2 73993, 2003.

Bragg, Billy. *Pressure Drop*. London: Bragg Central Ltd., BB5111, 2010.

Bragg, Billy. *Reaching to the Converted (Minding the Gaps)*. Burbank, CA: Rhino Records, R275962, 1999.

Bragg, Billy. *Talking with the Taxman about Poetry*. London: Go! Discs, 1AGOCD 6, 986.

Bragg, Billy. *The Internationale*. New York: Elektra Records, 9 60960-2, 1990.

Bragg, Billy. *The Internationale/Live and Dubious*. Chapel Hill, NC: Yep Roc Records, YEP2604, 2006.

Bragg, Billy. *The Peel Sessions*. Rockville Centre, NY: Strange Fruit, SFPS 027, 1987.

Bragg, Billy. *The Peel Session Album*. Rockville Centre, NY: Strange Fruit, SFRCD117, 1991.

Bragg, Billy. *Try this! Try That!* St Laurent, PQ: Polygram, CDP 559, 1991.

Bragg, Billy. *Victim of Geography*. London: Cooking Vinyl, COOKCD061, 1993.

Bragg, Billy. *William Bloke*. London: Cooking Vinyl, COOK CD 100, 1996.

Bragg, Billy. *William Bloke* (Reissue). London: Cooking Vinyl, COOKCD350, 2006.

Bragg, Billy. *Workers Playtime*. London: Go! Discs, AGOCD 15, 1988.

Bragg, Billy and The Blokes. *Mermaid Avenue Tour*. London: BillyBragg.co.uk, BB5108, 1999.

Bragg, Billy and The Blokes. *England, Half-English*. New York: Elektra Records, 627432, 2002.

Bragg, Billy and The Blokes. *Take Down the Union Jack*. London: Cooking Vinyl, RYCD131, 2002.

Bragg, Billy. Martin Carthy, and Eliza Carthy. *"England, Half-English Meets John Barleycorn."* On *Folk Against Fascism, Vol. 1*. Various Artists. London: Folk Against Fascism, FAF1CD, 2008.

Bragg, Billy. Simon Emmerson, The Young Copper Family, and Eliza Carthy. "Hard Times of Old England Retold." On *The Imagined Village*. Various Artists. Wiltshire, UK: Real World Records, CDRWDJ147, 2008.

Bragg, Billy and The Red Stars. *Live Bootleg/No Pop, No Style, Strictly Roots*. London: No label, BB5107, 1995.

Bragg, Billy and Wilco. *Mermaid Avenue*. New York: Elektra Records, 7559-62204-2, 1998.

Bragg, Billy and Wilco. *Mermaid Avenue Vol. II*. New York: Elektra Records, 62522, 2000.

Less than Jake featuring Billy Bragg, *"The Brightest Bulb has Burned Out."* On *Rock Against Bush, Vol. 1*. Various Artists. San Francisco: Fat Wreck Chords, FAT6752, 2004.

Rosetta Life featuring Billy Bragg. *We Laughed*. London: Cooking Vinyl, FRYCD252, 2005.

Chapter 6

Sinéad O'Connor: The Collision of Bodies

Marcy R. Chvasta

It is two weeks past the deadline for submitting this chapter to the editors. I am panicked. Most obviously, this psychological and physical condition is the result of simply being late. I find being late intolerable. But I am also panicked over the reason for my lateness. Right now, as I type these words, Sinéad O'Connor is suffering a crisis of mental health. I do not want to write about someone who is in the throes of psychological distress. It feels exploitive. It is the work of entertainment or tabloid journalists, a kind of drive-by reporting of the here-and-now. Concerns about the effects such reporting may have on the involved subjects—the people—be damned.

Writing about O'Connor right now feels premature. For months, O'Connor has been very active in the media, submitting letters to the Irish press, blogging, Tweeting, and doing television interviews. Just when I think I can stop collecting "data," more appears. Generally speaking, this is the trouble with writing about the living. They do not sit still for the purposes of the biographer. However, in the case of writing about O'Connor, right now, it seems I cannot avoid committing the very acts she currently is decrying. And I feel terrible. But I continue, even though I have lost the plot.

Losing the Plot

According to the *Oxford English Dictionary*, to "lose the plot" is "to lose one's ability to understand or cope with events; to lose one's touch; to go off the rails." In this colloquialism, "plot" is synonymous with "storyline." On 14 January 2012—that date, for me right now, is today—O'Connor uses that phrase five times in a blog post to describe her reaction to criticisms of her and her husband leveled by the media as well as people close to her husband.[1] These criticisms have centered on O'Connor's behavior of the past six months. In brief, beginning in the earliest days of August 2011, O'Connor began to advertise—on her website, in newspapers, and on television—for a sexual partner. On 8 December, her 45th birthday, she married Barry Herridge, a man she met through her public search. Then, on 26 December,

---

[1]   Sinéad O'Connor, "In Answer to a Sweet English Journalist Regarding 'Mental Health' Perceptions in Ireland and My Self," *Sinéad O'Connor*, 14 January 2012. http://www.sineadoconnor.com. The "Sweet English Journalist" is Niamh Horan.

she announced plans to divorce him, citing the disapproving "behaviour of certain people in my husband's life. And also by a bit of a wild ride i took us on looking for a bit of a smoke of weed for me wedding night as I don't drink."[2] On 3 January 2012, she "Tweeted" their reconciliation.

She "lost the plot." The most serious result of which was two suicide attempts over the course of three days: the first in Los Angeles on 5 January and the second in Ireland on 7 January. On 8 January, *The Irish Independent* published an article by Niamh Horan entitled, "Sinéad O'Connor: 'Do Not F**k with Me or My Husband'."[3] The titular quotation, Horan reports, was directed at Horan by O'Connor after Horan contacted Herridge's workplace to discuss what Horan believes is a "conflict of interest between her [O'Connor's] husband's job—counseling drug-addicted teenagers—and pictures of him being splashed all over the tabloids last week after being re-united with the woman [O'Connor] who took him on her 'wild' search for marijuana on their wedding night."[4] Three days after the article was published, O'Connor tweeted that she needed help: "does any1 know a psychiatrist in dublin or wicklow who could urgently see me today please? im really un-well … and in danger."[5] She lost the plot, and her loss has caused my own.

In the spring of 2011, when I enthusiastically proclaimed that I would write a chapter about Sinéad O'Connor, she had been lurking in the shadows of the United States limelight for quite some time. I saw my endeavor here as an opportunity to educate and remind folks about the significance of O'Connor's musical and political contributions. I meant to offer O'Connor as an example of the empathic singer-activist, a singer-activist who creates change through her ability to effect empathy from others and her visible empathic reaction to others. I had a plot from which to write. That was in the beginning.

The trouble with writing about the living is the whole "living" thing. Beyond wishing my "subject" would just *sit still*, O'Connor's behavior during the last third of 2011 irritated me. Some of her proclamations even shook my admiration for her. Indeed, O'Connor's website activity during the last third of 2011 catapulted in me a crisis of faith—in her. All this I experienced before O'Connor's suicide

---

    [2]   Sinéad O'Connor, "26.12.11," *Sinéad O'Connor*, 26 December 26 2011, http://www.sineadoconnor.com. NB: I choose not to correct any grammatical or typographical errors in O'Connor's blog post and Tweets. I want to preserve the form—intended or not—of her expressions.

    [3]   Niamh Horan. "Sinéad O'Connor: 'Do Not F**k with Me or My Husband'," *Irish Independent*, 8 January 2012. http://www.independent.ie/national-news/sinead-oconnor-do-not-fk-with-me-or-my-husband-2982612.html.

    [4]   Ibid.

    [5]   O'Connor has since removed the Tweets requesting help; however, you can find reproductions in news reports such as "Sinead O'Connor: Fears For Fragile Singer As She Makes Plea For Help On Twitter," 11 January 2012, http://www.huffingtonpost.co.uk/2012/01/11/sinead-oconnor-fears-for-singer-plea-for-help-twitter_n_1198629.html.

attempts. In the here and now, days following the reports of the suicide attempts, my perception of her has shifted again. I reinterpret her recent behavior with empathy rather than irritation. I fear for her. I fear for her children. I fear what I may read every morning when I check her blog and Tweets.

I realize by writing this I may appear to be a bit melodramatic. Furthermore, by writing this, I am freezing in time my current, rather immediate, reaction to O'Connor's behavior. It is quite possible that you are reading this ten years—even one—after I wrote it and saying to yourself, "Wow. Chvasta got herself all riled up over something that turned out to be so utterly forgettable." I am not so worried about that; it cannot be helped. Certainly, all authors risk suffering the unforgiving glare of hindsight. We can only speak from where we are. What does worry me is that I am freezing "Sinéad O'Connor" in this here-and-now. Writing about her current state memorializes it. I can only hope that my doing so serves a purpose that O'Connor holds dear: breaking the debilitating silence that surrounds mental health and suffering. But I hate not being sure.

I am having difficulty here and now because I cannot get any distance. I am having trouble zooming out from my myopic view of O'Connor's latest ubiquitous headlines. I cannot stop having a visceral reaction to O'Connor's non-musical performances. I have lost the plot and I am panicked. Yet, it is precisely this felt crisis that strengthens my conviction in the usefulness of conceiving of controversy as *the collision of bodies*.

So, dear readers, this is what I offer you: an exploration of others' and my own reactions to (some of) Sinéad O'Connor's controversial behavior. I do this, recognizing that people and our perceptions of people may change over time—and may remain the same—and may be fortified. I do this to *illustrate* such changes, stagnations, and reinforcements in the context of rock politics. In my discussion and through my analysis—despite my periodic sense that I have lost the plot in storyline and psychological stability—I offer O'Connor as a case study of controversy as the collision of bodies.

The Vitals

Sinéad Marie Bernadette O'Connor, the third of five siblings, was born on 8 December 1966, in Glenageary, County Dún Laoghaire-Rathdown, Ireland. Her parents, Sean and Marie, separated when O'Connor was eight years old. O'Connor and her two older siblings lived with her mother and, according to O'Connor, suffered grievous abuse. In O'Connor's words, she was "abused from the moment [she] was conceived" (Brown 1992). In 1979, O'Connor moved in with her father. In her adolescence, she attended three different schools, the second of which was a Magdalene asylum, the Grianan Training Center, run by Sisters of Our Lady of Charity. While there, she was introduced to the Irish rock band In Tua Nua. At 14, she wrote and recorded the band's debut single. Although her time with them was brief (they deemed her, at the age of 15, too young to tour with them), it was the genesis of her professional music career.

The year 1985 contained several major events for O'Connor: her mother died in a car accident; she left the band Ton Ton Macoute that she co-founded the year before; and she signed on with Ensign Records. By the time she was 21, she had written and recorded her first album, *The Lion and the Cobra* (1987). Though far more popular among international audiences than US audiences, the album did reach #36 on the Billboard 200 chart of 1988, and the Recording Industry Association of America certified the album Gold. It was her second album, *I Do Not Want What I Haven't Got* (1990) that reached the #1 spot on Billboard and made her world-famous—with the help of fans and music critics alike, of course.

Around the time the album became available, so did two book-length biographies of O'Connor (Guterman 1991, Hayes 1990). She denounces both. As will become clear in this essay, O'Connor frequently vocalizes her displeasure with the ways that professional writers describe her and her life. However, it appears that O'Connor has granted her blessings upon a journalist to tell her story. On 30 December 2011, O'Connor announced that she has commissioned a biography:

> Have asked a writer i think is fucking amazing called Olaf Tyaransen (google) to write my 1st official biography. Since so many other fuckers have done them and got everything arse-ways. Book isn't going to be about personal stuff like boyfriends or husbands and such.. maybe touch on growing up but only glimpses. [...] he's cool. wont be a like 'oh isn't Sinead fucking great and perfect' or anything. it will be 'warts and all'. but focussing on career/artistic issues. not personal. Explaining various escapades from my point of view. so the great-great grandchildren can know why "we don't mention your great great grandmother."[6]

I want to avoid getting everything "arse-ways," so I will conclude this section with a tracing of her musical accomplishments since her sophomore album.

Over the years spanning from 1992 to 2007, O'Connor completed six studio albums. *Am I Not Your Girl?* (1992) is a compilation of torch song covers and one original track, "Success Has Made a Failure of Our Home." In addition to a cover of Kurt Cobain's "All Apologies," *Universal Mother* (1994) contains 14 original songs and was produced by John Reynolds, O'Connor's first husband. Showcasing O'Connor's penchant for collaboration, *Faith & Courage* (2000) includes contributions from diverse artists and producers such as Wyclef Jean, David Stewart, and Brain Eno. O'Connor's last three albums further exemplify the range of her musical interests and talents. *Sean-Nós Nua* (2002)—translation: "new old-style"—is a collection of traditional Irish songs. *Throw Down Your Arms* (2005) features reggae. *Theology* (2007) is comprised of two discs: "Dublin

---

6   Sinéad O'Connor, "Biography," Sinéad O'Connor, 30 December 2011. http://www.sineadoconnor.com.

Sessions" contains acoustic songs; "London Sessions" contains the full-band versions. None of these albums achieved the widespread audience recognition like O'Connor's second album. However, O'Connor's soon-to-be-released album *How About I Be Me (And You Be You)?* (2012) is generating more positive buzz for O'Connor than I have seen in 20 years—despite the negative responses to her recent behavior online.

Body Count

I am a performance studies scholar. As such, I am interested in how, who, where, when, what, and why people perform in everyday and aesthetic contexts. Scholars within the field of performance studies find axiomatic the notion that an individual is a compilation of selves, some existing in harmony, some discordant. Whether in aesthetic or mundane realms, an individual is a complex compilation of selves. For example, a person can be a student, a mother, a girlfriend, and a farmer. In performance terms, all of these selves are roles to perform. They are *bodies* that dwell within particular discursive domains. Each of these bodies acts differently than other bodies, yet all of these bodies continuously implicate, affect, and effect each other.

This is not to say that a person *simultaneously* performs all of their constitutive bodies across all contexts. Using the example above, it would be very difficult for a person to execute the actions of a farmer while tending to a toddler. However, that farmer does not stop being a mother even when she is milking cows. Furthermore, the fact that this farmer is also a mother has some impact on where, when, how, and why she milks these cows. Because she is a farmer, she tends to her toddler in particular ways and at particular times. Depending on the context, a person may more prominently perform one role over all others. What interests me here, and in general, are the moments when a person performs roles that may appear to be in conflict with each other and in conflict with others' roles. I am interested in the moments when bodies collide.

Central to my perception of constitutive bodies is David Graver's 1997 essay "The Actor's Bodies" (Graver 1997, 221–35). Despite the title of his essay, Graver applies his typology to a range of performers that extends beyond the actor you would find in a play. In fact, another performance studies scholar, Philip Auslander, cites Graver's work in his own proposed tri-part typology of the musical performer (Auslander 2006, 100–19).

According to Graver, there are seven bodies that constitute the actor's body: characters, performers, commentators, personages, representatives of socio-historical groups, physical flesh, and loci of private sensations (Graver 1997, 222). In the following section, I apply Graver's seven bodies to O'Connor in her music video performance of "Nothing Compares 2 U" (1990). On the O'Connor Scale of Controversy, this video ranks at the low end. You may have forgotten by now, but her hairstyle was a bit shocking back in the day. Nevertheless, O'Connor's performance was—and continues to be—widely acclaimed. It marks O'Connor's entry into celebrity status. It is the performance that set her apart from other artists, inviting us to consider what it is about her complex self that demanded the attention of so many.

O'Connor's Bodies in "Nothing Compares 2 U"

O'Connor first entered the consciousness of the US mainstream with the release of the song "Nothing Compares 2 U" off her second album, *I Do Not Want What I Haven't Got* (1990). It was not just the song that enthralled audiences, but O'Connor's performance in the accompanying music video. Trying to write a description of the video of "Nothing Compares 2 U" makes me look like a plagiarist. I have read hundreds of descriptions, from posts on *YouTube* to articles and interviews in major publications, and the language used across all of these media is remarkably similar (for example, "close-up"; "heartbreaking"; "lament"; "tear"). *Time* included this video in their chronologically ordered 2011 list, "The 30 Best Music Videos of All Time." From the author's description and review, we get a sense of the character, performer, commentator, group representation, personage, flesh, and private sensations of O'Connor. In the following quotation, I have italicized the language that implicates O'Connor's various bodies and inserted in brackets the various bodies that are implicated.

> It's one of the simplest music-video concepts ever: a close-up of *elfin Irish singer* [flesh; personage; group representation] Sinéad O'Connor, sporting a *crew cut* [flesh] and a black turtleneck, *singing directly to the camera* [performer]. It's also the most heartbreaking. Written by Prince, the song is a lover's lament. As such, *the look on O'Connor's face* [performer; sensations] pinballs between nostalgia, anger, and sadness, a temporary schizophrenia familiar to anyone who has ever experienced a significant breakup. Near the end, when O'Connor sings, "All the flowers that you planted, mama/in the backyard/all died when you went away," two tears roll down her cheeks—the result, *said O'Connor later* [commentator], of her tempestuous relationship with *her own mother* [private sensations]. (When Prince sings the song, he replaces "mama" with "baby.") You're a robot if you don't follow suit. It's raw and intimate and unforgettable (Cruz 2011, emphasis is my own).

Each of these bodies requires some "fleshing out." In part, the popularity and critical acclaim of O'Connor's performance as a singer and music video performer attest to her ability to *embody a character*. O'Connor is not the author of the lyrics. However, the "I" of the song both is and is not O'Connor. The "I" of the lyrics both is and is not the author, Prince. However, a typical audience member, while enjoying a musical performance, does not usually consider these complexities of "Who is speaking?" A typical audience member tends to consider the singer to be the only "I" of the song. In his analysis of music television, Andrew Goodwin argues similarly: "When a pop singer tells a first-person narrative in a song, he or she is simultaneously both the character in the song and the storyteller. Often the two positions become confused for audiences" (Goodwin 1992, 75). Auslander further addresses this distinction and confusion in his tri-part typology of the singer. Following the lead of Simon Frith (Frith 1996, 211)—and Graver to a very limited extent—Auslander identifies a singer's three "layers": "the real person (the performer as a human being), the performance persona (which corresponds to Firth's star personality or image [and Graver's personage]), and the character (Firth's song personality)" (Auslander 2004, 1–13). Although the distinctions among the three may be blurry, Auslander argues that they must be attended to for a full understanding of the music performer. I agree; however, Graver's bodies provide for an even more usefully nuanced analysis of the music performer than Auslander's three layers.

Regarding again that confusion between character and "the real person," one might say that it may only be the result of a successful performance. That is, if an audience believes that the singer is singing autobiographically, the singer has done his or her job. The singer is a skilled *performer*. O'Connor performed this character beautifully. And she clearly recognizes a difference between her character and, in Auslander's terms, herself as a "real person." In an 11 September 2011 letter printed in the *Irish Independent* and posted on her blog, she provides her interpretation of "Nothing Compares 2 U":

> There's a hugely beloved song in this world. Sung from the point of view of a lover who has lost reciprocation. It describes the minutes of the days becoming like hours. And how one counts them, as one would if it was days without fags [i.e., cigarettes]. It describes the loneliness and anguish and crying and self-bashing we all do when a relationship, particularly a marriage, fails. The narrator tells of utter in-ability to even live and sleep at the times expected by 'normal' society. He or she (depending upon who wrote and or sang it) seeks medical help but very unwisely ignores it. It being a song very close to my own heart I'm inclined to pay attention to what the doctor says and I lately decided to put his advice into practice.[7]

O'Connor is calling attention to the *character* of the song as a body that is "other" than herself.[8] By using phrases such as "the point of view of a lover" and stating,

---

[7]   Sinéad O'Connor. "This Week's Un-cut Version of *Irish Sunday Independent* Piece." *Sinéad O'Connor*, 18 September 2011. http://www.sineadoconnor.com.

[8]   And here is where I want to diverge from Auslander's conceptualization of "character." For Auslander, "character is an optional element that comes in primarily when the musician is a singer performing a song that defines a character textually" ("Performance Analysis," p. 7). Textually defined characters are common elements of certain genres of music, such as opera or rap; but Auslander is interested in non-dramatic musical

"It describes" rather than "I describe," O'Connor distances herself from the persona of the lyrics, as well as the author of the lyrics. We see here the work of the *performer*. As a performer, one must recognize that one both is and is-not the character one performs (Schechner 1985). Though O'Connor explicitly separates herself from the character of the song, she also takes on the role by stating that she—as if she were the character of the song—is "inclined to pay attention to what the doctor says [to her]." By offering her interpretation and noting the contingency of "depending upon who wrote and or sang it," she is engaging her *commentator* self, commenting on "the ongoing discussion of the possibilities of the role" (Graver 1997, 223).

Less explicitly, the above quotation reveals portions of O'Connor's *personage*, her celebrity status, in two ways. First, by noting that the song is "hugely beloved," she implicates her popularity as a music performer. Second, by disclosing that she will "put [the doctor character's] advice into practice," she is engaging in behavior that the public has come to expect of O'Connor. I know of no other rock musician who has worked as hard as O'Connor has to control and remediate the ways in which the mass media present her to the public. As early as 1990, in a *Rolling Stone* interview, O'Connor repudiated the role of the mass media in creating a musician's personage: "It's important to make people aware that you're a person and you're not what people read in the newspapers" (Rogers 1990). The public has heard similar assertions from celebrities for as long as celebrities have existed. However, O'Connor both continuously refutes media portrayals of her, as well as discloses the way media portrayals make her feel. Again, from the 1990 *Rolling Stone* article:

> "I used to get really, really upset by negative press," O'Connor says, reclining on a chaise lounge, clad in a purple spandex unitard rolled down below the waist and a blue bra. "They really insulted me as a person and continually made me out to be some sort of real bastard. It used to really hurt my feelings. I'm not the most secure person on the planet, you know. It's very, very difficult to deal with being seen as a celebrity by practically everyone you meet. I like the fact that a lot of people like my records, but I don't like being famous." (ibid.)

This excerpt is noteworthy for its disclosive nature and for its consistency with O'Connor's most current statements to the media. Being forthcoming about her private life and private sensations has become a significant part of her personage.

The remaining two bodies Graver identifies are group representation and flesh. The first of these bodies encompasses "a corporeal identity linked to race, class, or

---

performances in which "musicians do not usually portray fictional characters" ("Musical Personae," p. 102). I understand wanting to a keep a distinction between narrators and characters—as performance studies and literature scholars will tell you, they are different personae. However, I find it more important to use "character" as a label to signify that the singer is not singing autobiographically.

gender and constructed within the socio-historical discourse of culture" (Graver 1997, 228). Membership in a particular group is the deciding factor in whether a person is subjected to oppression or invested with (and invested *in*) privilege (ibid.). Discourse is a powerful force that has material effects on a body, the multiplicitous whole Self. For example, in the US, a person's skin color can signify expectations in others that determine a person's life experiences. Racism, in other words, can affect a person socially, mentally, and physically. Group representation can be the most powerful defining body of a person.

Graver argues that another body, the body of *flesh*, exists beyond discourse. According to Graver, the exterior is comprised of "simply skin and hair," whereas the interior is made up of "muscle, fat, blood, and warmth" (ibid., 230). Though it is easy to do, Graver argues that we should not confuse the fleshy body with others. That is, even if we are seeing the flesh of a naked body on stage, we are more inclined really to be seeing the flesh of a character or the flesh of a performing body engaged in the task required to execute the performance. Graver claims: "The fleshy body is the aspect of animate life free from volition. One can see it when contemplation reaches an absolute zero where the eye gazes without a purpose beyond the simple joy of seeing, and the object displayed has no purpose or plan beyond being seen" (ibid.). I will be honest with you: I have a very hard time imagining how one can see—a body or anything—without engaging discourse. Graver anticipates that response by noting that flesh is "really only a small part" of the multiplicitous body on stage: "flesh is seldom displayed in and for itself exclusively" (ibid., 231). Despite my misgivings, the notion of "flesh" is useful to my thinking about O'Connor.

Recall *Time*'s description of O'Connor cited above: O'Connor is an "elfin Irish singer [...] sporting a crew cut." In these few words, aspects of O'Connor's group representation and flesh are highlighted—and the highlighting is noteworthy for its ubiquity. Chances are, if you have read any description of O'Connor, it includes a nod to her nationality, her physical size, and hair (or lack thereof). All of these descriptors guide us in how we think of O'Connor, specifically as a seemingly harmless (elfin) yet unusual (woman who wears a crew cut) singer from Ireland. I cannot help but wonder if the author felt compelled to describe O'Connor as "elfin" to counter the associations people make with crew cuts on women. O'Connor herself commented on such associations when asked about her hair in a *Rolling Stone* interview:

> I don't really know why it's such a big deal to people. I suppose it's because it's not like anybody else's. It has certain associations as well. It has the whole fascist association. It has the whole lesbian association. And it has the whole aggressive-woman association, which, of course, everybody hates. (Ritts 1991)

The interviewer countered her negative assessments by asking, "Are you aware of people trying to look like you?" O'Connor replied: "I've seen people with shaved heads, but I wouldn't flatter myself by assuming it was because of me." Perhaps she is right. Perhaps people tried to look like her because journalists described her in harmless and flattering terms.

These are descriptions of O'Connor derived from evidence beyond her actual performance. Hearing "Nothing Compares 2 U" and seeing the video gave me no indication that O'Connor is Irish. I heard no accent and noted no dialect in her performance of that particular song. In the years since the release of the song and video, I have heard and watched O'Connor perform countless times, often hearing traces or the full force of her brogue. (One also could hear her brogue in other songs from the album, such as "I am Stretched on Your Grave.") O'Connor herself has thoughts regarding a singer's accent. Years after the release of "Nothing Compares 2 U," she claimed: "I used to sing in an American accent; now I sing in my own. The freedom you get from that is indescribable" (Goldman 1997). Engaging her commentator body, she offers three "commandments of singing," the first of which is "Sing in your own accent" (Long 2011).[9] This indicates that, for O'Connor, being an *Irish* singer is as important to her as being a singer. But in the video for "Nothing Compares 2 U," it is not her nationality that is the most prominent indicator of her group membership. It is her gender.

More specifically, what struck us then—and stays with us now—about O'Connor's performance was—is—her *mis*-performance of gender. We first met O'Connor as a closely shorn woman. Though there were other female celebrities who wore tightly cropped hair—for example, Annie Lennox, Grace Jones, and Linda Evangelista—I was not as struck by their appearances as I was by O'Connor's. Perhaps this is because the masculine cuts worn by Lennox, Jones, and Evangelista accompanied the strong, sharp—more masculine—facial features of these women. O'Connor's face, in contrast and in close-up, appears delicate, even when she scowls through certain lines in the lyrics. This appearance is due partly, I am sure, to the filter used in the filming; O'Connor's face softly glows against a black background. Nevertheless, the contrast of the culturally determined femininity of her face and the historically masculine haircut presents the audience with a striking contradiction. If an audience member believes that gender roles are clearly distinct and must be followed according to one's sex, that audience member may experience that striking contradiction as a collision of bodies. O'Connor is mis-performing her gender. That mis-performance collides with a viewer's expectations of how gender should be performed. Whether one viewed O'Connor's head exposure as an affectation or affront, fans and critics alike have come to identify O'Connor with that haircut. That haircut has been a part of her personage since we first "met" her over 20 years ago.

In fact, the association of O'Connor with her lack of hair has become so strong that audiences will not tolerate any other follicular style upon her head. Nor do

---

[9]   The other two commandments reveal the importance O'Connor places on integrating the body of private sensation into one's performance. The second commandment is "Don't sing a song that you don't identify with emotionally." The third is, "Don't think about the notes, think about the feelings within a song."

they—we—take kindly to the rest of her body changing. The images in the video for "Nothing Compares 2 U" were so seared into our brain that, for some, any deviation is unacceptable. Such a reaction is exemplified in recent media stories such as, "What's Happened 2 U? Rocking Sinead O'Connor is Barely Recognisable in Long Hair and Mumsy Trouser-Suit" (Owen 2011), and, "Sinead O'Connor Appears On Stage, No Longer Bald or Skinny" (Johnson 2011). The titles alone make clear the tone of these news stories, perhaps best described as mocking dismay. (I admit to laughing through a cringe when I read the first title. I admit to laughing right now.) Not all journalists or readers, however, shared such a reaction. For example, *Salon* ran a piece entitled, "Sinead O'Connor's Latest Shocker: Not Being 20 Anymore," with the byline, "The Irish singer blows the Internet's mind by getting older" (Williams 2011). Audiences seem willing to accept only the "Sinéad O'Connor" of the 1990 video performance of "Nothing Compares 2 U." That video branded her and burned into our memory an unsustainable body. Whether one found that body pleasurable or repugnant, that body—as character, performer, personage, group representative, and flesh—became beholden to our expectations and the only acceptable embodiment of "Sinéad O'Connor."

I hope what I have made clear in this explication and application of Graver's bodies to O'Connor's performance of "Nothing Compares 2 U" is the usefulness of the typology in making sense of our perceptual process when audiencing a performer both on and off the stage. In the next section, I focus on O'Connor as a singer-activist, demonstrating how the controversies she has sparked over the years can be understood as collisions of bodies—her own with others'. Being a singer-activist does not mean one is necessarily controversial. However, "controversial" is what the media have branded[10] O'Connor's behavior—and her—now and for the past 20 years.[11] Very few singer-activists have elicited the amount of scorn, derision, and ire that O'Connor has from her political interventions. We should tend to that distinction. Furthermore, I feel compelled to tend to her for what she has suffered in speaking out—acting out—against what so many hold dear. Rare among her contemporaries, O'Connor has sacrificed well-being for the sake of showing us the profanity of the sacred.

O'Connor's Colliding Bodies Colliding with Others' Bodies

Over the past two decades, Sinéad O'Connor has presented herself as the embodiment of seemingly striking contradictions: an abject beauty; a vehement

---

[10] The term "branding" has become cliché in this context; however, I use the term for two reasons: (1) to conjure the association of burning flesh to demarcate ownership; and (2) to refer to the marketing practice.

[11] For an example dating 20 years ago, see Pareles. For an exemplary 2011 headline, see Devlin. For a sense of the pervasiveness of this characterization, Google "Sinéad O'Connor controversial" and you will get about 7,360,000 hits.

pacifist; a devout blasphemer; and a heterosexual torch singer who is "no man's woman." She is both a victim of child abuse and a victor in the war against it. Arguably, she is a martyr for the very Church she demonizes. O'Connor writes of herself: "I'm a very strong woman. But I am also over-sensitive by nature of what I do for a living and I, like every other human on earth am a kaleidoscope of sometimes glorious, sometimes agonizing contradictions."[12] Critical reactions to O'Connor usually fall within the scope of "She's crazy." It seems that Western audiences do not easily process embodied contradictions. However, embodied contradictions alone do not necessarily generate controversy.

We can identify 3 October 1992 as the point of conception of O'Connor's internationally recognized controversial self, the date when O'Connor tore up an image of Pope John Paul II on *Saturday Night Live*. That was the night she first became known as a singer-activist. That event alone would have sustained at least a chapter of analysis, but O'Connor lived on to be the center of more controversy by, for example, refusing to sing the national anthem at a 1992 concert in New Jersey, getting herself ordained a priest by a splinter-sect of the Catholic Church in 1999, and in 2000, pronouncing herself a lesbian then retracting. Even if academics have not paid her much attention, the mainstream international media certainly have "written her up" *ad nauseam*. Arguably, such coverage has helped and hurt her causes.

From the release of "Nothing Compares 2 U" in 1990 to 3 October 1992, the media helped establish O'Connor's personage as an unusual but hardly controversial pop musician. It was not until 3 October 1992, that O'Connor collided with the mainstream, transforming herself from unusual to, in the eyes of many, unconscionable. Her performance on *Saturday Night Live* is a complex embodiment both driven by and received with forceful emotions. Declaring the head of the Catholic Church "the real enemy" in the fight against child abuse caused such cognitive distance, in Catholics and non-Catholics alike, that people sought to silence both message and messenger by any means necessary.

There are two primary ways in which critics in the public realm attempted to silence O'Connor. The first way was—and continues to be—through invalidation on the grounds of insanity. In particular, critics deemed—and continue to deem—her insane. This was the chosen rhetorical strategy of at least one Catholic Church official. On 6 October 1992, the Associated Press circulated the following reaction: "'The Holy Father would be the first one to want to say a prayer for her,' said Frank DeRosa, a spokesman for Brooklyn Bishop Thomas V. Daily. 'She's more to be pitied than condemned. ... She needs some professional help" ("O'Connor Draws Criticism" 1992). After O'Connor spoke to the press about the violence perpetuated by the Catholic Church over the centuries, the spokesperson for the Catholic League for Religious and Civil Rights responded: "'This poor woman not only needs a good historian, she also needs a psychiatrist,' said [Kathleen] McCreary. 'It's difficult to get angry at these statements because she obviously

---

[12]   Sinéad O'Connor, "This Week's Un-cut Version *of Irish Sunday Independent* Piece," *Sinéad O'Connor*, 18 September 2011, http://www.sineadoconnor.com.

has a compulsion for notoriety. ... These are just rantings'" (Morse 1992). Such indictments effectively silence the accused for there is no response the accused can offer that is not immediately deemed suspect or incredible.

The second silencing strategy was threatening physical violence: 3 October 1992 was not the first time public figures responded to O'Connor with violent speech. The first time occurred on 24 August 1990 when O'Connor, right before she was scheduled to take the stage at New Jersey's Garden States Arts Center, refused to perform if the "Star Spangled Banner" was to be played. The following night on that stage, Frank Sinatra is reported to have said to the audience: "She should leave the country. Her behavior is unforgivable. For her sake, we'd better never meet" ("Sinatra Takes Verbal Swipe at O'Connor" 1990). Another publication reports that Sinatra suggested O'Connor should "have her ass kicked" (Sinatra, quoted in Brown 1992). Still another reports that Sinatra himself wanted to "kick her ass" (Sinatra, quoted in Peachey 1992). And, finally, from the folks in Australia, we can read that Sinatra believed O'Connor "deserved 'a kick up the ass'" (Nunah 1992).

In this case, however cited by journalists, it is clear that Sinatra experienced a multi-bodied collision. In the most prominent sense, Sinatra lashes out as a representative of the United States, thereby implicating negatively O'Connor's nationality. However, even more implicit though no less significant, Sinatra is decrying the presence of O'Connor's commenting body. By refusing to perform if the national anthem were played, O'Connor makes a statement about a performer's choices. In engaging her commenting body, she contributed to the development of her personage as a singer who performs according to her convictions rather than the demands of others'—including those of the music industry, fans, and critics. Sinatra was so insulted by the affronts to his national identity and performing identity that he could not contain his own commenting body in wishing to cause harm to O'Connor's locus of private sensations. Arguably, his violent reactions did not violate the public's expectations of him. Over decades he established a 'tough-guy" personage.

Perhaps it was because Sinatra had already blazed a bully trail that Joe Pesci felt emboldened to do the same following O'Connor's *SNL* performance. Or perhaps Joe Pesci was just being "Joe Pesci," another beloved tough-guy celebrity. While hosting *SNL* on the Saturday following O'Connor's performance, Pesci displayed for the audience a mended photograph of the Pope and stated that "she was very lucky it wasn't my show, because if it was my show, I would have gave her such a smack." The audience cheered approval ("Wait! Sinead Believes in God" 1992). I was not in that audience, but I imagine that, to many people in that audience, it felt like "Tommy DeVito" of *Goodfellas* was their host for the evening (Scorsese 1990).

Just as Goodwin and Auslander note the ease with which audiences confuse a singer's bodies (that is, we often confuse character with "the real person"), we can say the same of audiences who view actors. It is not fair of me to suggest an equation of Pesci and his mobster character DeVito. But I cannot help myself. What Pesci said sounds like something DeVito would say—and it may be the case that DeVito says things Pesci would say.[13] What I can say about Pesci's reaction is this: O'Connor's performance collided with his Catholic body. We should wonder, however, if Pesci felt threatened in other ways, by other bodies. Furthermore, I must make clear that Sinatra's and Pesci's reactions can be considered consistent with and representative of a multitude of critics, whether they expressed themselves in the media or at the water cooler—or from the seats of Madison Square Garden.

On 16 October 1992 at a Bob Dylan tribute concert, O'Connor was scheduled to perform Dylan's "I Believe in You"; however, mixed with cheers, the crowd's deafening "Boos" silenced her—but only for so long. Steve Morse of the Montreal *Gazette* reports: "After freezing at the microphone for nearly a minute, O'Connor was assisted by emcee Kris Kristofferson, who came out to say quite audibly, 'Don't let the bastards get you down'" (Morse 1992). After stopping the band from playing the introductory notes of Dylan's song, O'Connor belted out her *SNL* version of "War." The jeers were relentless. After finishing with a defiant pose, O'Connor walked off the stage into Kristofferson's arms.[14] It is the bravest performance I have ever seen.

At that point in her life, she had been threatened countless times with physical violence and accused (I use that word purposefully) of being insane—all of these acts sanctioned by and perpetuated by various journalists, artists, representatives of the Catholic Church, and members of the general public. Regardless of what ultimately happened on that stage, she already had accepted courageously an invitation to honor her adored Dylan while the press was still pummeling her for her *SNL* protest. In the face of hatred, she stood her ground and reiterated her stance. For some, in shouting her war cry, she reinforced her personage as an activist. For others, her actions were seen as further evidence of insanity. Yet others interpreted her actions in the context of trouble-making rock stars. Two examples of this type of contextualizing are worth noting.

The first can be found in a Canadian publication dated 16 days after O'Connor's *SNL* protest and 3 days after O'Connor re-performed "War" at Madison Square Garden:

> O'Connor has fast become a new kind of pop antagonist—a loose, venom-spewing cannon whose scattergun brand of rebellion is a lot more unnerving than Madonna's contrived eroticism, Prince's macho narcissism or Axl Rose's self-indulgent, bad-boy ravings. O'Connor ripping up the pope's picture was probably the single most enraging pop act since John Lennon said the Beatles were more popular than Jesus—a statement surely less deliberate than O'Connor's. (Morse 1992)

---

[13]   For a sampling, see the character's quotation page on *Internet Movie Database*, http://www.imdb.com/character/ch0002627/quotes.

[14]   See, for example, "Sinead O'Connor: 'War' live at the Bob Dylan Tribute," *YouTube*, http://www.youtube.com/watch?v=TKeJifOXAnA.

In his comparison of O'Connor to other "pop antagonists," Steve Morse identifies authenticity as the differentiating factor. While other pop antagonists perform well-known roles—familiar rock-star personages characterized by predictable unpredictability—O'Connor is creating a new role, one that is volatile. On the one hand, Morse's description is a concession to O'Connor's power as an activist. On the other hand, his description is easily interpretable as condemnation on the basis of insanity. He paints her as a violent lunatic, someone to be feared. What I find most remarkable about O'Connor's performance at Madison Square Garden is how not-performance it is. She does not *perform* fear, anger, and suffering. She *is* fearful, *is* angry, and *suffers* before our eyes. She may even be reciprocating the hatred of the audiences (present and otherwise). But I cannot tell for sure—and I would not blame her if she were.

The second description of O'Connor from this time period that I want to note was published in *The New York Times*. It is noteworthy not only for the journalist's characterization of O'Connor, but for the justification he offers for the enraged responses:

> Anti-authority sentiments raise hackles highest when the challenge comes from insubordinate blacks (like Ice-T with "Cop Killer") or women, like O'Connor. If a heavy-metal band took a picture of the Pope, hung it on an upside-down cross and burned it, the act would likely be greeted with yawns—that old bit again? But waifish female 25-year-olds like O'Connor don't have the same prerogative. While bullies like Axl Rose are lionized as rock-and-roll rebels simply for lashing out at the press—like so many losing political candidates—O'Connor draws real outrage because she doesn't know her place. (Pareles 1992)

Leaving aside the specificity of O'Connor's message—that the Catholic Church is aiding and abetting child-abusing priests—Pareles concisely argues that the "real" problem with O'Connor's actions are that they are embodied by a "waifish female 25-year-old." This particular body—in its smallness, in its youth, in its femaleness—has no place in the political arena. That this particular body is also white exacerbates the ire from the majority. In a racist society, in the eyes of the dominant, being black is, by default, being insubordinate. Being white and resistant is seen as a betrayal.

O'Connor's flesh, her performing body, her personage, her commenting body, her representation of her gender and nationality, and her private sensations combine and present themselves in ways that are perceived to be contradictory to each other and contradictory to the status quo. O'Connor, on and off the stage, challenges us to see and hear her in all her "sometimes glorious, sometimes agonising contradictions."[15] Even when she sings the words of others, because she is such a skillful performer so adept at empathizing and embodying the other, I, along with other fans and critics alike, willfully interpret these character performances as performances of her self.

---

[15]   O'Connor, 18 September 2011.

On the importance of empathy in her artistic endeavors, O'Connor once said, "I wouldn't give a flying fuck if it was God himself who wanted to hear a song. [...] If I didn't identify with it emotionally, I wouldn't sing it."[16] O'Connor succeeds in her singer-activist agendas because of her ability to empathize and evoke empathy. Perhaps more important, she does not fail when she enrages. However problematic, O'Connor is remarkable for her apparent authenticity. She is efficacious because she—as a multitude of bodies—crashes into us, making us confront the ways that our existence is always in conflict with others'.

Reverberations

I am acutely aware that, thus far, I have presented O'Connor to you primarily as the target of violent expression, rather than contemplating her as the perpetrator. Her performance on *SNL* was symbolically violent. She cries for war and destroys an image of a human being. Moreover, she appropriates Marley's song for her own purposes—an act that, in effect, simultaneously erases and alludes to Marley's intent. In addition to "tending to" the various bodies that comprise the controversial self, we must attend to the contexts from which these bodies were born. We must ask, what are the circumstances that brought these bodies into being? What are the generating events? What—and who—provided this multi-bodied performer with motives to behave in these particular ways?[17]

As an abused child, O'Connor suffered a most literal collision of bodies, the reverberations of which she will suffer the rest of her life. However, it is not only the continued pain of the memories of abuse that she must endure. Like she and many others argue, "A child of violence and abuse is not allowed a voice."[18] O'Connor must suffer repeated collisions as she speaks out about her experiences and the experiences of others to hostile audiences. O'Connor blames all the incessant and injurious silencing—from childhood on—for her poor mental and physical

---

[16]   Long, 2011.

[17]   I must credit the work of two other theorists who inform my thinking here. One is Victor Turner and his theoretical frame of the social drama, "a sequence of social interactions of a conflictive, competitive, or agonistic type," including the stages of breach, crisis, redress, and reintegration or schism (Victor Turner, *The Anthropology of Performance*, New York, PAJ Publications, 1988, p. 33). The other is Kenneth Burke and his dramatistic analysis, dependent upon the Pentad—Act, Scene, Agent, Agency, Purpose—and the ratios between and among the elements (Kenneth Burke, *A Grammar of Motives*, Berkeley: University of California Press, 1945). Both of these theoretical lenses are useful for understanding controversy. However, neither emphasizes to my satisfaction the ontological features of controversy—hence, my use of Graver.

[18]   This quote is from a full page that O'Connor purchased from the *Irish Examiner* after being criticized and scorned for publicly advertising for a sexual partner. Sinéad O'Connor, "I Am Exercising My Right," *Irish Examiner*, 24 September 2004, p. 7.

health. Furthermore, her pain is worsened each time she attempts to redress the continuous abuse. So often, journalists rebuff all attempts O'Connor makes to take control of the way people perceive her.

For example, journalists for news organizations ranging from *The Guardian*[19] to *The Huffington Post*[20] assert that O'Connor is bipolar—despite O'Connor explicitly and frequently denying the condition. Here is an example:

> I would like to clear up another mis-understanding. Almost eight year go I was dignosed with Polar Disorder. This diagnoses was thrown into dispute over the last few years and I have undergone three separate sets of intense re-assessments and been very clearly told I do not in fact suffer from bi polar disorder but from regular 'situational depression'. I would like this clarified so as to stop people dismissing me as 'insane' wether to my face or behind back.[21]

To be fair, after O'Connor was diagnosed with bipolar disorder, she discussed her condition with print and television journalists. In one instance, during a 12 November 2007 interview with a United Kingdom talk show, ITV1's *This Morning*, O'Connor addresses her mental health in terms of multiple selves:

> I never really had a chance to form a personality of my own. The big issue with child abuse is it takes your personality and then suddenly you're this famous thing and you know you're not that either for real. You're in some spiritual gap or something. [...] You don't know who you are so it's not much fun but I've found getting older to be fantastic, you know.[22]

Although explicitly asked about bipolar disorder, O'Connor describes a condition that is not necessarily indicative of bipolar disorder. Although she currently claims to suffer from "situational depression," her description above seems to indicate an enduring condition. But what do I know? I know only that she continuously struggles with making sense of herself while struggling against the ways others make sense of her.

In addition to her ongoing survival of her mother's unspeakable abuse, O'Connor claims an ongoing fight for survival of—and from—her Motherland,

---

[19] Sean Michaels, "Sinéad O'Connor Explains Twitter Suicide Claims," *Guardian*, 19 September 2011, http://www.guardian.co.uk/music/2011/sep/19/sinead-o-connor-twitter.

[20] Stephanie Marcus, "Sinéad O'Connor Recovering from Suicide Attempt, Pleads for Help on Twitter," *Huffington Post*, 12 January 2012, http://www.huffingtonpost.com/2012/01/12/sinead-oconnor-pleads-for-psychiatric-help-on-twitter--suicide-attempt_n_1201626.html.

[21] Sinéad O'Connor, "Polar Disorder," *Sinéad O'Connor*, 26 September 2011. http://www.sineadoconnor.com.

[22] "Sinéad O'Connor Talks about Her Bipolar Diagnosis." *YouTube*. http://www.youtube.com/watch?v=zeENabygTco&feature=related.

Ireland. According to O'Connor, Ireland makes her suffer as a woman and as singer-activist. Ireland as a theocracy invalidates and condemns her with accusations of insanity. For O'Connor, Ireland is as abusive a home as the domicile she shared with her mother:

> I wrote on twitter on my way home from the visit as I was crying my face off that I have been so traumatised over the years by this treatment of me as if I'm a mad-woman it has often made me wish there was a way I could die without my children knowing it was on purpose. By choice I would rather not live in Ireland. But am here because it is what is best for my children. If Ireland wasn't still in the grip of the dregs of theocracy a woman like me could live here happily. Without disrespect or humiliation.[23]

Despite her righteous anger at the debilitating forces of her nation and the church within which she was raised, she chooses not to leave or ignore these realms. For the sake of her own children and the children of Ireland, she talks back to power. More than choosing, as an artist, she feels *obliged* to do so. She expects the same from her artist compatriots and publicly decries Bob Geldof and Bono for not joining her efforts for the sake of Ireland and Ireland's children:

> Neither Geldof, Bono, nor other internationally massive, influential Irish artists are vocal on ANY Irish issues. This is un-Irish in the extreme, and a great let down to Joyce, O'Brien, Yeats, Pierce, Behan, all of them. All of what they suffered so that we could be free Irish artists. They hoped we would care. There is a stunned silence in the people of Ireland on so many issues. I am convinced that this is in enormous part because the artists, the very people who should be shouting from the rooftops, are silent. [. . .] On the south side in our rock-star mansions we roll over in our beds and our only problem is what fucking wankers we are. Ireland is heading towards the end of the first republic. All structures are down. Including spiritual. All we have left is our artistry. We need it. We spiritually need it. Ireland need[s] spiritual support and upliftment. And to speak and be heard and valued. The artists are the ones who need to be doing this work because no one else is doing it.[24]

For decades, O'Connor has used the press and now, increasingly, her website and Twitter account to engage her commenting body—to state what she think artists should do. Her own consistency with her imperatives should be expected. But given the costs she has paid—her situational depression and the blows to her self-esteem caused by journalists—for the path she has forged, O'Connor is to be admired. All of this—from the beginning of my analysis to this point here—is not

---

[23]   O'Connor, 18 September 2011.

[24]   Sinéad O'Connor, "*Irish Independent* article and Sinead's addendum," *Sinéad O'Connor*, 23 November 2011. http://www.sineadoconnor.com.

to say that I always agree with her. In fact, given who I am—as a performance studies scholar—I have had my own collision with O'Connor.

My Collisions with Sinéad

I write "Sinéad" in this section rather than "O'Connor" because that is how I think of her—as "Sinéad," not "O'Connor." Is that not how everyone thinks of her, if they think of her at all? I hesitate even to share this with you, especially as I near the end of my chapter. I have worked so hard to present Sinéad in a particular halo of light. But I know that no one is an angel—not I, certainly—and I would be remiss if I were not completely honest in sharing with you my own experience of colliding with Sinéad. After all, one of the purposes of this volume is to offer explorations of the relationships between artists and authors/fans.

A couple months after I committed to writing this chapter, Sinéad decided her website would be a fine place to bemoan her loneliness and disclose her libidinal yearnings. In a post dated 2 August 2011 and entitled "Is Sinéad about to Hump Her Truck?" she writes:

> My shit-uation sexually/affectionately speaking is so dire that inanimate objects are starting to look good as are inappropriate and/or unavailable men and/ or inappropriate and/or unavailable fruits and vegetables. I tell you yams are looking like the winners.[25]

"My goodness," I thought, "This is something different!" I was excited to see some action on the site that moved beyond tour dates and links to official reports on the sexual abuse scandal and the Vatican (not that these are not *very important* bits of information). This post promised to be a much more explicit evocation of what I hoped would be the "real person" behind "Sinéad O'Connor."

But as I read on, I continuously thought, "I don't believe this"—first in the "I'm shocked!" sense, then in the literal sense. What first had me reeling was not the disclosure of desires; rather it was O'Connor's misrepresentation of Karen Finley. After her consideration of yams as a sexual partner, O'Connor writes:

> I actually do know a woman who is a performance artist from America. I have a photo of her being escorted arm in arm by two uk police man onto a plane back home cuz she humped a yam in the middle of her show. I just know that's going to happen to me if I don't take drastic action.[26]

---

[25]   Sinéad O'Connor, "Is Sinéad about to Hump Her Truck?," *Sinéad O'Connor*, 2 August 2011, http://www.sineadoconnor.com.

[26]   Ibid.

Granted, O'Connor does not say the name "Karen Finley"; however, I know a couple things that lead me to this conclusion. First, I know that O'Connor collaborated with Finley on a remix of "Jump in the River" (O'Connor and Finley 1988). Second, I know that many people mistakenly believe that Finley inserted a yam into her anus during a performance. Knowing these things, I cannot believe that O'Connor would be among the many who mis-characterize Finley's actions—especially because so much of Finley's work (including the one alluded to by the reference to yams) is about and against abuse—especially toward women. Finley has repeatedly and explicitly debunked the myth that she inserted a yam into her anus during her performance, *Yams Up My Granny's Ass*, which she first performed in February 1986.[27]

"I don't believe it!" I think. I am shocked. Then I rationalize: "She must be referencing some other 'American performance artist' who actually *did* hump a yam." But a quick investigation told me otherwise. In an interview, O'Connor characterizes her relationship with Finley, as well as mischaracterizes Finley's work:

> I got to do loads of amazing collaborations over the last ten years. My favourite one was with a woman named Karen Finley. She was this mad performance artist who, before I met her, had been escorted out of the city of London by the police for stuffing yams up her hole at a gig. As it turned out, on a personal level, she was really normal—but as an artist she was mad, completely mad. So we did this version of 'Jump In The River', with MC Lyte, and it was very funny, cos Karen's just completely insane. (90s: Lion's Daughter 2002)

I am simultaneously certain and incredulous. I do not want to believe Sinéad is capable of engaging—on two occasions—in the careless characterization of another person—let alone another woman performer dedicated to fighting abuse—as "mad." It smacks me as hypocritical. I wonder if I am holding Sinéad to too high of standards. I wonder if Finley would even be bothered by Sinéad's characterization. I wonder if this wondering matters at all. Perhaps the only thing that matters is that Sinéad's commentary struck me. "I don't believe you," I whisper to the computer screen, to this new "Sinéad."

"I don't believe you," despite its common usage, is a terribly powerful statement. It is the expression of confrontation. It is used in two ways, with equal epistemological and ontological force. In the epistemological sense, it is literal and used to characterize what someone has said as being untrue. In another way, in the ontological sense, it is used to express shock at someone's expressions or actions—and hence, their performance of self. In both ways, it is an act of invalidation. I do not want to join the parties that have sought to invalidate Sinéad for so long. But I stand my ground in this particular disappointment.

---

[27]   For example, see the 1997 interview conducted by Jeanne Carstensen of *The Gate*, http://www.sfgate.com/eguide/profile/arc97/1297finley-interview.shtml.

My Here and Now is Your There and Then

As I write this, Sinéad O'Connor's ninth studio album, *How About I Be Me (And You Be You)?* is not yet available.[28] Nevertheless, thanks to *YouTube* and its posters, I have seen multiple versions of her performing three of the tracks: "Take off Your Shoes"; "4th & Vine"; and her cover of John Grant's "Queen of Denmark."[29] I listen to her. I watch her. I read her title album and, again, I do not believe her. At least, I do not believe the title. (I can say the same for her 1990 breakout album, *I Do Not Want What I Haven't Got*.) If the titular "You" is, say, the Vatican or Bono, I am confident she does not want "You" to remain who "You" are. O'Connor makes herself very clear on this point in two songs: "Take Off Your Shoes" (sung as the Holy Spirit addressing the Vatican) and "V.I.P." (volleyed at Bono) (Sweeney 2011). I have seen Sinéad perform the former. It chills my Catholic body as the tune and her voice—*her incomparable voice*—reverberates from my tummy to the top of my head and the tips of my toes. Sinéad awes me, angers me, frightens me, and inspires me. She makes me lose the plot. But when I stop to consider her in her wholeness, in her compilation of colliding selves in relation to my own, I begin to find my way.

I like to say that I am not a violent person. But the truth is, I work very hard at not being a violent person. I want to say that I do not condone violence of any sort. But the truth is, I admire O'Connor for her actions—actions that can be characterized as violent. As someone who has experienced silencing in its many forms, I empathize with O'Connor and I believe her behavior to be rational responses to the misdeeds of others. I have no doubt that her actions are powerful; however, to this day, right here and now, her actions have yet to overpower the violence of the dominant structures that debilitate so many. I am grateful for the collisions O'Connor endures and for sacrificing herself, her body as a compilation and collision of bodies, in the name of controversy.

---

[28] The album release date is 20 February 2012. Until October 2011, the album was titled *Home* upon the suggestion of O'Connor's brother Joseph. O'Connor changed the title in response to the negative responses to O'Connor's public proclamations of sexual desire. See Nadia Mendoza, "'I was Getting Too Much Abuse': Sinéad O'Connor Quits Twitter After Her Followers Took Stories about Sex 'Too Seriously,'" *Daily Mail*, 12 November 2011, http://www.dailymail.co.uk/tvshowbiz/article-2060495/Sinead-OConnor-quits-Twitter-followers-took-stories-sex-seriously.html.

[29] Go to YouTube, http://www.youtube.com. For a sampling of footage from her summer tour, in the "Search" box, enter following phrase: "Sinéad St. Petersburg 2011." For a peak at her November tour, enter "Sinead St. John at Hackney 2011." Following this process will be easier for you than if you were to type in any *YouTube* URL I were to supply here.

Postscript

It is now 21 January, 2012. Sinéad, now home after a few days in the hospital for her depression, tweeted a request for jokes. She hoped for bawdy ones and lots of folks complied. I opened a Twitter account solely to follow Sinéad during my writing process. I do not plan to become an enthusiast of this particular social medium; but today I figured sending Sinéad a joke is the least I could do as a gesture of thanks for all she has done for me in the past and as I write this chapter. I tweeted: "Q: How do u catch a polar bear? A: Cut a hole in the ice; line it w peas. When he goes 2 take a pea, kick him in the icehole." To my amazement and giddy-fan delight, Sinéad responded: "My 8 yr old loved that :)))) Many cackles were had." Then she retweeted that silly little joke, the only joke I know, and I am profoundly moved—not through collision, but by the ease with which humans can make joyous connections.

Bibliography

Auslander, Philip. "Musical Personae." *The Drama Review* 50, 1 (2006): 100–19.

Brown, M. "Sinead's Fight for Her Convictions." *Sunday Herald Sun*, 25 October 1992.

Burke, Kenneth. *A Grammar of Motives*. Berkeley, CA: University of California Press, 1945.

Cruz, Gilbert. "MTV's 30th Anniversary: The 30 Best Music Videos of All-TIME." *Time*. 28 July 2011. http://www.time.com/time/specials/packages/article/ 0,28 804,2085389_2085358_2085385,00.html.

Devlin, Martina. "Sinéad: Always Controversial but Still Incomparable." *Belfast Telegraph*, 10 December 2011. http://www.belfasttelegraph. co.uk/opinion/news-analysis/sinead-always-controversial-but-shes-still-incomparable-16088771.html.

Frith, Simon. *Performing Rites: On the Value of Popular Music*. Cambridge: Harvard University Press, 1996.

Goldman, Vivien. "Sinéad O'Connor." *Rolling Stone*, 13 November 1997.

Goodwin, Andres. *Dancing in the Distraction Factory: Music Television and Popular Culture*. Minneapolis: University of Minnesota Press, 1992.

Graver, David. "The Actor's Bodies." *Text and Performance Quarterly* 17, 3 (1997): 221–35.

Guterman, Jimmy. *Sinéad O'Connor: Her Life and Music*. New York: Grand Central Publishing, 1991.

Hayes, Dermott. *Sinéad O'Connor: So Different*. London: Omnibus Press, 1990.

Johnson, James. "Sinéad O'Connor Appears On Stage, No Longer Bald or Skinny." *Inquisitr*, August 9, 2011. http://www.inquisitr.com/133380/sinead-oconnor-appears-on-stage-no-longer-bald-or-skinny-pic/.

Long. Siobhán. "Home Truths." *Irish Times*, 26 August 2011. http://www.irishtimes.com/newspaper/theticket/2011/0826/1224302969258.html.

Marcus, Stephanie. "Sinéad O'Connor Recovering from Suicide Attempt, Pleads for Help on Twitter," *Huffington Post*, 12 January 2012, http://www.huffingtonpost.com/2012/01/12/sinead-oconnor-pleads-for-psychiatric-help-on-twitter--suicide-attempt_n_1201626.html.

Mendoza, Nadia. "'I was Getting Too Much Abuse': Sinéad O'Connor Quits Twitter After Her Followers Took Stories about Sex 'Too Seriously.'" *Daily Mail*, 12 November 2011. http://www.dailymail.co.uk/tvshowbiz/article-2060495/Sinead-OConnor-quits-Twitter-followers-took-stories-sex-seriously.html.

Michaels, Sean. "Sinéad O'Connor Explains Twitter Suicide Claims." *Guardian*, 19 September 2011. http://www.guardian.co.uk/music/2011/sep/19/sinead-o-connor-twitter.

Morse, Steve. "Sinéad O'Connor's Career at Risk as Fans Respond to Her Anger with Their Own." *The Gazette* (Montreal), 19 October 1992.

Nunah, J. "Sinéad is a True Believer." *Sunday Mail*, 25 October 1992.

"O'Connor Draws Criticism, Pity," *Daily News*, 6 October 1992. http://news.google.com/newspapers?id=1SsbAAAAIBAJ&sjid=KkgEAAAAIBAJ&dq=sinead-o-connor%20saturday-night-live%20pope&pg=6761%2C1191830.

O'Connor, Sinéad. "Biography." *Sinéad O'Connor*. 30 December 2011. http://www.sineadoconnor.com.

O'Connor, Sinéad. "I Am Exercising My Right," *Irish Examiner*, 24 September 2004.

O'Connor, Sinéad. "*Irish Independent* article and Sinead's addendum." *Sinéad O'Connor*. 23 November 2011. http://www.sineadoconnor.com.

O'Connor, Sinéad. "Polar Disorder." *Sinéad O'Connor*. 26 September 2011. http://www.sineadoconnor.com.

O'Connor, Sinéad. "This Week's Un-cut Version of *Irish Sunday Independent* Piece." *Sinéad O'Connor*. 18 September 2011. http://www.sineadoconnor.com.

Owen, Pamela. "What's Happened 2 U? Rocking Sinead O'Connor is Barely Recognisable in Long Hair and Mumsy Trouser-Suit." *Mail Online*, 2 July 2011. http://www.dailymail.co.uk/tvshowbiz/article-2010532/Sinead-OConnor-barely-recognisable-long-hair-mumsy-trouser-suit.html.

Pareles, Jon. "Why Sinead O'Connor Hit a Nerve." *New York Times*, 1 November 1992, http://www.nytimes.com/1992/11/01/arts/pop-view-why-sinead-o-connor-hit-a-nerve.html?src=pm.

Reuter, A.P. "Wait! Sinead Believes in God." *Toronto Star*. 25 October 1992.

Ritts, H. "Sinéad O'Connor." *Rolling Stone*, 7 March 1991.

Rogers, Sheila. "Sinéad: Face to Face." *Rolling Stone*, 4 October 1990.

Schechner, Richard. *Between Theatre and Anthropology*. Philadelphia: The University of Pennsylvania Press, 1985.

"Sinatra Takes Verbal Swipe at O'Connor." *The Globe and Mail*, 30 August 1990.

"Sinead O'Connor: Fears For Fragile Singer As She Makes Plea For Help On Twitter." *Huffington Post*, 11 January 2012. http://www.huffingtonpost.co.uk/2012/01/11/sinead-oconnor-fears-for-singer-plea-for-help-twitter_n_1198629.html.

Sweeney, Ken. "Slimmed Down Sinéad O'Connor: I've Lost Two Stone Since Coming off the Wrong Medication." *Independent.ie*, 23 November 2011. http:// www.independent.ie/entertainment/music/slimmed-down-sinead-oconnor-ive-lost-two-stone-since-coming-off-the-wrong-medication-2942537.html.

Szendrey, Roman. *The Sinéad O'Connor Website*. http://www.sinead-oconnor.com.

Turner, Victor. *The Anthropology of Performance*, New York, PAJ Publications, 1988.

"Wait! Sinead Believes in God." *Toronto Star*, 25 October 1992.

Williams, Mary Elizabeth. "Sinead O'Connor's Latest Shocker: Not Being 20 Anymore." *Salon*, 10 August 2011. http://www.salon.com/2011/08/10/sinead_oconnors_latest_shocker/.

Discography

O'Connor, Sinéad. *Am I Not Your Girl?* Ireland: Ensign/Chrysalis, CDP 521952, 1992.

O'Connor, Sinéad. *Faith & Courage*. New York: Atlantic, 83337-2, 2000.

O'Connor, Sinéad. "4th & Vine." *How About I Be Me (And You Be You)?* London: One Little Penguin, TPLP1122CD, 2012.

O'Connor, Sinéad. "Take Off Your Shoes." *How About I Be Me (And You Be You)?* London: One Little Penguin, TPLP1122CD, 2012.

O'Connor, Sinéad. "V.I.P." *How About I Be Me (And You Be You)?* London: One Little Penguin, TPLP1122CD, 2012.

O'Connor, Sinéad. "I Am Stretched On Your Grave." *I Do Not Want What I Haven't Got*. Ireland: Ensign/Chrysalis, F2 21759, 1990.

O'Connor, Sinéad. "Nothing Compares 2 U." *I Do Not Want What I Haven't Got*. Ireland: Ensign/Chrysalis, F2 21759, 1990.

O'Connor, Sinéad. *Sean-Nós Nua*. New York: Vanguard, VSD 79724-2, 2002.

O'Connor, Sinéad. *Theology*. New York: Koch Records, KOC-CD-4244, 2007.

O'Connor, Sinéad. *Throw Down Your Arms*. Los Angeles: That's Why There's Chocolate and Vanilla, THCVLP001, 2005.

O'Connor, Sinéad. *Universal Mother*. Ireland: Ensign/Chrysalis, 7243 8 30549 2 3, 1994.

O'Connor, Sinéad with Karen Finley, "Jump in the River." *Jump in the River*. United Kingdom: Ensign Records, ENYCD 618, 1988.

Videography

Goodfellas. Directed by Martin Scorsese. United States: Warner Bros. Pictures, 1990.

Chapter 7

Steve Earle: The Politics of Empathy

Mark Mattern

Many people believe popular myths and stereotypes about marginalized others, and politicians sometimes enact policy based on those myths and stereotypes. These include, for example, the belief that success is available to anyone who works hard; all crimes are committed by bad people who should be punished harshly; and people who are struggling have only themselves to blame. Each of these platitudes reveals an inability to see the world from others', especially marginalized people's perspectives. When enacted into policy, they harden inequalities based on factors such as class, race, and gender. Each represents a failure of empathy. This chapter addresses the music of Steve Earle as an antidote to that failure of empathy. Many of the characters who populate his songs face difficult challenges and live in marginalized circumstances. His music plays a valuable role of cultivating empathy for those whose lives little resemble the dominant narrative of the American Dream.

Martha Nussbaum argues that the arts play a special role in cultivating empathy. They are particularly useful for helping us understand the world from the perspective of "those whom their society tends to portray as lesser, as 'mere objects'." They help us grasp "what it might be like to be in the shoes of a person different from oneself." The arts refine our "capacity to see the world through another person's eyes." Sometimes this involves breaking through "demeaning stereotypes" in order to appreciate and understand the lived reality of another person. Without empathy, we may demonize others who are different, rather than recognize their truth; we may attempt to marginalize and stigmatize them rather than work with them to solve shared problems (Nussbaum 2010, 45, 95–96, 107, 51).

How does art enable empathy? Art captures human experience and makes it meaningful to others; art provides a window into others' lives, identities, and histories. According to philosopher John Dewey, experience "becomes a conscious common possession" through art, "more than by any other means." Compared to other forms of communication, this sharing of experience occurs relatively directly. Language only signals experience, while art creates a direct experience. Art expresses meanings that are not accessible through words, and it does this through creation of a new experience. This is especially clear in music, which is more obviously physical than other forms of art. We experience music with our bodies, as sound waves. "Sound agitates directly" and carries the "power of direct emotional expression." Musical instruments "stir the atmosphere or the ground," and we experience these stirrings as physical sensations. Art plays to our affective as well as cognitive selves. It does not segment the intellect from emotion and affect. In that sense it is not simply a more powerful form of communication, but also a more realistic form in that it deliberately engages the whole person (Dewey 1980, 286, 215–6, 237–8, 158, 208).

The capacity of art to convey others' identities and experiences allows it to play a role in breaking through barriers to understanding. Dewey called art the best form of communication that can occur in "a world full of gulfs and walls that limit community of experience." Art "strikes below the barriers that separate human beings from one another." Art helps people recognize common experiences, and potentially helps them understand and adapt to different experiences of different people (ibid., 105, 270). Having access to others' lives through art gives us a critical foothold in examining our own lives and experiences: it helps us to see ourselves differently. This potentially forces us to rethink our assumptions and beliefs. The "function of art," according to Dewey, "has always been to break through the crust of conventionalized and routine consciousness" in order to see more clearly and critically (Dewey 1954, 183). This is the "moral function" of art: "to remove prejudice, do away with the scales that keep the eye from seeing, tear away the veils due to wont and custom, perfect the power to perceive" (Dewey 1980, 324–5).

Steve Earle's music illustrates these ties between art and empathy. He has made a career of singing about marginalized and stigmatized people whose lives do not follow the stereotypical path to the American Dream, who encounter seemingly insurmountable challenges and acquire physical and emotional scars. There is a deep strain of empathy for these people running through his music, a strain that predates and later accompanies his increasingly overt political activism. This empathy helps him challenge the facile truths of his time, and forces us to think more carefully about our beliefs and assumptions about other people and their lives. He uses his music to help cross boundaries walling off worlds of experience, and this helps us understand the lives of other people.

My relatively recent introduction to Earle also illustrates some of these themes. My wife and I had just finished watching a movie we had rented from the local video store entitled *You Can Count on Me* (Lonergan 2000), starring Mark Ruffalo, Laura Linney, Matthew Broderick, and Rory Culkin. The film portrays a young drifter named Terry Prescott (Ruffalo) who pauses in his wandering to visit his sister Sammy Prescott (Linney), a single mother, and ends up staying. Terry embraces the role of uncle to Linney's pre-teen son Rudy (Culkin), and begins to plant some roots. Eventually, however, he runs into trouble by taking his nephew to a tavern to play pool. Sammy scolds Terry, accusing him of bad judgment and irresponsibility. Terry feels bad about it, and his dismay and shame drive him back to the open road. At the conclusion of the movie, Terry boards a bus and leaves town, opting once again for the open road over immediate family connections. As the bus leaves town, this beautiful, haunting song played. The song, very simple and unadorned, featured sparse lyrics with simple lines repeated multiple times. It told of a pilgrim who constantly travels a lonely, sometimes-rocky highway, the only home the pilgrim knows. Though deeply poignant, wistful, and sad, a third verse injected a note of hope, as the traveler looks forward to meeting again somewhere down the road, with stories to share and songs to sing together. The song, slow but not plodding, opened with a dobro playing lead, and a fiddle playing just behind it. These two instruments are noted for the lonely, mournful feelings they can summon. They were quickly joined by mandolin, guitar, and bass. The lead singer's voice was rough and worn; the voice of someone who had himself traveled a rocky road. It effectively brought to life the sadness and pain of the lyric. Toward the end of the song, a full chorus joined the lead singer, amplifying the already-powerful affective dimension of the tune and, perhaps, offering communal solidarity for the lonely wanderer.

I felt bad for Terry. I wanted to stop the bus, shake Terry, and tell him to stay with his sister and nephew; to opt for connection and family ties over the loneliness of the road. The music helped me *feel*—in a very direct physical way— the loneliness and sadness Ruffalo's character projected on the screen. It helped me sit beside him on that bus, sharing in his pain, offering solidarity.

I don't usually wait for the movie credits. This time, however, I remained glued to my seat, eagerly watching the credits roll until the music credits appeared. "Steve Earle," I said to my wife. "Who's that?" Then I rewound the film and listened again to "Pilgrim." Then I did it again. And again.

In "Pilgrim" (1999), Earle channels the pain and sadness of anyone who has ever felt like they don't belong, who feel like outsiders and so have to keep moving, who feel rejected and excluded, alienated and lonely. It helps the listener share in a deeply painful experience of loneliness and separation. Yet, that note of hope that Earle adds in the third verse helps ward off despair. It speaks to our deep need for a lifeline in the depths of loneliness and desolation.

After this memorable introduction to his music, I began noticing Earle's name and music in various and sometimes surprising places. His music has been covered countless times, and various tunes have been included on movie soundtracks. As this is being written in 2011, he has recorded 14 original albums and counting, and released several compilations and live albums. He has also published a book of short stories, *Doghouse Roses*; a full-length novel, *I'll Never Get out of This World Alive*; and a play, *Karla*. Earle has written numerous haiku poems, and acted in hit TV dramas, including *The Wire* and *Tremé*. For most of his career, he has toured incessantly, suggesting a deep affinity for pilgrims on the road. His career reflects a restless spirit that has crossed, bent, and blended many musical genres including rock, rockabilly, country, bluegrass, folk, and a host of ethnic influences. This genre-bending and genre-busting complements and supports the empathic dimension of his work. It shows a deliberate and natural inclination to break through walls separating worlds of experience. Never one to let conventional walls stop him, he has used his art to listen to others, including and especially marginalized and stigmatized others, and to convey their experiences creatively and affectively to others. He reminds us that those walls are artificial, and that we have much to gain by following his lead in breaking through them.

In the following, I first briefly describe Earle's biography, with special attention to the aspects of his life that help him appreciate the difficult circumstances and challenges of the characters that populate his music and literature. I then examine Earle's music, focusing on songs that best illustrate the theme of empathy. Earle earned his empathy the hard way, by experiencing the alienation, loneliness, and hard times about which he writes and sings.

A Pilgrim on the Road

Steve Earle was born on January 18th, 1955. By the time he reached eighth grade, his family had moved nine times, mostly in Texas near San Antonio. In short, his wandering days began early. Earle read a lot of books as a youngster, but his disinterest in school began to show by the fifth grade. As a junior high student, Earle sometimes spent the night wandering around the city rather than resting up for school. He was eventually expelled from ninth grade for failing to turn in any work.

Earle acquired his first guitar from an uncle, and it quickly became the central focus of his life, driving out whatever interest in schoolwork might have remained. His father attempted to remedy this by locking the guitar in a cupboard. Earle tore the cupboard door off the hinges, grabbed the guitar, and ran away briefly. By age 14, Earle was playing solo gigs at coffeehouses around San Antonio. Like coffeehouse scenes throughout the US during the 1960s, this one featured a cast of activists, hippies, folkies, and radicals who exerted early influence on Earle's political interests and leanings. Earle also began experimenting with drugs in this scene. Apparently recognizing the fruitlessness of attempting to force Earle's hand about school, his parents paid for an apartment in San Antonio for him at age 16. From there, he hitchhiked to gigs in San Antonio, Houston, and Austin.

Earle soon moved to Houston, where he was exposed to rock, rockabilly, honky tonk, folk, country, and the newer strains of country, including the outlaw country of Waylon Jennings, Willie Nelson, Gram Parsons, Jerry Jeff Walker, Kris Kristofferson, Guy Clark, and Townes Van Zandt. In Austin, he latched onto Van Zandt, whom Earle would later cite as one of the most important influences on his own songwriting. Soon after meeting Van Zandt, Earle was opening for him. Like many of the outlaw musicians of the era, Van Zandt was a dubious role model, living on the edge, drinking heavily.

In 1975, at age 20, Earle got his first job with a studio, Sunbury-Dunbar, a division of RCA, writing songs for $75 a week. He also experienced his first studio session there as a background chorus singer for a Guy Clark recording. At this point, it appeared that Earle was taking the fast track to success. However, it would be eight more years before he landed his first record deal, and another two before he actually made his first record.

Earle was married for the first time in June 1974, to Sandra Jean Henderson. Soon after their marriage, while Sandy was gone with her family, Earle unexpectedly took off for Nashville. At first, he crashed on people's floors and couches. The troubled musician was drinking heavily, and using mescaline, LSD, and other drugs. Eventually he took his own apartment, and Sandy joined him. Constantly on the road, however, he saw little of his wife, and the marriage did not last long. In January 1977, he married Cynthia Hailey Dunn. On a whim, they moved briefly to San Miguel de Allende in Central Mexico. Earle's frequent change of homes as a child seems to have established a pattern. By now, it seemed, he was constantly in motion.

Earle experienced a bad cocaine trip in 1977, ironically while playing a benefit gig for the National Organization for the Reform of Marijuana Laws (NORML). He experienced a partial meltdown on stage, lost coordination, forgot some lyrics, and became dizzy and disoriented. After this occurred a second time, Earle stopped performing live, and briefly gave up alcohol and drugs. He finally also gave up Cynthia, whose drug habits threatened his own sobriety. The two divorced in 1980. In March 1981, he married Carol-Ann Hunter, his third wife. In 1982, they had a baby, Justin Townes Earle. Justin would eventually follow his father into the music business.

During his two-year hiatus from performing, Earle went to work for High Chaparral music publishing company as a staff songwriter. Johnny Lee recorded one of his songs, "When You Fall in Love," and it became a Top 10 hit, Earle's first, at the age of 26. Earle eventually began performing again, this time in a rockabilly genre. He and some musician friends, collectively named the Dukes, cut four songs in one night. The songs, released as *Pink and Black* in February 1983, established some of the themes that would characterize much of his subsequent work. "Continental Trailways Blues," Earle's first recorded road tune, featured a man down on his luck, stuck in a bus station eating crappy food, broke, trying to get home to his sweetheart. "Nothin' but You" and "Open up Your Door" both revealed an emerging class consciousness in which rich folks get the good stuff and working-class people make do. Earle began touring again in 1983, traveling a whopping 77,000 miles that year. He also returned to drinking and prescription meds, while continuing his chain smoking and an overall disinterest in hygiene. While still married to Cynthia, in 1984 Earle met and courted Lou-Anne Gill.

Although *Pink and Black* did not sell well, it did help Earle land a recording deal with CBS to do rockabilly. CBS never promoted him, however, so he left CBS to sign with MCA in 1986 to record seven albums over seven years. His breakthrough album, *Guitar Town* (MCA, 1986), reached #1 on the country charts, and led to his appearance on the *Tonight Show* with Johnny Carson. *Rolling Stone* named him Country Artist of the Year, and he was nominated in early 1987 for two Grammys as Best Male Country Vocal Performance and Best Country Song for "Guitar Town." Like *Pink and Black*, *Guitar Town* established or solidified some of the themes that would appear repeatedly in Earle's career: hard times, alienation and the felt need to keep moving, blue collar roots, heartache, lost love, and hope for something better down the road. It also helped establish the genre of alternative country and earn Earle the title of "Godfather of alt-country" (Collins 2011).

Meanwhile, Gill became pregnant, and gave birth in 1987 to their son, Earle's second, Ian Dublin Earle. After finally divorcing Hunter, he married Gill, though by this time he was in love with Teresa Ensenat. He showed up at his bachelor party with Ensenat. Immediately after his marriage ceremony, Earle walked to a pay phone and called Ensenat. Unsurprisingly, Earle and Gill separated in November of the same year. Meanwhile, a band groupie named Theresa Baker gave birth to his third child. Earle's standard response to questions about his serial marriages—"I'm not afraid of commitment" (quoted in McGee 2005)—may strike some as comic, others as surreal.

Earle wanted to use his own band for his second album, to name it *Exit 0* after a freeway exit between Nashville and Louisville, and to feature a photograph of the exit sign on the cover. Earle's MCA producers, however, wanted him to use Nashville studio musicians, to change the front cover, and (for marketing purposes) to release the album under the solo title of *Steve Earle*. Earle refused, insisting that his regular bandmates would record the album with him, that the album cover would stay, and that the album would be released as Steve Earle and the Dukes. Earle eventually prevailed on all counts. This is telling of Earle's loyalty to the Dukes, his sense of fairness, and his willingness to buck the Nashville trends and powers. It also helped cement his reputation as the "class hoodlum" among the "Class of '86" among country musicians (Corcoran 1993). His "innate rebelliousness," on vivid display in this struggle with the Nashville power structure, would manifest itself throughout his subsequent career in part as an unwillingness to stay put within any particular musical genre or any definitive category of performer. Within the first decade of his career, he morphed through several identities: as a "hard-knocked troubadour, rockabilly punk, tattooed arena-rocker, real-life outlaw," and more (Friskics-Warren 1999). Continuing a trend that would mark his entire career, and illustrating the costs of trying to break barriers, *Exit 0* (1987) ran into genre troubles from the outset. Was it country and western? Rock'n'roll? Partly as a result, *Exit 0* did not do as well in the US as his debut album had done. However, it went platinum in Canada.

By the time Earle got to the third album, *Copperhead Road* (1988), his life was spinning out of control. By now he was deeply into heroin, in addition to his other menu of drugs, and he is reported to have been high throughout the recording sessions. He was living with Ensenat, but sometimes sleeping with wife Gill. Eventually he divorced Gill and married fifth wife Ensenat in early 1989, turning up late for the ceremony in front of a judge. By 1988, Earle was paying $4,000 a month in child support and alimony; by 1990, this figure had doubled. Despite the turmoil in his personal life, *Copperhead Road* proved more successful than *Exit 0*, primarily as a rock record.

Friends and family members attempted a drug intervention in 1989, but Earle caught wind of it in advance and did not show up. By the time *The Hard Way* (1991), Earle's fourth album, was released, the "hardcore troubadour" had added guns and motorcycles to his list of vices. During a tour as opener for Bob Dylan, he shot two holes in the bus floor.

The Hard Way failed to crack Billboard's Top 100 Albums chart; one single, "Back to the Wall," made it to #37. Earle released *Shut Up and Die Like an Aviator* (1991), a live album featuring previously released selections recorded over two nights, 5 and 6 October 1990, in London, England and Kitchener, Ontario. The album opens with an homage to the Mohawk Indians blockading a bridge into Montreal in protest of a land dispute with Canadian authorities; another about an inmate on Wyoming's death row; and another about Iraq's invasion of Kuwait. Earle's voice showed the strain of drug abuse and a lifestyle spinning out of control. His self-destructive behavior "made life for him and those around him excruciatingly unbearable" (Krewen 2003).

In the depth of drug addiction, Earle went approximately four years without writing any songs, playing only an occasional gig. Yet, his activism, especially anti-death penalty activism, continued. He wrote to several death row inmates. "Billy Austin," released in 1991 on *The Hard Way*, about a death row inmate, brought him to the attention of Amnesty International. Amnesty staff asked him to support the cause. For a period, Earle went through a methadone treatment program, causing him to gain considerable weight.

Meanwhile, Teresa Ensenat filed for divorce, and it was finalized in 1992. He then married Lou-Anne Gill for the second time in 1993. He continued to rack up a list of petty crimes such as failing to appear before a judge, failure to report for jury duty, and driving without a license. He was finally sentenced to 11 months and 29 days in jail for failing to appear at an earlier hearing. Earle was jailed, but suffered such severe withdrawal that he was moved to a hospital in Fayetteville, Tennessee, to a detox program. After 28 days of treatment, he was returned to jail. He was released in November 1994, after serving only part of his sentence, thanks to a letter-writing campaign on his behalf that included letters from such luminaries as Johnny Cash, Waylon Jennings, and Emmylou Harris.

After jail, Earle managed to clean up his act in most ways. He abandoned his love affair with guns, and stayed off drugs. He divorced Gill for the second time in mid-90s, but maintained alimony and child support for previous wives and his children. Earle also returned to songwriting and recording. *Train a Comin'* (1995), recorded with folk and bluegrass stalwarts Norman Blake, Peter Rowan, Roy Huskey, and Emmylou Harris, was released to critical acclaim, garnering both a Grammy nomination and a Nashville Music Association nomination for Best Folk Album. He also played live to favorable reviews, and received an invitation from filmmaker and actor Tim Robbins to write a song for *Dead Man Walking*, a movie about a man on death row. The result was "Ellis Unit One." *I Feel Alright* (1996) arrived the following year. In 1996, Earle was introduced to members of Journey of Hope: From Violence to Healing, an organization that sought to exonerate death row inmates and included many of their relatives in its membership.

El Corazon (1997) combined many of the genres Earle had been steeped in: rock, country, bluegrass, grunge, rockabilly, and more. The album included "Christmas in Washington," in which Earle calls for some real heroes to fix the mess he observes in Washington and the country. The song includes references to some of his own heroes: Joe Hill, Malcolm X, Martin Luther King, and Emma Goldman. The album shot to #1 on *No Depression*'s Top 40 chart, ahead of Bob Dylan's *Time Out of Mind*. It also reached #1 on Gavin's Americana chart, and the top five on the Triple AAA chart. The single "Telephone Road" hit the top of the Country Music Radio charts. *El Corazon* was also nominated for a Grammy. Following *El Corazon*, Earle mined a bluegrass vein on *The Mountain* (1999), recorded with the Del McCoury Band. This album featured several songs true to the "blues" motif in "bluegrass," including the title track of the same name about a miner forced not only to watch the destruction of his beloved mountain but also, forced by economic necessity, to participate in it.

Earle's romantic odyssey continued. He lived briefly with Kelley Walker, but this was cut short when Earle met Sara Sharpe, a death penalty activist, in 1998. He eventually moved in with Sharpe. *Transcendental Blues* (2000), Earle's next album, included a tune dubbed "Steve's Last Ramble," allegedly referring to his determination to stay with Sharpe. Eventually, in 2002, Earle and Sharpe founded the nonprofit Broadaxe Theater in Nashville, and staged a play written by Earle, entitled *Karla*, about Karla Faye Tucker, the first woman executed in Texas since 1863. Earle's staggering creative output in the six-year-period after emerging from jail in 1994 and getting clean from drugs included 85 songs, 365 haikus, a collection of short stories packaged as *Doghouse Rose* (Earle 2001), several draft chapters of a book about Hank Williams' doctor, published in 2011 as *I'll Never Get Out of This World Alive* (Earle 2011), co-production with Ray Kennedy of dozens of records through their company E-Squared, and the play. He had also participated in many anti-death penalty events, the Campaign for a Landmine Free World, and other activist causes.

"The Revolution Starts Now"

Earle's *Jerusalem* (2002) brought him a new kind of attention: sharp criticism from a chorus of conservatives snarling about its single, "John Walker's Blues," Earle's empathetic treatment of John Walker Lindh, the young American who volunteered for the Taliban. The conservative backlash included headlines such as "Twisted Ballad Honors Tali-Rat" (Sujo 2002) and similar reactions published or aired in the *Wall Street Journal*, *Fox News* and *CNN*, from the usual roster of conservative radio, television, and print commentators. Even former President George Herbert Walker Bush joined in the attack. Despite—or perhaps in part because of—the uproar over "John Walker's Blues," *Jerusalem* rose to the top of *Billboard*'s Top Independent Albums chart, peaked at #7 on *Billboard*'s Top Country Albums chart, and at #12 on *Billboard*'s Top Internet Albums chart.

The Revolution Starts ... Now (2004) was Earle's attempt to intervene directly in electoral politics. Writing in the liner notes, Earle admitted that "me and my boys had a deadline to meet." That deadline was the November election pitting the incumbent President George W. Bush against Democratic challenger John

Kerry. Nine of the 11 songs were recorded within a day after Earle began writing them. *The Revolution Starts ... Now* was nominated for Grammy Awards in the categories of Best Contemporary Folk Album and Solo Rock Vocal Performance (illustrating once again the difficulty of categorizing his music within a single genre), and won in the former category, Earle's first Grammy as a solo artist after ten nominations (he and Ray Kennedy had won in 1999 for producing Lucinda Williams' album *Car Wheels on a Gravel Road*). In this same year, Earle began deejaying a radio show on Air America that would air for approximately three years. The UK's BBC Radio 2 also awarded him a Lifetime Achievement Award for songwriting in 2004.

Washington Square Serenade (2007) included "City of Immigrants," his paean to his new home, New York City, and featured Allison Moorer, with whom Earle has lived since 2004. He married her in 2005, his seventh marriage, and they have one child together. Suggesting their melding of personal and political, nine days after their marriage ceremony they played a concert in support of Cindy Sheehan, the Iraq War soldier's mother protesting Bush's war in Iraq. In 2007, he began deejaying a show on Sirius Satellite Radio entitled "Hardcore Troubadour" on their Outlaw Country channel.

Earle's long-standing admiration for Townes Van Zandt finally resulted in an homage album, *Townes* (2009), that featured Earle's covers of Van Zandt tunes. It won a Grammy Award, his third, for Best Contemporary Folk Album. In 2010 Earle was awarded the National Coalition to Abolish the Death Penalty's "Shining Star of Abolition" award for his ongoing activism against the death penalty. *I'll Never Get Out Of This World Alive* (2011), named after a Hank Williams song, garnered Earle another Grammy Nomination (his 14th), this time in the Best Folk Album Category. The album features "This City," written by Earle for the HBO series, *Tremé*, in which Earle also appeared as an actor. "This City" earned both a Grammy nomination (in 2010) and an Emmy Award nomination in the Music and Lyrics category. In 2011, the City University of New York (CUNY) School of Law granted Earle an honorary degree.

Throughout his career, Earle has participated in many activist causes including the campaign to abolish the death penalty, Farm Aid, Stop Landmines, and various other political and charitable causes. A "self-defined socialist" (Ratliff 2009) and an "unapologetic leftist" (quoted in McGee 2005, 270), Earle has been a staunch critic of the US political economy for allowing and inducing deprivation among so many of its residents. He endorses the idea that some can have more than others, due to talent and effort; however, he says, "when it comes to people being allowed to just flat-out starve to death and go without medical attention in a country like the United States, that doesn't make sense to me" (quoted in St John 2002, 206). Although early in his career Earle refused to write advertising jingles, he later (in 2005) sold "The Revolution Starts Now" to General Motors for use in a commercial for Chevy trucks. The same song was used to promote *Fahrenheit 9/11*, Michael Moore's anti-war documentary film. It is also featured on the album

Songs and Artists That Inspired Fahrenheit 9/11. Finally, the song opened Earle's weekly Sunday-night show on Air America Radio.

Earle routinely excoriates politicians for their attentiveness to the interests of the rich and powerful while ignoring the plight of struggling US residents. His "Christmas in Washington" (*El Corazon* 1997) is a plea for leaders who will reverse that order of priority. Yet, he does not blame the ills of the world entirely on politicians. Reflecting a democratic sensibility, he refuses to blame the country's problems solely on "them." "There's always a 'them'," Earle argues. "I blame it on us; I think we quit participating in large enough numbers to be significant and surrendered the field to them" (McGee 2005, 271). Democracy, Earle believes, "is hard work." It "requires constant vigilance to survive and nothing short of total engagement to flourish." Voting is important, according to Earle, but especially in difficult times, "voting alone simply isn't enough." The real struggle begins after the election (Earle 2004).

Empathy in Earle's Songs

In this section, I highlight some of Earle's songs that illustrate the theme of empathy. The section is organized into categories of the death penalty, hard times, alienation and loneliness, marginalization and exclusion, hope for a better future, and war.

Death Penalty

Among Earle's political commitments, perhaps his best known is his opposition to the death penalty. "I'm against the death penalty on every level," he says. "It is nothing more than about pain" (St John 2002, 29). Earle cites Truman Capote's *In Cold Blood* as an early influence on his attitude toward the death penalty. In Capote's rendition, the condemned man feared he would soil himself when hanged, so requested one last trip to the bathroom. Initially, his executioners refused. The attending priest intervened, and permission was granted. Then they hanged him. Earle concluded from this that it all seemed so "inhuman" (Poe 2004, O'Hehir 2002, quoted in McGee 2005, 21). Earle also opposes the death penalty because "in a democracy, if the government kills somebody, then I kill somebody, and I object to the damage that does to my spirit. Period." (Poe 2004)

Given how strongly and explicitly Earle condemns the death penalty in interviews, it is noteworthy how non-judgmental and non-pedantic are his songs that address the death penalty. "Over Yonder (Jonathan's Song)," from *Transcendental Blues* (2000) relates the final day of Jonathan Wayne Nobles, on death row for murder. Earle had corresponded with Nobles over a period of approximately ten years, after Nobles contacted him. Nobles eventually asked Earle to witness his execution in 1998. Earle spent nearly two weeks in Huntsville, Texas, visiting Nobles every day, then witnessed the execution (McGee 2005,

221). Written and sung from the perspective of the condemned, the song focuses on Nobles' musings in his last day. Nobles offers no excuses, even admitting that he probably deserves to die and that living would not enable him to repay his crime. Yet, this song is a powerful statement, from the perspective of a man who is not patently bad, facing his death at the hands of the state. In that last day, he mails off a letter, and meets with the chaplain who will accompany him to the death chamber. Nobles tells us that he'll cross into the next life where his suffering will end and where he hopes to be set free. He gives instructions to divide up his meager possessions among his fellow prisoners, and to send his Bible home to his mother. He concludes with a statement of hope that his execution will bring peace to those who hate him. Overall, the song offers a strong message of acceptance and forgiveness, of accepting his guilt and his fate. Yet, without pointing any fingers, it works as a powerful indictment of an inhumane enactment of vengeance. The song opens with Earle finger-picking an acoustic guitar alone, eventually joined by bass, mandolin, harmonica, and a light percussion. Earle's voice conveys sadness and pain; his voice strains on the chorus, conveying Nobles' straining to escape to a better place beyond the pain and sadness. The words are powerful enough as poetry, but adding the music brings the story fully to life for the listener.[1]

Earle's empathy and compassion for the condemned is apparent in this song. Earle appears drawn to "the kind of character he evidently was himself—that is, someone of tainted decency and fouled potential" (Weber 2005), yet capable of reform and rejuvenation. He carefully avoids attacking supporters of the death penalty, opting instead to convey a great sadness, pain, and longing experienced by many surrounding an execution. This arguably works better than a more accusatory approach, which could be expected to alienate listeners who are more sympathetic to victims and their families. By representing the condemned and their basic humanity, without invective or accusation, he is able to connect with both sides more effectively.

Hard Times

Hard times are one of the most prominent and consistent themes in Earle's music throughout his career. His songs are populated with a steady procession of people who struggle daily against long odds, and who are on familiar terms with insecurity, hardship, and suffering. Earle wrote "The Rain Came Down" for his second album *Exit 0* (1987), after participating in Willie Nelson's Farm Aid. He

---

[1]   For other songs by Earle about the death penalty, see especially "Billy Austin" from *The Hard Way* (MCA 1990), written from the perspective of a 29-year old quarter-Cherokee named Billy Austin who sits on death row for killing a filling station attendant during a robbery; and "Ellis Unit One," written for the movie *Dead Man Walking* at the invitation of Tim Robbins, the movie's director, and issued on *Sidetracks* (E-Squared/Artemis Records 2002) in which Earle adopts the perspective of a prison guard who relates the last days of the condemned in human, sympathetic terms.

adopts the point of view of a farmer who, facing foreclosure, recalls the struggles of his dirt-poor grandparents and great grandparents to carve out a new life in the west. They loaded everything they owned into a wagon and headed west, where they settled on 40 acres and struggled to feed six hungry children. The narrator recalls their struggle as he faces his own: the appearance at his door of the sheriff who represents the efforts of a bank to seize his land and equipment. The narrator defiantly tells the sheriff that the auctioneers may seize his equipment, but he will not let them take his land. Musically, this tune is in familiar country-rock territory, with instrumentation of electric guitars, drums, piano, and synthesizer. Earle's voice is at times angry and defiant as he channels this family's efforts to keep their farm; it grows increasingly defiant when the narrator tells the sheriff he will not get his land. Augmenting the defiance and anger in his voice are occasional shouts and hoots, suggesting energy for the upcoming fight.

Some of Earle's songs are bluntly critical and confrontational.[2] For example, "Snake Oil" (*Copperhead Road* 1988) connects the hard times of its characters to the economic policies of the Reagan Administration, bluntly characterizing the promises embedded in Reaganomics as "snake oil." The song's narrator is a traveling salesman who visits towns whose inhabitants are experiencing hard times and promises them relief if they will just buy his snake oil. If your crops are suffering from drought, the salesman tells them, a little snake oil will open the skies and soon it will be raining. If you lose your farm or the factory you work at shuts down, a little snake oil will fix you right up. The last verse makes the connection to Reagan explicit by sarcastically touting the imperial accomplishments of the "President" in Grenada and Libya. The song ends with the snake oil salesman saying that his show and the President's will make a good team. The tune opens appropriately with a dominant honky tonk piano that one might hear at a carnival or in a saloon. Earle's voice adds to the carnivalesque feel, as he projects confidently like a carnival barker with something he wants to sell. Joined by electric guitars and drums, the tune becomes a hard-driving country rock tune that would appeal to many country and western fans. Since many and perhaps most of them are likely Reagan supporters, the tune works on the one hand to draw them in, to appeal to conservative listeners, while on the other hand challenging them with its critical message.[3]

---

[2] For additional illustrations of Earle's direct criticism, see for example "Ashes to Ashes" (2002), an attack on US imperialism; "Amerika V. 6.0 (The Best We Can Do)," (2002), a direct attack on US conservativism; "Justice in Ontario" (*The Hard Way* 1991) about lynch mobs in two different eras; "Taneytown" (*El Corazon* 1997) about a black boy who nearly gets lynched; and "Conspiracy Theory" (*Jerusalem* 2002) about the lies told to get the US into the Vietnam War.

[3] See also, especially, "Tecumseh Valley," on *Train a Comin'* (1995) which relates the story of a miner's daughter whose life, marked by a struggle to find work and make ends meet, ends in senseless tragedy; and "The Mountain," from Earle's album of the same name (*The Mountain* 1999), relating the difficult life of a miner who watches his beloved

Alienation and Loneliness

As an exercise in empathy, Earle set the bar high on "John Walker's Blues" (*Jerusalem* 2002), which adopts the viewpoint of John Walker Lindh, the American teenager who joined the Taliban. In this song, Earle attempts to understand the youth from his own point of view, rather than simply excoriating him. Earle reminds us in this song that even Taliban fighters have mothers and fathers who love them and feel anguish when their sons and daughters take missteps. The song opens with Lindh insisting that he is just a typical American kid who was raised on the standard fare of MTV and its commercials. However, he says, none of them look like he does. He did not fit in, so he started seeking elsewhere for meaning and direction. When he encountered the words of Mohammed, they made sense in a way other things did not. So he converted. He notes that his father would likely find it hard to understand how and why he took the path he took. But, he says, a man must stand up and fight for what he believes. And, he says, I believe in a Muslim God. He admits that he expected to die fighting for the Taliban, but discovered instead that Allah had other plans for him, including getting captured and jailed. The song ends with a verse from the Koran. Musically, the tune exudes alienation. Earle's voice is cold, angry, foreboding, and dark. The electric guitar in the background produces dissonance and distortion, using dark chords and electronic overtones, accentuating the grating dissonance of Earle's voice and the dark topic of the lyric.

Asked what he was trying to accomplish with the song, Earle replied "certainly, empathizing." When he saw Lindh on the television news, he "saw something a little bit different than what others saw." He saw "a twenty year old kid who hadn't eaten in a long time." Earle notes that Lindh has parents, and "they must be just sick" (Poe 2004). In a separate interview, Earle explained that "I'm trying to make clear that wherever he got to, he didn't arrive there in a vacuum." Earle noted that he does not condone the actions of Lindh, but can't help thinking of his own son, Justin, who was almost exactly the same age and who, like most young adults, was capable of making grave mistakes. According to Earle, "there are circumstances" leading to Lindh's mistake that help understand his actions, even if we can't condone them (British Broadcasting Corporation 2002).[4]

---

mountain deforested and strip-mined and then abandoned by the mining company after it was no longer profitable.

[4] See also, for example, "I Am a Wanderer," from *I'll Never Get Out of This World Alive* (2011), in which Earle empathizes with three separate characters: a refugee, a laborer, and a prisoner; "Long, Lonesome Highway Blues," from *The Mountain* (1999), which combines his woefulness about a lost love with two other themes that run like threads through Earle's work: loneliness, and hitting the road in search of relief.

Marginalization and Exclusion

Related to the theme of alienation and loneliness, some of Earle's songs highlight characters that are marginalized and excluded. His "What's a Simple Man To Do" (*Jerusalem* 2002) presents a sympathetic portrait of illegal immigrants who come to the United States, sometimes having been deceived, hoping to catch a break and find a way out of deprivation and insecurity. Earle adopts the standpoint of an immigrant who is writing a letter from a US jail to his "Graciela," trying to explain how he came to such unfortunate circumstances. He is alone and lonely, writing in the middle of the night, heartbroken about being so far from home. He explains that he lost his job at a maquiladora sweatshop, just south of the US-Mexico border, and felt desperate, so he accepted the invitation of a man he met in Tijuana to earn some quick money in the US peddling drugs on a street corner. Unfortunately, the police caught up to him before he could pocket any money and return to Mexico. He asks Graciela to forgive him and pray that he might someday be able to come home. Far from demonizing illegal immigrants, even those who engage in illegal activities, Earle sympathetically describes a man propelled by desperate circumstances beyond his control, who is simply trying to survive long enough to reunite with his lover.[5]

Hope for a Better Future

From *Guitar Town* (1986) to *I'll Never Get out of This World Alive* (2011), many of Earle's songs are infused with hope and yearning for a better future. He is a survivor, and his music reflects this. While the characters that populate his songs endure hardship, sadness, loneliness, lovesickness, and insecurity, and often take a beating, most refuse to give up or succumb.

Some of Earle's most eloquent expressions of hopefulness can be found in his most political music. "The Revolution Starts Now," on *The Revolution Starts ... Now* (2004) offers hope that the problems of the world can be turned around, but adds emphatically that it is up to each of us to make it happen. We have to rise above our fear to break through walls preventing change. Our role must be active, and it must occur not just in a voting booth but also in our workplaces and our leisure lives and where we shop. Everything we say and do must build on our acceptance of a responsibility to make change happen. Start the revolution, Earle tells us. Start it in our own backyards, in our homes and hometowns. Earle expresses his utopian vision that, if people take responsibility for change, great things can happen. He dreams that the efforts pay off, that the world moves in a more positive direction, and our hopes are realized. The song is a straightforward rock tune, using electric guitars, drums, and rhythmic clapping to accentuate the

---

[5] See also, especially, "City of Immigrants," from *Washington Square Serenade* (2007), Earle's paean to New York City and its immigrant culture; and "The Truth" (*Jerusalem* 2002) about an incarcerated person.

beat. The chorus insistently proclaims "the revolution starts now." A chorus effect is applied to Earle's voice, perhaps suggesting the need for collective action. This song, and others like it by Earle, speaks eloquently to the deeply felt human need to rise above difficult circumstances, to hope for a better future. He defiantly refuses to succumb to despair, insisting instead that we recognize the possibility of a better time and place.[6]

War

Earle has written several songs relating the experience of war or its aftermath. There is little doubt where Earle stood on the Iraq War initiated by President George W. Bush in 2003; he and his bandmates proclaimed it on stage. Bold, stenciled letters on the bass drum demanded "No Iraq War." Given his own strong disinclination to support the war, it is even more impressive how sympathetically he portrays some of the characters who find themselves involved directly in the war effort. "Rich Man's War" (*The Revolution Starts Now* 2004) manages to express Earle's empathy for three different characters caught in the war: a poor man, a patriot, and a Muslim suicide bomber. Like so many others, "Jimmy" joined the army partly as a desperate move. Unable to find decent work (the jobs had migrated to Mexico, according to Earle's lyric), he had no other good options. Now he finds himself unexpectedly fighting a "rich man's war" in a country far away from home. Earle's second verse switches perspectives to "Bobby," with an eagle and American flag tattooed on his arm, indicating his patriotism. He had to leave a wife and baby girl when he went to Iraq, along with a stack of unpaid bills and a bank repossessing his car. Finally, "Ali," who grew up amid deprivation in Gaza throwing stones at the Israeli tanks, answered the call for suicide bombers. A fat man drove him to his suicide in a Mercedes. Earle sympathizes with his three main characters, each one caught up in a class structure in which the rich push the war from the sidelines while the poor shed the blood. Earle is also clear about the futility and injustice of war. He asks: when we will learn to say no to these stupid foreign ventures? Until we do, he sings, we are not free.[7]

---

[6] See also, especially, "Jerusalem," from Earle's album of the same name (2002), a song in which Earle offers hope that the ongoing conflict in the Middle East can be resolved.

[7] See also, especially, "Johnny Come Lately," from *Copperhead Road* (1988), which recounts the experiences of veterans returning to the US from different wars; "My Uncle," *Sidetracks* (2002), Earle's cover of a Gram Parsons and Chris Hillman tune that sympathetically portrays a draft evader; and "Home to Houston," *The Revolution Starts ... Now* (2004), a sympathetic portrait of a civilian truck driver in Iraq.

Empathy as a Resource for Democracy

Earle portrays difficult lives torn by deprivation and worn down by sadness, suffering, and loneliness. His songs open a window into the daily lives of people whose stories do not match those found in the promises of the American Dream. Having done so himself, Earle knows that people make mistakes. They encounter bad luck and unanticipated obstacles. Earle gives musical voice to these people. His empathic renditions help listeners cross boundaries, break through walls of misunderstanding. They open new avenues of communication, bringing new messages and new experiences to new and different audiences. Especially at a time in US history when empathy for outsiders seems so scarce, his songs offer the possibility of change, of mutual recognition, compassion, and empathy. Earle's songs substitute empathy and forgiveness for revenge; he gives people the possibility of second and third chances.

Despite the difficult lives of his characters, hope for a better future remains prominent in Earle's music. His insistence on effort and action by average people adds a strong democratic element to his work. Empathy helps us cultivate the mutual respect that supports honest deliberation and peaceful resolution of conflict, both necessary in a healthy democracy. To the degree that we listen to Earle and heed his messages, empathy becomes a transformative resource for democratic change.

Most of Earle's songs avoid direct criticism; yet, critique is often implied. Earle clearly believes that much of the deprivation and suffering experienced by the characters in his songs can be alleviated through better, more humane public policy. By engaging his listeners through empathy rather than confrontation, Earle arguably is more likely to induce them to support his agenda for democratic change. On the other hand, as we have seen, at least some of Earle's songs express their politics more directly, explicitly, and bluntly. These songs, if delinked from empathy, may widen differences and reinforce or erect walls, rather than break through them.

Bibliography

British Broadcasting Corporation. "Earle Defends 'American Taliban' song." *BBC News*, World Edition, 24 July 2002, http://news/bbc.co/uk/2/hi/americas/2148674.stm.

Collins, Robert. "Untitled." *SteveEarle.net*, 27 June 2011.http://www.steveearle.net/articles/articles3.php?action+view_record&article_id+1126.

Corcoran, Michael. "Back in Business: Braced by great new song, a languishing Steve Earle finds his authentic voice." *The Dallas Morning News*, 1 August 1993.

Dewey, John. *Art as Experience*. 1934. Reprint. New York: Perigee Books, 1980.

Dewey, John. *The Public and Its Problems*. 1927. Reprint. Denver: Swallow Press, 1954.

Earle, Steve. *Doghouse Rose*. Boston and New York: Houghton Mifflin Company, 2001.

Earle, Steve. *I'll Never Get out of This World Alive*. Boston and New York: Houghton Mifflin Harcourt, 2011.

Earle, Steve. *Karla*. Directed by Bruce Kronenberg. 2005.

Earle, Steve. *The Revolution Starts ... Now*. Liner notes. Artemis/E-Squared 2004.

Friskics-Warren, Bill. "Steve Earle, Picking Up on Bluegrass; With 'Mountain,' Rocker Scales Skepticism of His Turn to Tradition," *The Washington Post*, 14 March 1999.

Krewen, Nick. "Against all odds." *Toronto Star*, 16 February 2003.

McGee, David. *Steve Earle: Fearless Heart, Outlaw Poet*. San Francisco: Backbeat Books, 2005.

Mitchell, Greg. "Steve Earle: Still a Leading 'Hard-Core Troubadour' Against the Death Penalty." *The Nation*, 27 September 2011. http://www.thenation.com/blog/163651/steve-earle-still-leading-hard-core-troubadour-against-death-penalty.

Nussbaum, Martha. *Not for Profit: Why Democracy Needs the Humanities*. Princeton: Princeton University Press, 2010.

O'Hehir, Andrew. "The Salon Interview: Steve Earle." *Salon.com*, 13 November 2002.http://www.salon.com/2002/11/13/earle_7/.

Ratliff, Ben. "Songs About the Common People, Performed in an Uncommon Setting." Music Review of Steve Earle and Allison Moorer. *The New York Times*, 10 January 2009.

St John, Lauren. *Hardcore Troubadour: The Life & Near Death of Steve Earle*. London and New York: Fourth Estate, 2002.

Sujo, Aly. "Twisted Ballad Honors Tali-Rat." *New York Post*, 21 July 2002.

Weber, Bruce. "Hard-Living Singer Gives Voice to the Executed." *The New York Times*, 22 October 2005.

Discography

Earle, Steve. *Copperhead Road*. Universal City, CA: Uni/MCA, UNID-7, 1988.

Earle, Steve. *Exit 0*. Universal City, CA: MCA, MCAD 5998, 1987.

Earle, Steve. *El Corazon*. Burbank, CA: Warner Bros., 9 46789-2, 1997.

Earle, Steve. *Guitar Town*. Universal City, CA: MCA, MCD 01888, 1986.

Earle, Steve. *I Feel Alright*. Burbank, CA: Warner Bros., 9362-46201-2, 1996.

Earle, Steve. *I'll Never Get out of This World Alive*. Los Angeles, CA: New West Records, NW 165, 2011.

Earle, Steve. *Jerusalem*. New York: E-Squared/Artemis, DMCG 6095, 2002.

Earle, Steve. *Sidetracks*. New York: E-Squared/Artemis, 751 128-2, 2002.

Earle, Steve. *Townes*. Los Angeles, CA: New West Records, NW6165, 2009.

Earle, Steve. *The Hard Way*. Universal City, CA: MCA, DMCG 6095, 1990.

Earle, Steve. *The Mountain*. Nashville: TN, E-Squared, 1064-2, 1999.

Earle, Steve. *The Revolution Starts ... Now*. Liner notes. New York: Artemis/E-Squared, ATM-CD-51565, 2004.

Earle, Steve. *Train a Comin'*. Nashville, TN: Winter Harvest Entertainment, 9 46355-2, 1995.

Earle, Steve. *Transcendental Blues*. New York: E-Squared/Artemis, 498074 2, 2000.

Earle, Steve. *Washington Square Serenade*. Los Angeles: CA, Near West Records, NW6128, 2007.

Videography

Lonergan, Kenneth. Writer and director. *You Can Count on Me*. Paramount Classics, 2000.

Poe, Amos. *Steve Earle: Just an American Boy*. Writer and director. E-Squared/Sheridan Square Entertainment, 2004.

Robbins, Tim. Director. *Dead Man Walking*. Polygram Filmed Entertainment, 1995.

Chapter 8
Kim Gordon: Ordinary, Feminist, Musician

Norma Coates

I write and teach about gender and popular music for a living. When people hear that, especially people who consider themselves hip and in the know, they often ask me if I've interviewed or want to interview Kim Gordon. Gordon is a founding member of archetypal noise band Sonic Youth and feminist role model to a generation of younger women (and probably some young men) who identify strongly with indie music and culture. It's certainly possible; I know for a fact that I'm but one degree of separation from her several times over. I was even in Northampton, Massachusetts, where she lives, last summer! But no, although I wouldn't pass up the opportunity, I'm not sure that I want to. For one, she's way too cool for me. I'm afraid that I couldn't measure up or that I'd lapse into my best Chris Farley-meets-Paul McCartney behavior, stumbling for intelligent or any words and thoughts in her presence. I recognize that Gordon's coolness may be a shield, and/or a mechanism for surviving in a cultural formation that clings to, or is clung onto by, its common-sense meaning as a space of heterosexual white masculinity, despite visual and sonic evidence to the contrary. I'm afraid I'd fall back onto the clichéd and out-of-date, if we go strictly on numbers and surface appearances, question that she's even critiqued in a song: "What's it like to be a girl in a band?"

She's answered and critiqued that question, a lot, even in song. She even provides a non-answer of sorts in "Sacred Trickster," the first song on what may well be Sonic Youth's final album, 2009's *The Eternal*: "I don't quite understand. That's so quaint to hear." "Quaint" is an odd word choice. On the one hand, in part because of Gordon's model as one of the few "women in rock" who have actually admitted to being, gasp, a feminist, and who has dared write a feminist analysis into her music (as well as her writing, art, and fashion), she's not as much of a rarity anymore. Besides, she's written about it, a few times. And really, it's an unimaginative question. Gordon's lyrics, combined with her delivery, her style, and her stage presence as part of Sonic Youth have consistently answered that question for almost 30 years.

If I had to answer the question for her, I'd say, "it depends." In "Boys are Smelly," reprinted in the important collection, *Rock She Wrote*, Gordon makes being the girl in a band seem like being the girl in any sort of homosocial, normatively masculine space, that is, kind of gross, fun, and infuriating all at once. She captures the sense of being in it, but not of it, that so many of us women who love rock music feel and experience, but more so. And less so, because she's not with the band, she's in the band and is an integral contributor to it. Anyway, she answered the question of what it's like to be a girl in a band in a 1994 interview for Liz Evan's collection, *Women, Sex and Rock'n'Roll In Their Own Words* (and probably countless other interviews since):

> So I like being in a band with men for the most part. Although sometimes it's hard because no matter how much of a new man someone thinks they are, they're just not! There's always some prejudice there. I think that in general there's a preconception about indie rock, that it's not sexist and that it's very accepting of women, but I see the mainstream of it as pretty conservative, like college rock or something. (Gordon 1994, 175)

Popular music scholar Marian Leonard, in her book-length examination of gender in indie rock, confirms Gordon's perception (Leonard 2007). Leonard did much of her research in the 1990s, perhaps indie rock's finest hour, especially in terms of women being allowed onto the figurative and literal front of the stage. What she found, via ethnography and discourse analysis (that is, reading lots of rock magazines and criticism), is that indie rock is not less patriarchal than other rock genres, despite a greater number of female performers in the genre (ibid., 63). Granted, almost 20 years have passed since Gordon made the statement quoted above, and since Leonard performed much of the research for her book, but a quick scan of band membership, writing about music, and images of bands indicate that numbers do not necessarily add up to major change. A more appropriate question may be: why is the question still being asked?

This is not to say that Gordon's feminism falls on deaf ears. For one thing, she's never denied it, which is a statement unto itself. I love Patti Smith and always will, but she didn't embrace feminism, if she even has, until well after a 15-year-absence from the stage. British feminist bands like the Slits and the Raincoats were heard by the few of us who identified as punks back in the day, but languished in obscurity until indie rock merged with the mainstream for a while in the 1990s. They did not even rate a display in the Rock and Roll Hall of Fame's recent "Women Who Rock" exhibit. Gordon, in fact, was partly responsible for getting Sonic Youth's record label, Geffen, to reissue the three original Raincoats albums in 1993, and contributed liner notes to the reissue of the group's second album, the wonderful *Odyshape*. Gordon and the rest of Sonic Youth rankled guardians of indie purity when they signed with major label Geffen in 1990, but their deal, which gave them a form of A&R responsibility for finding and signing other bands, helped them to retain their credibility and help other groups, from the Raincoats to the then up-and-coming Nirvana. Further, their Geffen deal signaled that earning enough money to live an "ordinary" life was not antithetical to being a rock musician, and that "selling out" was not an aesthetic or ideological crime.

Gordon, the daughter of a professor and a seamstress, was born in upper-state New York and grew up in Los Angeles, where her father taught sociology at UCLA. She was an artistic tomboy who grew up listening to her father's jazz records and her older brother's rock'n'roll. After attending progressive elementary and secondary schools in Los Angeles and a year at Santa Monica College, she enrolled in York University in Toronto, Canada, to study dance and art. While there, she played in her first band with high-school friend, William Winant, now an avant-garde percussionist. In that band Gordon, according to biographer Peter Browne, danced and screamed along to "noisy no-wave songs," a herald of musical things to come for Gordon. After a year Gordon returned to Los Angeles, enrolling in and graduating from the Otis College of Art and Design. With her degree in fine art in hand, Gordon went east to New York City in 1980. Upon her arrival Gordon reconnected with conceptual artist Dan Graham, who she met during a lecture at Otis. Graham's work, like that of many others in lower Manhattan at the moment, led him to make connections between art and rock'n'roll. Gordon, through Graham, became involved in the nascent SoHo art scene. She curated art shows and wrote a few articles about rock'n'roll and art for *Artforum* magazine (Browne 2008, Gaar 2002).

Gordon arrived in New York after the initial florescence of CBGB's punk, but in time to fully participate in another, more important movement, sonically as well as in terms of gender politics. The No Wave bands that emerged on the Lower East Side of Manhattan in the 1970s were more experimental and gender-mixed than any rock music since the mid-1970s. That scene and the emergent art and new music (avant-garde classical) scenes in the same downtown neighborhoods intermingled and merged, musically, personally, and politically. Noise was their palette and their aesthetic weapon. Gordon played guitar in a "one-off" band called CKM. One of her bandmates took her to see a group called the Coachmen and introduced her to one of its members, guitarist Thurston Moore. They soon became a couple, and by mid-1981 had formed a band that, with the addition of guitarist Lee Ranaldo, would become Sonic Youth. As guitarists, Moore and Ranaldo relied upon unusual guitar tunings, feedback, and distortion, often manipulating their instruments with household tools and drumsticks. Gordon took up the bass and sang vocals and often overtly feminist lyrics over the noise.

No Wave Noise, and the sounds that bands like Sonic Youth and others would make afterwards, raged against the dawning encroachment of neoliberal global political realignment. A big part of that terrain was popular culture, something that informs Gordon and Sonic Youth's work. Sonic Youth has, since forming, brought politics and popular culture into its music, especially, in Azerrad's words, a "refusal to ignore harsh realities" (Azerrad 2001, 249). The not-so-subtle damage wrought by patriarchy is one of those realities, but not usually a topic for a rock band, especially given the gender politics of popular music.

Gordon has confronted the gendered "rules" of indie and other rock genres by bringing important feminist issues and topics, often those with significant cultural ramifications, into Sonic Youth's music. For example, "Tunic (Song for Karen)," released on Sonic Youth's Geffen debut *Goo* in 1990, is about Karen Carpenter of soft-rock superstars The Carpenters. In the early 1970s, the Carpenters were the antithesis of "authentic" rockers exalted in rock culture. In a 1997 interview for

Rolling Stone's "Women in Rock" issue (it only took them 30 years to realize that "women in rock" were deserving of an issue devoted to them), Gordon described her motivation for writing and recording the song:

> I wanted to put Karen Carpenter up in heaven playing drums and being happy. This whole thing about teenage girls cutting themselves and that being associated with anorexia and girls being conditioned to having such a big desire to please— I'm just curious, because of Coco [her then 3-year-old daughter], at what point do girls start getting their sense of self-worth and [need to please] people, and why don't they have anything else. (O'Dair 1997, 143)

There's so much going on here, in this song and in Gordon's description. Gordon brings an issue and source of secrecy and much shame for teenage and older girls into the open here. In the 1970s, when Karen Carpenter began fading away in public, anorexia was only just beginning to enter consciousness, mainstream or otherwise. We all knew girls, often very bright, who exhibited odd eating behaviors and who exercised constantly, even in the days before it became a cultural mandate. There was little medical attention paid to it until it seemed to reach epidemic proportions. Girls suffered for generations before that. When Karen Carpenter died, in 1983, collapsing in her closet when her heart gave way from years of anorexia and bulimia, her death became a pop culture joke, up there with Mama Cass and her ham sandwich, and Marianne Faithfull and a Mars Bar. Why is it always a joke when a female rocker dies because of a relationship to food, real or imagined? Gordon implicitly asked that question, and those of us who were sensitive to being on the wrong side of rock's gender divide recognized what she was doing.

But beyond the obvious feminist issues articulated in "Tunic (Song for Karen)," Gordon and the band recorded a song about the Carpenters, the epitome of early 1970s' mainstream soft/schlock rock that cool middle- and high-schoolers of the era ran screaming from. This was mainstream music, mom music, secretary music, television special, and variety show music, the "pablum" that our mothers wanted us to listen to instead of those nasty Rolling Stones or worse (or better, depending upon the point of view you were coming from). Sure, we might find ourselves secretly listening to "Close to You" on our transistor radios held close to our ears, or humming it in the shower, because there was something inside the schlock that drew you in and was hard to resist, but to admit to liking them, the most mainstream of mainstream bands, especially if you fancied yourself a rocker, was anathema.

The "mainstream" is the Other to the rock "authentic." If authenticity, in the words of music historian Keir Keightley, "mingles aesthetic evaluation (is this music beautiful?) with ethical judgments about the degree of music's complicity with the alienating aspects of mass society (is this music compromised?)," then the mainstream is the dumping ground for that compromised output (Keightley 2001, 133). The common sense definition of the mainstream, especially when tossed around by rock and popular music tastemakers, is that it's a commercial, feminized and therefore aesthetically invalid space. The (dumping) ground of the mainstream can shift, often under the cover of irony or for more arbitrary reasons such as justifying a new taste cohort. The elevation of The Monkees (the band, not necessarily the television show) out of the mainstream dreck by a rogue group of rock critics beginning in the 1970s, or the rehabilitation of 1960s' and early 1970s' "Sunshine Pop"—something I'll wager most people didn't even know existed— by academics exemplifies this operation (for example, see Keightley, 2011). With "Tunic (Song for Karen)," along with their quasi-tribute to Madonna, *The Whitey Album*, credited to "Ciccone Youth," and numerous songs throughout their long recording career, Gordon and Sonic Youth use their conferred hipness and cool to unsettle the articulation of the mainstream to the commercial and feminized. This move is often cited by the rock press as "ironic," but it can also be read as strongly feminist. It also reflects the band's artistic and generational background. As Azerrad observed, the core band members, including Gordon, all grew up with pop radio in the 1960s and 1970s (Azerrad 2001, 262). Their aesthetic pluralism merged well with their artistic postmodernism, and lifted "feminized" popular culture out of the garbage bin and back into artistic discourse.

Women, I contend, are culturally tracked, in a way, toward softer and less challenging or confrontational pop music as they get older. Part of this is due to the idea of the "pink collar" jobs in which, for a long time, women were congregated and to some extent confined. Another is due to strict formatting that governs what is played on corporate, homogenized, de-regionalized radio in the last couple of decades. Most insidious may be the entrenched idea bordering on article of faith that rock music is for the young, and that one rightly "grows out" of it once she or he begins her or his real job. Men get more of a pass, as playing in a rock band or a continuing involvement with rock music of some sort is characterized as an appropriate "escape" from the constrictions of a day job and family responsibilities. These subtle cultural imperatives are particularly pernicious for women, especially if and once they become mothers, as, even with feminism's advances, they are still often held responsible for the moral and physical well-being of their children. After all, it was a group of well-connected political wives who started the Parents Music Research Council in the 1980s, resulting in "warning labels" on music. Gordon's enduring presence and influence on the indie scene and the edges of the mainstream, including Sonic Youth's major label contract, posing for a Gap ad, and agreeing to interviews with *People* magazine, are very visible statements against this type of tracking. They provide evidence that a woman can mature and integrate into "adult" society without leaving behind her passions or sublimating them along more socially acceptable lines.

Gordon's enduring presence in a 30-year-old working band leads to discussion of another one of her important interventions in cultural politics, especially, but not limited to, popular music, around age and aging. Gordon was part of the same working band for 30 years. They never broke up or reformed; nor have they gone on hiatus, even when Gordon and her now estranged husband, Thurston Moore, were new parents. (Gordon and Moore announced their separation in October

2011; the band is, as of this writing, on hold and may be over.) Gordon may be unique among rock women from the punk era in that respect. Gordon has therefore aged and matured in indie rock public. So have her male counterparts in the group, but age operates on a much different register for women in rock, and arguably most spaces of popular culture, than for men. From the start, Gordon was an equal member of the band; their usual compositional process is to create songs as a band, then to write lyrics for them later. Works are credited collaboratively. Guitarists Thurston Moore and Lee Ranaldo generate the feedback and noise for which the group is known, but Gordon's bass, combined with Steve Shelley's drums, tethered it for years and, in my opinion, provides it with much of its power. In later years, Gordon contributed a third guitar, with bass duties going first to James O'Rourke and later to Mark Ibold. That's not to say that Sonic Youth's sound is grounded, but that the rhythm section keeps the noise from roiling away into nothing; it channels it for effect and purpose.

Unlike other groups with a female member, it's hard to think of Gordon as only "the girl in the band." Gordon has had to talk about and defend her age since she was in her 30s, something her male bandmates never had to do (and still don't). In her 1994 interview with Liz Evans, she was very aware of a double standard, observing that male critics had license to say "some really mean things" about her, and that "all these guys writing about music only seem to like women who sing nice little melodies and pop princesses" (Evans 1994, 180).

Gordon, again exhibiting her ability to operate on many intellectual levels at one time, soon moves the discussion beyond the misogyny of young male rock critics to the politics of age and popular music, acknowledging that she understands the resentment of younger people toward older musicians like the Rolling Stones and Eric Clapton and the like who were at that time beginning to reap the benefits of their second careers (ibid.) (Curiously, the same crew is still reaping benefits, and probably will long after they are available to perform in holographic form only.) She then linked aging to authenticity in a powerful way, by comparing the way she was treated in terms of her age to how Neil Young was treated, thereby showing the gender biases and binaries built into that important ideological tenant of rock culture.

But that was almost 20 years ago. The politics of age and rock have changed a bit, but not much. The younger generation moans a bit about "dad rock" and "mom rock," in order to differentiate "their" rock music from that of their parents (especially fathers?). At the same time, punk and post-punk bands have reformed and sell out clubs, filled in some cases with balding and expanding male fans from "back in the day," and in others with trendy hipster kids with a curatorial view toward music. One would think that it's 1982 rather than 2012 when reading a list of upcoming concerts in any big city. For example, over the last nine months I've seen Gang of Four, the Raincoats, and Prince in concert. What year is it again? Moreover, the Rolling Stones are rumored to be considering a 50th anniversary tour. The Raincoats played to a room full of young people; I was one of the very few middle-aged people there, and the other women my age in attendance were the band. Older women are still an anomaly, as audiences and performers. Artists run the risk of being ignored, trapped in the amber of their youthful personae, or relegated to an oldies circuit. Some just give up. Or older women in rock are described and depicted as MILFs. To be called a MILF can seem like a compliment, but it is a form of objectification that transfers power from the woman to the younger man who is making the assessment. Nevertheless, Gordon continues to stay relevant and committed to rock performance, creating dissonance in her music and her onstage style that undermines attempts to objectify her or place her in a category not of her choosing. Style has multiple meanings here. Gordon's stage presence has never played on or up her sex. Her stage attire has, for decades, often consisted of form-hugging, 1960-ish short dresses. She's worn them long after an age where women are "supposed to." Her stage attire also challenges rock convention by appearing to conform to it. Her short skirts signal comfort with her sexuality despite or even in celebration of her age. At the same time, her studied coolness signals that she's not interested in being objectified. Her comfort in her sexual subjectivity sends a powerful message to both younger women and women in her age cohort. Gordon transcends the MILF designation, and, in my opinion, flips it, drawing attention to the sexual insecurity of the younger men who confer the title on her and other older women. To call an older woman a MILF may just be a sign of unresolved Oedipal tension and/or anxiety.

Gordon's contributions to a feminist politics of age go beyond the rock stage and culture. Gordon has an enduring interest in fashion, and over her career has started two fashion lines, X-Girl in the 1990s (launched while she was pregnant with her daughter) and Mirror/Dash in 2008. Both lines were designed with older women in mind—not necessarily middle-aged women, but those old enough to supplement their thrift-store finds with clothing that expressed a different take on female maturity. Mirror/Dash, a line introduced in 2008, was designed to fill a need for "clothes for cool moms," in Gordon's words (Pulse 2008). Mirror/Dash clothing was available through Urban Outfitters, usually not a retailer of choice for the 50-something woman, but not entirely out of the ken of the possible. To articulate a market need for cool clothes for moms is to make a statement against the dominant visual representation of the middle-aged mother donned in age-appropriate, desexualized clothing such as "mom jeans," cut a bit wider in the rear with some stretch material added to the fabric. Although the relationship between fashion and feminism is often thorny, fashion can send potent political messages. A middle-aged mom in hip clothing is not necessarily trying to look younger; she may just be refusing to submit to cultural mandates. Gordon clearly recognizes this. As an aside, Urban Outfitters is notorious for exploiting female workers in offshore sweatshops. Like most of us who operate from a position of privilege, Gordon likely makes conscious or unconscious trade-offs in terms of her political investments, just like the one I am making while writing this on an Apple computer, given the poor working conditions in their Chinese factories.

Gordon accepts her role as a model for girls and women who want to be in bands, to age in an interesting manner while not succumbing to not-so-subtle cultural dictates, or who want to balance an "ordinary" life with a career that's considered out of the mainstream. She doesn't like the title conferred upon her in many articles, "Godmother of Grunge." As she told *Rockrgrl* founder Carla DeSantis Black in 2000, "The literally means I'm delivering the generation to Jesus Christ! Too bad I'm an atheist. I find that one particularly offensive." Of course, conferring that and similar titles upon her is a way of putting her in a particular box and frame in order to marginalize her, as is the term "woman in rock" (DeSantis 2000, Coates 1997, Kearney 1997). Her "ordinariness" may be her most important political contribution. Returning again to her 1994 interview with Evans, she stated that: "I've always tried to be as ordinary as possible, because for me it's really important for some other girl to see that I don't have to be a freak or a drug addict or have a Siouxsie Sioux persona and can still be creative, and I can still express myself in a powerful way— just by being myself" (Evans 1994, 176–7).

Indeed, she's managed to live a somewhat ordinary life, albeit a heightened, and yes, cooler, version of ordinary, on her own terms. For example, Gordon moved, with husband Thurston Moore and daughter Coco, to Northampton, Massachusetts, a quintessential liberal college town, in the mid 2000s. Sonic Youth biographer David Browne reports that Gordon and Moore hadn't thought of leaving New York City before they became parents, but that changed. Browne quotes Gordon as saying that, "We didn't want to raise a kid in Manhattan and constantly have to hover over her," and that living outside of New York City would enable Gordon and Moore to focus more on being parents than when surrounded by the city's diversions. Gordon and Moore kept their apartment in lower Manhattan, but their lives revolved around Northampton. They toured during school vacation periods. Browne describes the Volvo in the driveway and the propane grill on the porch, staples of middle-class suburban life (Brown 2008, 310, 370). Gordon did not single-handedly make living and raising a child in a college town "hip," but her example forces a rethinking of the articulation of a quasi-suburban lifestyle to a perceived mainstream emptiness or sameness. Cool does not just reside in major metropolitan areas, and not all "soccer moms," if any, conform to the political and media shorthand created for them.

Gordon was likely not a stereotypical stay-at-home mom, but, really, who is? The stereotypical stay-at-home mom is a media creation and an increasingly out-of-reach economic goal. Gordon had her daughter "late in life," at 41, still depicted as somewhat of an aberration despite growing numbers of women waiting to have children, stating that she wasn't ready before then. Voicing such concerns is a feminist move, given that to do so grates against mythologies of the maternal. Gordon speaks for many of us who have waited. By the time her daughter was born, in 1994, older mothers and rock'n'roll had both been around the mainstream for a while. Women were not "in rock" no matter their age.[1] She was in the middle

---

[1]   See, for example, Norma Coates, "Mom's Don't Rock: The Popular Demonization of Courtney Love," in Molly Ladd-Taylor and Lauri Umansky (eds), *"Bad" Mothers: The Politics of Blame in Twentieth-Century America* (New York: 1998), pp. 319–33.

of launching her first fashion label, X-Girl, when her daughter Coco was born, has since launched another label, and also restarted her art career in the recent past. She has also released a couple of albums with her second band, the noisy and feminist Free Kitten, since Coco's birth, and revived her art career. This is not to reiterate hackneyed and politically suspect advertising slogans claiming that women can "have it all," but that Gordon has found a way to balance the many artistic and personal endeavors in her life without having to deny some or others.

Gordon and Moore seemingly dashed the dreams of many younger indie fans—hopeful that, too, they could form a union based on personal and artistic commonality while remaining consummately cool—when they announced their separation in October 2011. That move that will probably also end Sonic Youth. The break-up of a long-term marriage is an ordinary occurrence. It can happen to your mom and dad, and it can happen to indie rock royalty. The relative coolness of the couple has no role to play. Thankfully, the couple requested privacy and so far their request has been respected. That Gordon and Moore's marriage broke up does not obviate the over-30 years they spent and worked together as a couple. As Nitsuh Abebe wrote in a recent *New York* article about the break-up, Gordon, by example, showed that, among other things, "coming to be a feminist, punk, or artist would not cut you off from normal people and force you into huge compromises in your domestic affairs but might actually lead you to someone who'd share all of those commitments" (Abebe 2011). Relationships are hard, and they get harder the longer they go on. Life is ordinary, even for indie rock icons.

Gordon has managed to balance a rock'n'roll life and an ordinary life, thereby setting a model for a rock'n'roll lifestyle that does not conform to the masculinized "sex, drugs, and rock and roll" myth, but that creates a new template. This template could be even more important as musicians, female and male, work to use new technologies and other means to construct a middle-class musician lifestyle, given the decline of the conventional record industry, one that did not have much space or use for women to begin with. Moreover, Gordon's embrace of the "ordinary," including things like living outside of a major city and being a visible mother and parent in a cultural formation in which parental status is either hidden or ignored, presents an alternative way of imagining musical adulthood. Rock exceptionalism, the idea that the genre somehow transcends everyday life and crass commercialism, is an ideological construct that continues to valorize certain groups and beliefs while marginalizing others. It also provides validation for industrial and discursive structures that reproduce the status quo and foreclose other possibilities. Noise and dissonance do not just reside in sound, but also in the challenging of norms, including those created by so-called non-mainstream communities and cultural formations. Gordon's ordinary choices, mixed with her feminism and vital cultural presence, may hold the key to new articulations of what it means to live a life in rock, as a band member, as an enthusiast, as a woman, as an adult.

Bibliography

Abebe, Nitsuh. "They Struck a Chord: Sonic Youth's impossible domestic ideal." *New York*, 31 October 2011.

Azerrad, Michael. *Our Band Could Be Your Life: Scenes from the American Indie Underground, 1981–91*. New York: Little, Brown and Company, 2001.

Browne, David. *Goodbye 20th Century: A Biography of Sonic Youth*. New York, Da Capo Press, 2008.

Coates, Norma. "(R)evolution Now? Rock and the Political Potential of Gender." In *Sexing the Groove: Popular Music and Gender,* edited by Sheila Whiteley, 50–65. New York: Routledge, 1997.

Coates, Norma. "Moms Don't Rock: The Popular Demonization of Courtney Love." In *"Bad" Mothers: The Politics of Blame in Twentieth-Century America,* edited by Molly Ladd-Taylor and Lauri Umansky, 319–33. New York: New York University Press, 1998.

DeSantis Black, Carla. "Kim Gordon: Sonic Warrior." *Rockrgrl* 32 (2000): 19.

Gaar, Gillian, *She's A Rebel: The History of Women in Rock & Roll*, expanded second edition. New York: Seal Press, 2003.

Evans, Liz. *Women, Sex and Rock'n'Roll In Their Own Words*. London: Pandora, 1994.

Kearney, Mary Celeste. "The Missing Links: Riot Grrrl—feminism—lesbian culture." In *Sexing the Groove: Popular Music and Gender*, edited by Sheila Whiteley, 207–29. New York: Routledge, 1997.

Keightley, Keir. "Reconsidering rock." In *The Cambridge Companion to Pop and Rock*, edited by Simon Frith, Will Straw, and John Street, 109–42. Cambridge: Cambridge University Press, 2001.

Keightley, Kier. "The Historical Consciousness of Sunshine Pop." *Journal of Popular Music Studies* 22,3 (2011): 343–61.

Leonard, Marian. *Gender in the Music Industry: Rock, Discourse, and Girl Power*. Aldershot: Ashgate Publishing Ltd, 2007.

O'Dair, Barbara. "Kim Gordon." *Rolling Stone* 773 (Nov. 13, 1997): 143–4.

"Pulse." *New York Times*. 5 September 2008. http://www.nytimes.com/slideshow/2008/09/05/fashion/20080907-PULSE_3.html.

Discography

Sonic Youth. *Goo*. Los Angeles: DCG, 9 24297-D2, 1990.

Sonic Youth. *The Eternal*. New York City: Matador, Ole 829-2, 2009.

Chapter 9
Ani DiFranco: Making Feminist Waves

Nancy S. Love

I mean why don't all decent men and women call themselves feminists? If only
out of respect for those who fought for this. (Ani DiFranco, "Grand Canyon")

Introduction[1]

Ani DiFranco is changing the meaning of feminism, giving it new life through her
music, politics, and sexuality. I first heard Ani perform over two decades ago as
the opening act for a Holly Near concert at the University of Pennsylvania. The
audience was mostly middle-aged women, folk music fans used to hearing feminist
truths in softer sounds. Like many, I found Ani's combination of righteous anger,
poetic lyrics, unpredictable melodies, and percussive guitar chords jarring, at best.
Her music disrupted my expectations, and ultimately in a good way. Ani DiFranco
sings of women's power to be creative, honest, joyous, loud, sexual, and wise, and
to be known for our work in the world rather than our image or income. Looking
back, I see now that I was witnessing more than a generational shift from second
to third wave feminism. Building on previous waves of feminist struggles, Ani
DiFranco was invoking a future feminism—a fourth wave, perhaps—that reclaims
the efforts of all women and men to create a more just world. Listening to this
self-proclaimed "Little Folk Singer" play a warm-up act, I now know that I was
hearing the early sounds of an ongoing transformation in feminist politics. In this
chapter, I explore Ani DiFranco's life and music as that continuing story.

Life Story: Songwriter, Musicmaker, Storyteller, Freak

Ani DiFranco was born in 1970 and grew up in Buffalo, New York. Her parents,
Dante and Elizabeth DiFranco, met at MIT where her father was an engineering
student and her mother studied architecture. Both parents were busy professionals
and Ani describes spending a lot of time on her own during her childhood. This
was a mixed blessing: "My mother and father afforded me a lot of independence
and just assumed I would rise to the occasion. It was a really good way for me to

---

[1]   I would like to thank Travis Smart for assistance with the research for this chapter
and the editors, Mark Pedelty and Kristine Weglarz, for their guidance and support.

be brought up—or not brought up, as the case may be—because I was always a very independent person, the stable one in a very fucked-up family…" (DiFranco, quoted in Quirino 2004, 24–5). Ani chose to live on her own at the age of 15 when her parents' increasingly troubled marriage ended in divorce. She worked odd jobs to pay the rent, playing guitar and singing in local bars and clubs, until she finished high school. During this time, Ani also got involved with an older man, became pregnant, and had an abortion, a story she tells in her "Lost Woman Song" (DiFranco 1990).

Ani decided that she wanted to play guitar when she was just nine years old. She chose her first music teacher, Michael Meldrum, who introduced her to the local folk music scene, including numerous folk musicians passing through Buffalo on tour. According to her resume, Ani also studied dance at The Buffalo Academy of Visual & Performing Arts and later painting at Buffalo State College. Her passion for dance carries over into live concerts: "I danced with some regional Buffalo companies … I love moving and expressing. Dance to me is so primal— you have no tools whatsoever except for your body, which has an immediacy that I love" (DiFranco, quoted in ibid., 28). In 1989, Ani moved to New York City where she studied poetry with Sekou Sundiata at the New School for Social Research for several years. She also began touring, first in New England and the Mid-Atlantic states and later throughout the Southwest. Once again, she performed in bars, at clubs and festivals, and also on college campuses. Her first international tours were to England in 1994 and Australia in 1995. Today she tours the globe. Since 1990 when she released her first album, Ani has produced 21 studio albums, 12 official bootlegs, and 11 CDs with other artists, all under her Righteous Babe Records (RBR) label. Her most recent releases are the CDs: *Which Side Are You On?* (2012), *Red Letter Year* (2008), and the compilation, *Canon* (2007).

Although the Do-It-Yourself (DIY) movement was already popular when Ani founded Righteous Babe Records in 1989, her financial success has given the movement increased credibility and prominence. Ani has consistently refused recording contracts from the corporate music industry. Her brief online biography explains that: "Early in her career, Ani made a choice that is now so obvious to so many people that it's hard to remember it was once considered brazen: to say no to every record label deal that came her way, and yes to being her own boss" (Righteous Babe Records 2012). Although Ani has lived in New Orleans for much of the past ten years, Righteous Babe Records has remained in Buffalo.

Today Internet downloads have decreased the sales of many DIY record companies, including Righteous Babe, so Ani's intense tour schedule provides most of the financial support for RBR (Bendery 2008). In a recent interview, she describes reaffirming her anti-corporate music industry stance daily: "… I have to wake up every morning and do my job, and a lot of mornings I just think, 'Why? Why don't I just sign a record deal? Fame and fortune, what's wrong with that?' So every day I have to make the decision that there is something wrong with it" (DiFranco, quoted in Mechanic 2010). Today Ani handles the musical side of the business, including selecting other RBR recording artists, who are affectionately known as "the Babes." Scot Fisher, her long-time business partner, manages the company. Another business entity, Little Folk Singer (LFS) Touring, works with a network of local supporters to manage Ani's tours.

The unique mix of folk/jazz/punk/rock that is Ani DiFranco's music has been called somewhat paradoxically "folk experimentalism." According to Charles Garret, Ani's core musical strategy—a mix of autobiographical stories and progressive politics—best aligns her with folk, even though her musical tactics vary considerably (Garrett 2008). Many have remarked on DiFranco's guitar sound, which she describes as "the rhythmic, chunky, pulling, pushing, ripping end of the guitar spectrum" (DiFranco, quoted in ibid., 381). She achieves this instrumental effect by using artificial fingernails wrapped with duct tape for guitar picks.

Ani also has an unusual vocal style. One commentator offers this apt description: "It is a mix of singing and spoken word, jazz scat and pop-star belting, growls and hisses and sighs all incorporated into melodies with indistinct pitches, unpredictable contours, and intervallic content unusual for the standard pop repertory" (Attias, quoted in ibid., 386). Along with her untraditional appearance, DiFranco's musical sound has prompted some critics to place her in the "angry female singer" category, a label she resists for reasons I discuss below. Of her place in the folk music scene, Ani simply says, "I'm never quite sure if I'm a freak at the folk festival or some chick with an acoustic guitar at a rock club" (DiFranco, quoted in Quirino 2004, 41).

Ani DiFranco also resists other labels. Although she self-identifies as bisexual, she consistently questions the binary categories used to classify sexualities. As she puts it, "I don't experience love or sex as sleeping with a woman or a man. It's a person" (DiFranco, quoted in ibid., 48). Some of her LGBT fans felt betrayed when she married Andrew Gilchrist in 1998. Their marriage ended in divorce and Ani married Mike Napolitano in 2009. He is also the father of her daughter, Petah Lucia DiFranco Napolitano, born in 2007. Ani speaks openly of how giving birth increased her sense of our human connections and changed her understanding of feminism:

> When you have a baby, there is no more question as to whether you are separate. The baby body comes out of your body and remains connected to your body for a long time. Any mother puts that relationship and the needs of her child, before anything else. The role of mother on this planet has some very, very deep wisdom. Taking part in that has really reblossomed my feminist understanding.
> (DiFranco, quoted in Baumgardner 2011, 143)

Marriage and motherhood have also changed her sound, which critics, fans, and DiFranco agree now conveys less worry and more joy.

These life experiences are reflected in Ani's definition of feminism as much "more complex than rights and opportunities" (DiFranco, quoted in ibid., 147). For DiFranco, feminism has never been solely about women's autonomy or liberation, though that aspect of the movement remains important. It is the feminine sensibility she describes above, the sense that "we only exist in relation to each other, and we couldn't exist without each other," that matters most for women, men, and the earth (DiFranco, quoted in ibid., 143). She traces many contemporary social problems, such as pollution, poverty, and war, to the loss of this basic sense of human connection. According to DiFranco, there is no tension between feminism and this feminine sensibility or, for that matter, masculinity: "Feminism is simply the belief that a woman has a right to become herself, just as a man has a right to become himself. All decent people, male and female, are feminists" (DiFranco, quoted in Quirino 2004, 96). With this inclusive definition, DiFranco resists the internal divisions and identity politics that have undermined many feminist struggles and broadens her commitment to social justice beyond women's rights.

Although she recognizes the importance of her musical activism for feminism, DiFranco also refuses to let the movement define her role in it. When *Ms.* Magazine honored her among "21 Feminists for the 21st Century" for her business success, DiFranco responded with an open letter that extracted a promise: "If I drop dead tomorrow, tell me my gravestone won't read: ani d. CEO. Please let it read: songwriter musicmaker storyteller freak" (DiFranco 2003, 26–7). With these four words, Ani DiFranco sums up her life journey through the shoals of corporate capitalism, popular culture, and political controversy. In the next section, I discuss how she is reshaping feminism with her musical activism along the way.

Making Feminist Waves

We can position Ani DiFranco in the third wave of feminism, an ideological shift that began in the 1990s. However, it can be difficult to tell where a wave begins, especially when you are in it. The very concept of "waves" suggests a feminist movement that flows back and forth with overlapping and contending identities, images, and issues. Although some question the wave metaphor and argue that it inappropriately organizes feminist history around Western or, even more narrowly, American struggles, I find it useful as long as the various currents within waves, including their backflows and undertows, are acknowledged (Bailey 1997). An increasing number of activists and scholars now suggest that feminists began forming a fourth wave in the early 21st century; I think Ani DiFranco and her music are best understood as part of it.[2]

---

[2]   For discussions of a possible fourth wave of feminism, see Jennifer Baumgardner, "Is There a Fourth Wave? Does it Matter?," in *F'em! Goo Goo, Gaga, And Some Thoughts on Balls* (New York: Seal Press, 2011): 243–52; Pythia Peay, "Feminism's Fourth Wave," *Utne Reader*, March/April 2005. http://www.utne.com/2005-03-01/feminisms-fourth-wave.aspx; Jessica Ketcham Weber, et al., "A Dialogue on Action: Risks and Possibilities of Feminism in the Academy in the 21st Century," *third space, a journal of feminist theory*

A brief review of the first three waves clarifies why DiFranco belongs in the emerging fourth wave. In standard histories the first feminist wave began when American women organized to fight for the right to vote, own property, divorce, attend college, and become lawyers, doctors, and ministers at the Seneca Falls Women's Rights Convention in 1848.[3] At an earlier gathering, the 1840 World Anti-Slavery Convention, abolitionists Lucretia Mott and Elizabeth Cady Stanton were seated in the balcony behind a curtain and prevented from speaking. That experience convinced them that women could not liberate themselves or others until they had a voice in politics and it motivated them to gather at Seneca Falls. These early feminists narrowed their focus to the right to vote after the Civil War ended and the 14th amendment granted African American male suffrage. Other groups of women, such as the Women's Christian Temperance Union and the General Federation of Women's Clubs, continued to emphasize the larger social and economic issues included on the agenda at Seneca Falls. At the same time, anti-suffragists vigorously opposed giving women the vote, claiming women were not interested in or informed about politics and did not need or deserve the suffrage. The anti-suffragists also feared that immigrants and Negroes might outnumber white women among newly enfranchised voters and fundamentally change the electorate. Some suffragists shared this concern. American women—all of them— would not be granted the vote until the 19th amendment passed in 1920.

In the decades that followed, feminist struggles were less visible on the national political scene until the second wave of feminism formed in the 1960s. The main currents of this wave again flowed around calls for equal rights led by the National Organization for Women (NOW) founded by Betty Friedan in 1966. NOW fought for the Equal Rights Amendment (ERA) that reads "Equality of rights under the law shall not be denied or bridged by the United States or by any state on account of sex." In 1973 the ERA failed ratification by three states and since then NOW has focused on a number of other issues, including comparable worth, equal employment opportunity, reproductive rights, and electing women to public office. Given its liberal feminist rights-based strategy, NOW's attention to the concerns of LGBT women, working-class women, women of color, and men has waxed and waned. Although Betty Friedan originally worried that lesbians, whom she regrettably labeled the "lavender menace," would undermine mainstream support, in recent years NOW has fought for LGBT rights. Within this feminist second wave an alternative women's movement composed of many small groups sustained more radical anarchist and socialist visions of women's liberation.

---

and culture 8, 1 (Summer 2008). http://www.thirdspace.ca/journal/article/viewArticle/ weber/228.

[3] For a good brief history of feminism, see Jennifer Baumgardner and Amy Richards, *Manifesta, Young Women, Feminism and the Future* (New York: Farrar, Straus and Giroux, 2000), ch. 2, "What Is Feminism?." On the evolution of feminist theories, see Nancy S. Love, *Understanding Dogmas and Dreams: A Text*, 2nd. ed., (Washington, DC: CQ Press, 2006), ch. 7.

These groups of women articulated a feminism born out of the 1960s civil rights, environmental, and peace movements that focused more on grass-roots activism, community organizing, and holistic change. Some argue that the tensions within the second wave between NOW's emphasis on women's rights and the broader transformative agenda of these smaller groups replicate the earlier split between suffragists and social reformers in the first wave (McGlen and O'Conner 1995). Again, like the ebb of first wave feminism, feminist movements retreated from national politics after the 1960s, a retreat accompanied by antifeminist backlash against feminists as "angry, man-hating women." This stereotype persists today.

The third feminist wave emerged in the 1990s against the backdrop of this unflattering image of feminism that many women found disempowering (Gillis et al., 2004). Equally important for the third wave are continuing processes of globalization fueled by the fall of the former Soviet Union. Third wave feminism includes postcolonial feminist theories and transnational feminist organizations that challenge the "essentialism" of first and second wave feminisms, especially the idea that woman or man is a universal identity. Postcolonial feminists offer new opportunities for crossing borders and forming coalitions. These processes are also facilitated by the familiarity of a new feminist generation with a variety of social media. Yet the third wave also reconceptualizes feminism in ways that some earlier feminists argue are post- or even antifeminist. Here I refer to the rise of neo-liberal "lifestyle feminism," a consumer-oriented and image-based movement, and neo-conservative "power feminism," a movement that urges women to take responsibility for ourselves. In the process, it also often redirects attention from challenging patriarchal power to blaming female victims (Heywood and Drake 1997). Some third wave feminists have responded to conservative claims that feminism actually disempowers women by reasserting their "femininity" as "grrrl power." Others see "grrrl power" as just another form of media-driven "lifestyle feminism" with limited political impact (Munford 2004). What is most striking about the third wave is its emphasis on DIY feminism, a movement that encourages a variety of feminist identities and images. Missing, though, are the strong connections with larger struggles for social justice that marked the first two waves.

If a fourth feminist wave is emerging, it is gaining momentum and building strength from all three of the previous waves. Ani DiFranco, I argue, powerfully illustrates the features of this emerging fourth wave and, more generally, how waves advance and overlap. Although the crest of each feminist wave may seem distinct, beneath the surface their deeper values move and flow onward together. DiFranco challenges the superficial complicity with neo-liberal capitalist patriarchy that runs through many third-wave "wanna-be" feminisms; she does so without redrawing the ideological lines between liberals, socialists, and anarchists that often created splits within the first two feminist waves. The result is a feminism that is less compromised and less compromising than many third wave feminist varieties. Fourth wave feminism continues to celebrate strong, independent women and fight for social justice, but refuses to recreate an ideological and identity-based politics of "woman" versus "man" or other divisions of "us" versus "them." In the rest of this section, I focus on DiFranco's contributions to four features of this emerging fourth wave of feminism: 1) sexual ambiguity; 2) do-it-yourself; 3) feminist spirituality; and 4) social justice. I illustrate each feature with one or more of DiFranco's songs. Although these features define a fourth feminist wave, my primary purpose here is to use wave theory to show how past and future feminisms flow together.

1) Sexual Ambiguity or "not a pretty girl" (DiFranco 1995)

Many scholars agree that rock music plays a major role in constructing the sexual identities of its teenage listeners. Many also recognize that rock is a musical genre dominated by male performers and producers. Media images of rock stars—whether "cock-rock" or "teeny bop"—tend to feature men who control women sexually and/or emotionally.[4] Some scholars suggest that the driving rhythms, strong modulations, and hard-hitting sounds of rock music mirror an insistent male sexuality (Cox 1990, Whiteley 1990). Historically women have had few ways to enter this rock music scene, except as back-up vocalists or star-struck fans. Punk arguably offers more opportunities for women musicians because it cultivates ambiguity, including ambiguous sexual identities (Frith and McRobbie 1990, 384). Yet women musicians in the punk scene have also been limited by stereotypes of the diminutive "punkette" or the "angry female singer" (Feigenbaum 2005).

Ani DiFranco engages the sexual ambiguity of the punk scene and uses it to question a larger set of assumptions about beauty, femininity, and sexuality. Judith Butler, whose work was pivotal for third wave feminism, also offers a way of understanding how DiFranco plays with sex and gender categories. According to Butler, gender is something we "do" and its terms are articulated in advance by society. In a heteronormative society, gender (masculine/feminine) is most often presented as an extension of sex (male/female). Butler urges feminists instead to explore "what it might mean to undo restrictively normative conceptions of sexual and gendered life" (Butler 2004, 1–5). DiFranco discusses the positive effects her music has on the sexual identity of teenage girls in similar terms: "I think it's because my early songs came from a young woman trying to become herself. Other young women doing the same found good company and even comfort in that" (DiFranco, quoted in Hobart 2009). Her resistance to mainstream media images of female beauty and feminine behavior has earned her the gendered label "angry female singer" in some quarters. According to Anna Feigenbaum, some music critics still try to re-feminize DiFranco (and other "angry female singers")

---

[4]   The classic version of this argument is Simon Frith and Angela McRobbie, "Rock and Sexuality" in *On Record: Rock, Pop, and the Written Word*, Simon Frith and Andrew Goodwin (eds) (New York: Pantheon Books, 1990), 371–89. For a more recent discussion, see Andi Zeisler, *Feminism and Pop Culture* (Berkeley, CA: Seal Press, 2008), ch. 4.

by describing her as a goddess, kitten, siren, or muse—a term Ani occasionally uses herself.

Other critics contrast DiFranco's punk image with her actual beauty (Feigenbaum 2005). In a recent interview DiFranco said of her childhood, "I learned that pretty women are the best women and I'm not one of them, without any words spoken whatsoever" (Baumgardner 2011, 146). In "not a pretty girl," she affirms her appearance and refuses to play a "damsel in distress" or a "kitten up a tree" waiting for a man to rescue her. Instead, DiFranco is "punk," a woman who fights for what she believes and whose uncompromising honesty asks others to face their deepest fears about sexual identity. Regarding her anger, DiFranco maintains, "My songs were informed by my life, my gender, my identity, and that seemed to have no place in the world around me. Like my anger, for instance: if I included that in my songs, in my vocabulary of emotions ... then there was this whole contingent that [treated me as if] I were some kind of in-your-face, angry, screaming thrash band or something ... I'm not an angry person, I just have opinions" (Feigenbaum 2005, 43). Placed in a heterosexist category with negative connotations—"angry female singer"—DiFranco refuses to be defined by it and redirects attention to her politics (ibid.).

It is important here to note that DiFranco's music appeals emotionally to men as well as women. In her study of how people use music to explore emotions, a phenomenon called "depth listening," Danielle Bessett found that men and women use the music of "angry female performers," especially DiFranco, to vent their anger over failed relationships (Bessett 2006, 49–62). While women tend to identify with the singer as a model and to internalize the music, men more often "split" the female singer from the song lyrics. This allows them to hear a generic message of lost love and to see these female singers as role models for women. Some men also reported listening to "angry female singers" in order to better understand who women are or, as one respondent put it, to "get inside women's heads" (ibid., 58). By exploring how sex and gender shape the depth listening of men and women, Bessett illuminates the full reach of DiFranco's challenge to sexual binaries and gender stereotypes.

DiFranco's DIY feminism not only refuses to define people by stereotypes of female beauty and behavior. It also reaches out to listeners who may be searching for something beyond the binaries of sex and gender categories and trying to understand people as individuals. In an interview with Jennifer Baumgardner, DiFranco discusses the outcries of "Fraud! Sham!" from the queer community when she married her first husband. DiFranco criticizes this "us" or "them" orientation for denying "sexual fluidity" and responds, "I say to 'straight girl!' the same thing I say to 'dyke!': 'Whatever.'" (Baumgardner 2007, 149).[5] In keeping with the conscious ambiguity of musical messages in the punk scene, Ani

---

[5]   For a more extensive interview about DiFranco's sexuality, see "Bisexuality Now: The Ani Phenomenon" in Jennifer Baumgardner, *Look Both Ways, Bisexual Politics* (New York: Farrar, Strauss, and Giroux, 2007), ch. 4.

DiFranco offers her listeners what some have called an ethic of "ambisexuality" (McCarthy 2006).

2) Do-It-Yourself or "blood in the boardroom" (DiFranco 1993)

In her letter to *Ms.* mentioned above, Ani DiFranco expresses surprise that the magazine's 25th anniversary issue featured her among "21 Feminists for the 21st Century" and dismay that it emphasized her business acumen and financial success. As she puts it, "I'm glad I didn't sign on to the corporate army. I mourn the commodification and homogenization of music by the music industry, and I fear the manufacture of consent by the corporately-controlled media. Last thing I want to do is feed the machine" (DiFranco 2003, 27). Moreover, she has not. In "blood in the boardroom," Ani sings of getting her period while sitting in a corporate boardroom, bored by the lies, money, power, and suits that surrounded her. She also tells us of a corporate culture that mixes blood with death. She chose to maintain her independence and walked away, taking her life-giving music with her and leaving only a blood stain on an upholstered chair (DiFranco 1993). Other songs—"the million you never made," "napoleon," and "animal"—convey how her refusal to sign with the corporate music industry has changed her relationship to capitalism and other musicians, some of them her friends who later became "stars" (DiFranco 1995, 1996, 2004).

In *Small Giants, Companies that Choose to Be Great Instead of Big*, Bo Burlingham features Righteous Babe Records as a business that operates on a human scale and has a soul (Burlingham 2005). This is partly because the company remains deeply rooted in Buffalo, New York, Ani's hometown. RBR began with a small office in a rundown area of downtown Buffalo, but the company has now relocated to the former Ashbury Delaware Methodist Church. RBR restored the historic church that now houses its recording studio, a concert venue, a jazz club, and another business, Hallwalls' Contemporary Arts Center.

Like the other "small giants" Burlingham discusses, RBR stresses integrity, professionalism, and personal connections. Although Ani distances herself from the "women's music" scene, these qualities of RBR do resemble earlier independent women's record companies, such as Olivia and Redwood Records (Garrett 2008).[6] The company message is clear and consistent, without a lot of hype and marketing. In her letter to *Ms.* Ani writes, "I'm just a folksinger, not an entrepreneur. My hope is that my music and poetry will be enjoyable and/ or meaningful to someone, somewhere, not that I maximize my profit margins" (DiFranco 2003, 27). RBR prides itself on delivering what it promises and that includes more than concerts, recordings, and related paraphernalia, such as posters,

---

[6] For discussions of these second wave musical foremothers, see Nancy S. Love, *Musical Democracy* (Albany, NY: SUNY Press, 2006), ch. 4; Cynthia Lont, "Women's Music: No Longer a Small Private Party," *Rockin' the Boat: Mass Music and Mass Movements*, ed. Reebee Garofalo (Boston, MA: South End Press, 1992).

T-shirts, and so on. The company forms ongoing relationships with its customers, employees, and suppliers. Scot Fisher, who manages the business, says, "It's not enough for us to be good to customers … We want our relationships with them to be personal and real, not contrived" (Fisher, quoted in Burlingham 2005, 87). This means handwriting responses to letters, hiring live people to answer the phones, and addressing promotional materials to customers and friends, rather than fans. It also means hiring local suppliers, employing local talent, maintaining local networks of concert promoters, and putting the people who work for RBR first in business decisions (ibid.).

Burlingham claims that the success of RBR comes from its clarity about priorities: the business exists to support the art and not vice versa. Ani describes RBR as "People who incorporate and coordinate politics, art and media every day into a people-friendly, sub-corporate, woman-informed, queer-happy small business that puts music before rock stardom and ideology before profit" (DiFranco 2003, 27). Elsewhere she simply says, "I'm grossed out by the effect of capitalism on art" (Hobart 2009). As a result of this philosophy, RBR has challenged the supposed tension between art and business and succeeded at both. Ron Ehmke, an employee of RBR and Hallwalls, describes the collaboration between the two organizations, saying "[Scot] frequently says he's not an artist himself, but really he is. His art is helping artists make their work (quoted in Burlingham 2005, 210).

3) Feminist Spirituality or "the atom" (DiFranco 2008)

Feminism has long had a troubled relationship with organized religion and it comes as no surprise that Ani DiFranco describes herself as an "atheist." Why then associate her music with feminist spirituality? What DiFranco affirms are the life-giving powers of women; this includes reclaiming the female body, women's sexuality, and mother earth as sacred. To some extent, these powers are tied to women's capacity to give birth. In speaking about bearing and rearing her daughter, Ani invokes difference feminism and urges the "whole world to read that Carol Gilligan book" (Baumgardner 2011, 143). The book to which she refers is *In a Different Voice*: *Psychological Theory and Women's Development* where Gilligan distinguishes the different voices of a self, one defined by separation and another defined through connection. Although many associate a relational understanding with women and position Gilligan with second wavers' feminist "essentialism," Gilligan distinguishes these "voices" by theme, not sex or gender. Men also can experience the sense of interdependence that sustains life in its many forms (Gilligan 1992). However, in Western patriarchal societies that privilege the autonomous self, objective knowledge, and control over nature, including women's bodies, this relational voice speaks softly, if at all (McCarthy 2006). In "the atom," Ani challenges this dominant Western worldview. She sings reverently of the atom, the basic unit of matter, as a microcosm of the cosmos and the key to life on earth. She also condemns the arrogance and blasphemy of the "male" physicists, who split the atom to make a bomb, and she wryly suggests no "women" were present at its creation. Elsewhere DiFranco describes her experience of childbirth in terms that cry out for comparison: "The experience of childbirth, for me, ironically, was humbling instead of empowering ... You really feel small. You feel helpless. You feel insignificant—because you are. It's such a colossal, physical event. It's bloody, it's violent. Nature is unconcerned with your individual survival. Those are important blows to the almighty ego" (Baumgardner 2011, 145). For DiFranco, nature has its own creativity and divinity to which humanity might more appropriately respond with humility, awe, and wonder.

DiFranco's celebration of women's creative capacity is not limited to biological motherhood, though. She recognizes that the image of an essentialized (m)other has been and continues to be used to limit women's lives. In "Adam and Eve," she retells the story of the Garden of Eden as a bad date that ends with bad sex (DiFranco 1996). In the process, she affirms Eve's bodily knowledge (she enjoys apples) and sexual desires (she does not fear snakes). Here DiFranco mocks those who reduce female desire to sexual acts and she celebrates the female body as a source of deep wisdom and great power. Kate McCarthy draws a parallel between DiFranco's reclaiming of women's bodies and Audre Lorde's argument in her essay, "Uses of the Erotic: The Erotic as Power" (McCarthy 2006). Lorde celebrates the erotic as "a resource within each of us that lies in a deeply female and spiritual plane, firmly rooted in the power of our unexpressed or unrecognized feeling." She urges women to rediscover this, "our most profoundly creative source" that patriarchal societies have misnamed (as irrational or primitive) and distorted (as merely physical or even obscene) (Lorde 1984). McCarthy argues that DiFranco's music plays a role in this process of rediscovery by reconnecting "sexual desire with the largest, most socially and spiritually significant longings of human beings, the desire for the sharing of joy and opening to the divine" (McCarthy 2006, 89). As DiFranco sings in "joyful girl," human beings owe each other and the world nothing less than this life-giving creativity of the cosmos (DiFranco 1997).

4) Social Justice or "willing to fight" (DiFranco 1993)

Among her mentors and models, Ani DiFranco includes Woody Guthrie, Pete Seeger, Willie Nelson, Bob Dylan, and Thelonious Monk. Some have even called DiFranco the "female" Bob Dylan. The adjective "female" here arguably diminishes as well as acknowledges her contribution to a male-dominated music scene. Although folk music has long been associated with progressive causes and politics, for Ani DiFranco, it remains much too white (Eyerman and Jamison 1998).[7] In an interview for *Option Magazine*, DiFranco says, "It's amazing ...

---

[7]   Eyerman and Jamison (1998, 52) see the "active use of music and song by social movements" as "a natural outgrowth of the multilingual background of the American people ... This is especially visible in the case of white folk music, which was very early on used by movements of social reform for getting the message out."

you go to a folk festival and there's so many white people out in the field that it's hard to keep track of them all. I mean, I like folk music because it tends to span generations, but it does tend to be a white thing and that's kind of a drag. It's a drag that the world is so segregated ..." (DiFranco, quoted in Quirino 2004, 41).

As we have seen, DiFranco's experimental folk music shifts the genre both to desegregate it and to reach a Gen-X audience. Utah Phillips, with whom DiFranco collaborates, prefers to call younger listeners "the Y generation, because everybody is asking why" (Kupfer 2003). DiFranco insists, "Folk music is not an acoustic guitar—that's not where the heart of it is. I use the word *folk* in reference to punk music and rap music. It's an attitude, it's an awareness of one's heritage, and it's a community. It's subcorporate music that gives voice to different communities" (DiFranco, quoted in Rodgers 2000). In the song "willing to fight," she claims connections with a community that reaches across generations and around the globe, from her ancestors to the descendants she will never meet (DiFranco 1993).[8] Her life is a brief moment between this distant past and an uncertain future, and her time on this earth is precious. Ani asks her supporters to use their lives to fight for what matters, and the political causes she supports could not be more important. The RBR website includes a grass-roots action section with information on the following: "Media," "Peace and Justice," "Choice," "Arts and Education," and "Vote Dammit!" DiFranco has also spoken out against homophobia, racism, and the death penalty, and for historic preservation, environmental protection, and post-Katrina relief.

DiFranco's collaboration with Utah Phillips powerfully illustrates the cross-generational political bridges she would build. On *The Past Didn't Go Anywhere*, their collaborative CD, Ani gives Utah a musical makeover to reach a new generation (DiFranco and Phillips 1996). As she puts it:

> It was a very calculated move on my part ... because I can see people around me, people my age, who haven't had the experience I have of being thrown into folk festivals half their lives and coming into contact with all this crazy subcorporate music ... They would never find out that what he has to say does have something to do with them. So [the album] was taking Utah and putting him into a different context that somebody my age does have a vocabulary for, and then getting them to hear what he has to say. (DiFranco, quoted in Rodgers 2000)

DiFranco was motivated by the sense of social responsibility she shares with Phillips and a deep respect for the wisdom of her elders.

Her newest release, *Which Side are You On?*, also brings folk musicians together across generations (DiFranco 2012). Pete Seeger, to whom DiFranco refers as "my elder, my forefather in folk music and political song," joins her for

---

8   This song is featured in Paula Goldman, ed., *Imagining Ourselves, Global Voices from a New Generation of Women* (Novato, CA: New World Library, 2006).

the title song. On the RBR website, DiFranco acknowledges the bold(er) quality of these songs:

I'm testing deeper waters with the political songs on this album … I feel a little bit frustrated, politically desperate. After having written hundreds of songs over decades, I think, "Now what? How far can I go with this? Can you sing the word 'abortion,' can you sing the word 'patriarchy'—what can you sing and get away with?" I guess I've been pushing my own boundaries of politics and art. Seeing what people have the ears to listen to. How big is my mouth? What can I get out of it successfully? (RBR 2012)

Her music on this CD is more desperate because of the magnitude of the political challenges humanity faces today.

The feminist movement once again lacks visible leadership on the national political stage and this makes DiFranco's musical activism especially important. Jo Reger argues that activist musicians, like DiFranco, use their music to mobilize young listeners emotionally and align them politically with the feminist movement. As she puts it, "The music they create is political, far reaching, and empowering and allows their listeners to connect to feminist ideologies and communities, helping to emotionally mobilize contemporary feminism" (Reger 2007, 1364). This process occurs even—and perhaps especially—when those musicians resist direct leadership roles because of their critique of mainstream media and commitment to grass-roots politics (ibid.). For Reger, the cultural politics of activist musicians like DiFranco reflects the diffusion of feminism into women's everyday lives and represents the best of third waver's DIY feminist ethic. I agree that DiFranco shares these third wave qualities. But she refuses the consumer lifestyle and conservative power feminism that has co-opted many third wavers and instead joins their anti-essentialism with more holistic commitments to feminist spirituality and social justice. Through her anti-corporate, community-based politics, DiFranco shows how earlier progressive movements, including all of the earlier waves of feminism, can flow together into future struggles for peace and justice.

A Future Feminism?

Much has and has not changed since that evening over two decades ago when I first heard Ani DiFranco perform. Like many of my generation, I sometimes mourn our current post-feminist age and cringe at the high heels and mini-skirts of my "liberated" female students. I also laughed (not unkindly) when I read Claire Gordon's piece, "The patriarchy wears patent leather heels," in the *Yale Daily News* while researching this chapter (Gordon 2008). Gordon, the special events coordinator of the Yale Women's Center, reflects on how her post-feminist fashion statement—beautiful purple, patent leather, five-inch heels—resulted in a fall on black ice, a sprained ankle, too much Percocet, and a new sense of dependency and vulnerability. She asks, "If so much of the fashion marketed to women has roots in patriarchy, can a woman wearing it consider herself liberated? Can a feminist wear heels, painful heels, liability heels, as a valid form of self-expression?" (ibid.). In her drugged state, Gordon writes wryly that these very questions will open the door to "fourth wave feminism." Enter Ani DiFranco, righteous babe for a new millennium, whose music takes women back and moves all of us forward to a feminist politics that rings true(r) across generations. Giving her foremothers and forefathers credit where credit is due, she reaches beyond the political ideologies and identity politics that have shaped white, liberal, capitalist patriarchy and earlier feminist movements that resisted it alike.

When I teach the now classic texts of feminist theory to this new generation of students, I sometimes struggle to explain why their authors needed to use the binary categories they wanted to question in order to convey their arguments. In discussing DiFranco's music, we have already seen some examples of this problem: Gilligan relies on male/female to distinguish thematic "voices" and Lorde associates creativity with Eros and distinguishes it from obscenity. In *Giving an Account of Oneself,* Judith Butler explains how we are all "interpellated" into a "scene of address" without which we cannot make sense of ourselves and within which we are called on to act responsibly toward others (Butler 2005). Today this scene of address still includes the troubled and troubling categories of sex and gender. Butler comes closest to DiFranco's "ambisexual" ethic, and even she cannot speak, think, and write without using the binaries in question. Ultimately, the problem here is not false universalism (all women are not the same) or even over-generalization (age, class, gender, race intersect in important ways), but our all-too-human need for words. Often where language fails to explain, I invoke Ani DiFranco's music and suddenly my students understand.

According to Theodor Adorno, "music is a language, but a language without concepts" (Adorno 1988). Although DiFranco disavows the "women's music" of the 1970s, in some respects she follows in the footsteps of her musical foremother, Holly Near, for whose concert I first heard DiFranco play backup decades ago. Near also resisted the ideological and identity categories that marked many earlier feminist struggles, especially during the second wave. In her title song "Sky Dances," Near transcends the "grammatical fiction" of language on which the binaries of political ideologies and identity politics rely. She offers a pantheistic vision and sings of willows, women, snakes, fish, turtles, oaks, clouds, pines, seeds, water, and corn—all dancing as matter/energy in the mirror/storm of life.[9] Ani DiFranco brings this once nascent feminist sensibility to an emerging fourth wave of feminists whose categories are ever more fluid and mobile. It is no coincidence that she does so through music. Musical sounds flow and move, rise and fall, overlapping like waves in the ocean. What better way to bring multiple waves of feminist struggles to their political crest? In *Verses,* DiFranco reflects on

---

[9]   For a more extensive discussion of Near's music as queer, see Love, *Musical Democracy* (2006), ch. 4. Near writes about her changing roles in the lesbian feminist movement in her autobiography, *Fire in the Rain, Singer in the Storm: An Autobiography* (Near with Derk Richardson, 1990).

the difference between spoken, sung, and written words. She considered calling the book "transcript," but chose "*Verses*" to express "the overlap of poetry and song, while not ruling out the notion that all of these works could simply be verses in the one long rambling folk song of me" (DiFranco 2007, 95).

That "long rambling folk song" also tells a larger story of the evolution of feminism. Jennifer Baumgardner ends her portrait of fourth wave feminism with the following listserv exchange: "One aspect of the 'waves' metaphor that I kinda like," the historian Louise Bernikow wrote, "is the idea that waves recede and gather strength and come back stronger, don't they?" Roxanne Dunbar-Ortiz replies, "Tsunami! … Let's do it" (Baumgardner 2011, 252). Or, as DiFranco puts it, "Evolve!"[10]

Bibliography

Adorno, Theodor. *Introduction to the Sociology of Music.* Boston, MA: Continuum International Publishing Group, 1988.

Bailey, Cathryn. "Making Waves and Drawing Lines: The Politics of Defining the Vicissitudes of Feminism." *Hypatia: A Journal of Feminist Philosophy* 12, 3 (August 1997): 17–28.

Baumgardner, Jennifer. "Is There a Fourth Wave? Does it Matter? In *F'em, Goo Goo, Gaga, and Some Thoughts on Balls*, by Jennifer Baumgardner, 243–56. Berkeley, CA: Seal Press, 2011.

Baumgardner, Jennifer. "Bisexuality Now: The Ani Phenomenon." In *Look Both Ways, Bisexual Politics*, by Jennifer Baumgardner, 97–126. New York: Farrar, Straus, and Giroux, 2007.

Baumgardner, Jennifer and Amy Richards. "What Is Feminism?" In *Manifesta, Young Women, Feminism and the Future*, by Jennifer Baumgardner and Amy Richards, 50–86. New York: Farrar, Straus and Giroux, 2000.

Bessett, Danielle. "'Don't Step on My Groove!' Gender and the Social Experience of Rock." *Symbolic Interaction* 29, 1 (Winter 2006): 49–62.

Burlingham, Bo. *Small Giants, Companies That Choose to Be Great Instead of Big.* New York: Penguin, 2005.

Butler, Judith. *Giving an Account of Oneself.* New York: Fordham University Press, 2005.

Butler, Judith. *Undoing Gender.* New York: Routledge, 2004.

Cox, Renee. "A History of Music." *The Journal of Aesthetics and Art Criticism* 48, 4 (Fall 1990): 395–411.

---

[10]   After following DiFranco from afar for many years, I again heard her perform live in Asheville, North Carolina in February 2012. Echoing first wave feminists, DiFranco reminded the audience to register to vote and had volunteers in the lobby to assist her listeners with their voter registration forms.

DiFranco, Ani. "Ani DiFranco, Then and Now: Interview with Ani DiFranco," by Michael Mechanic. *Mother Jones*, 13 December 2010. http://motherjones.com/rif/2010/12/ani-difranco-righteous-babe-interview.

DiFranco, Ani. "SW Interview: Ani DiFranco on her New Album, Family Life, and Capitalism," by Erika Hobart. *Seattle Weekly*, 14 October 2009. http://blogs.seattleweekly.com/reverb/2009/10/an_sw_exclusive_interview_ani.php.

DiFranco, Ani. "A Righteous Babe in Uncharted Territory: An Interview With Ani DiFranco: Interview with Ani DiFranco," by Jennifer Bendery. *PopMatters*, 21 August 2008. http://www.popmatters.com/pn/feature/a-righteous-babe-in-uncharted-territory-an-interview.

DiFranco, Ani. *Verses*. New York: Seven Stories Press, 2007.

DiFranco, Ani. "Songwriter, Musicmaker, Storyteller, Freak: Open letter to *Ms. Magazine.*" *New Internationalist*. 359 (August 2003): 26–7. http://www.newint.org/features/2003/08/05/freak/.

Ron Eyerman and Andrew Jamison, *Music and Social Movements, Mobilizing Traditions in the Twentieth Century*. Cambridge: Cambridge University Press, 1998.

Feigenbaum, Anna. "'Some Guy Designed This Room I'm Standing In': Marking Gender in Press Coverage of Ani DiFranco." *Popular Music* 24, 1 (January 2005): 37–56.

Frith, Simon and Angela McRobbie. "Rock and Sexuality." In *On Record: Rock, Pop, and the Written Word*. Edited by Simon Frith and Andrew Goodwin, 371–89. New York: Pantheon Books, 1990.

Garrett, Charles Hiroshi. "The Musical Tactics of Ani DiFranco." *American Music* 26, 3 (Fall 2008): 278–97.

Gilligan, Carol. *In a Different Voice: Psychological Theory and Women's Development*. Cambridge, MA: Harvard University Press, 1992.

Gillis, Stacy, Gillian Howie, and Rebecca Munford, eds. *Third Wave Feminism: A Critical Exploration*. New York: Palgrave Macmillan, 2004.

Goldman, Paula, ed. *Imagining Ourselves, Global Voices from a New Generation of Women*. Novato, CA: New World Library, 2006.

Gordon, Claire. "The patriarchy wears patent leather heels." *Yale Daily News*, Wednesday, 5 March 2008. http://www.yaledailynews.com/news/2008/mar/05/the-patriarchy-wears-patentpleather-heels.

Heywood, Leslie and Jennifer Drake. "We Learn America Like a Script: Activism in the Third Wave; or, Enough Phantoms of Nothing." In *Third Wave Agenda: Being Feminist, Doing Feminism*, edited by Leslie Heywood and Jennifer Drake, 40–54. Minneapolis, MN: University of Minnesota Press, 1997.

Kupfer, David. "Utah Phillips," *The Progressive*, September 2003. http://www.progressive.org/mag/interview/utahphillips.

Lont, Cynthia. "Women's Music: No Longer a Small Private Party." In *Rockin' the Boat: Mass Music and Mass Movements*, edited by Reebee Garofalo, 241–54. Boston, MA; South End Press, 1992.

Lorde, Audre. "Uses of the Erotic: The Erotic as Power." In *Sister Outside, Essays and Speeches*, by Audre Lorde, 53–9. Freedom, CA: The Crossing Press, 1984.

Love, Nancy S. *Understanding Dogmas and Dreams: A Text*. 2nd ed. Washington, DC: CQ Press, 2006.

Love, Nancy S. *Musical Democracy*. Albany, NY: SUNY Press, 2006.

McCarthy, Kate. "Not Pretty Girls?: Sexuality, Spirituality, and Gender Construction in Women's Rock Music." *The Journal of Popular Culture* 39, 1 (2006): 69–94.

McGlen, Nancy S. and Karen O'Conner. *Women, Politics, and American Society*. Englewood Cliffs, NJ: Prentice Hall, 1995.

Munford, Rebecca. "'Wake Up and Smell the Lipgloss': Gender, Generation and the (A)politics of Girl Power." In *Third Wave Feminism: A Critical Exploration*, edited by Stacy Gillis, Gillian Howie, and Rebecca Munford, 142–53. New York: Palgrave Macmillan, 2004.

Near, Holly, with Derk Richardson, *Fire in the Rain, Singer in the Storm: An Autobiography* (New York: William Morrow, 1990).

Peay, Pythia. "Feminism's Fourth Wave." *Utne Reader* (March/April 2005). http://www.utne.com/2005-03-01/feminisms-fourth-wave-aspx.

Quirino, Raffaele. *Ani DiFranco: Righteous Babe Revisited*. Kingston, Ontario: Fox Music Books, 2004.

Reger, Jo. "Where Are the Leaders? Music, Culture, and Contemporary Feminism." *American Behavioral Scientist* 50, 10 (June 2007): 1350–69.

Righteous Babe Records, "Ani DiFranco Biography" and "Ani DiFranco Discography," Righteous Babe Records. http://www.righteousbabe.com.

Rodgers, Jeffrey Pepper. "Profile: Ani DiFranco and Utah Phillips." In *Rock Troubadours: Conversations on the Art and Craft of Songwriting with Jerry Garcia, Ani DiFranco, Dave Matthews, Joni Mitchell, and Paul Simon, and More*, edited by Jeffrey Pepper Rodgers, 157–80. New York: String Letter Publishing. 2000. http://www.jeffreypepperrodgers.com/difranco.htm.

Weber, Jessica Ketcham, Lisa Costello, Allison Goss, Regina Clemens Fox, and Lorie Jacobs. "A Dialogue on Action: Risks and Possibilities of Feminism in the Academy in the 21st Century." *thirdspace: a journal of feminist theory & culture* 8, 1 (Summer 2008). http://www.thirdspace.ca/journal/article/viewArticle/weber/228.

Whiteley, Sheila. *Women and Popular Music: Sexuality, Identity and Subjectivity*. New York: Routledge, 2000.

Zeisler, Andi. *Feminism and Pop Culture*. Berkeley, CA: Seal Press, 2008.

Discography

DiFranco, Ani. "Lost Woman Song." *Ani DiFranco*. Buffalo, NY: Righteous Babe Records, RBR 001-D, 1990.

DiFranco, Ani. "blood in the boardroom." *Puddle Dive*. Buffalo, NY: Righteous Babe Records, RBR 004-D, 1993.

DiFranco, Ani. "willing to fight." *Puddle Dive*. Buffalo, NY: Righteous Babe Records, RBR 004-D, 1993.

DiFranco, Ani. "not a pretty girl." *Not A Pretty Girl*. Buffalo, NY: Righteous Babe Records, RBR 007-D, 1995.

DiFranco, Ani. "the million you never made." *Not A Pretty Girl*. Buffalo, NY: Righteous Babe Records, RBR 007-D, 1995.

DiFranco, Ani. "Adam and Eve." *Dilate*. Buffalo, NY: Righteous Babe Records, RBR 008-D, 1996.

DiFranco, Ani. "Napoleon." *Dilate*. Buffalo, NY: Righteous Babe Records, RBR 008-D, 1996.

DiFranco, Ani. "joyful girl." *living in clip*. Buffalo, NY: Righteous Babe Records, RBR 011-D, 1997.

DiFranco, Ani. "animal." *educated guess*. Buffalo, NY: Righteous Babe Records, RBR 034-D, 2004.

DiFranco, Ani. "the atom." *Red Letter Year*. Buffalo, NY: Righteous Babe Records, RBR063-D, 2008.

DiFranco, Ani. *Which Side Are You On?* Buffalo, NY: Righteous Babe Records, RBR073-D, 2012.

DiFranco, Ani and Utah Phillips. *The Past Didn't Go Anywhere*. Buffalo, NY: Righteous Babe Records, RBR 009-D, 1996.

Chapter 10
Pearl Jam: The Conscience of Arena Rock

Kristine Weglarz

Maintaining a commercially successful band for almost two decades is no small feat, given shifting audience tastes and genre preferences on radio and television. This challenge becomes even more difficult when you face criticism for speaking out against a controversial president and controversial war. This is the reality faced by Pearl Jam, the Seattle band composed of Eddie Vedder, Stone Gossard, Mike McCready, Jeff Ament, Boom Gaspar, and a rotating series of drummers including, most recently, Soundgarden's Matt Cameron. After releasing their first album in 1991, Pearl Jam was one of a small but prominent group of musicians to speak out actively against the Bush administration and the Iraq War during a time when doing so could and did lead to charges of being unpatriotic, hypocritical, and even treasonous. As such, the band serves as a useful case study into contemporary American protest music. Additionally, the longevity of their career allows for a careful examination of how their protest efforts have changed (or alternatively, have not changed) in relation to changing political issues and events.

What recurring themes of protest music does Pearl Jam draw upon when engaging in protest? How has the nature of Pearl Jam's protest efforts changed over the last eight years? What is the relationship between Pearl Jam and live shows when performing as political rock artists?

At the heart of these questions is a concern with the "music of politics," which is relatively under-theorized and does not receive the same sort of academic attention as the "politics of music." The former, which I attempt to address here, represents musicians engaging directly, through song or activities, political causes, parties, candidates, and/or concerns. The latter generally looks at the political decisions behind the business of music, including considerations of genre and economics, and how communities use music to reinforce and redefine themselves. I do not wish to draw a clear line between the two, as from this brief description alone it seems clear that they are related and one may feed into consequences for the other.

In looking at Pearl Jam, I specifically highlight the role of protest music in fostering deliberative democracy. Amy Gutmann (2004) explains the purpose of deliberative democracy. Gutmann suggests that the purpose of deliberative democracy is to promote the "most justifiable conception for dealing with moral disagreement in politics" (ibid., 10). This is especially important given the relative power difference between performers and their audiences. I will add that for Pearl Jam, the act of protest is a good in itself. While the ends matter, the process is what remains crucially important and central for protest artists.

Pearl Jam's career is dotted with their continued commitment to a number of social and political causes. Rock for Choice, an organization committed to securing the right to abortion and the means to achieve it, got a very high-profile endorsement from Eddie Vedder during Pearl Jam's earlier years. Rock the Vote, a group committed to increasing young voter turnout (but was not associated with any particular candidate or party), also received considerable attention due to Pearl Jam's involvement with the cause. Pearl Jam's legal challenge against Ticketmaster represents the most publicized of their socio-political causes.

Pearl Jam vs. Ticketmaster: The Antitrust Complaint

In 1996, I managed to get tickets through Ticketmaster to see my first Pearl Jam show in Toronto. Sure, the seats were not great, but I was not complaining, particularly since my ticket only cost $25, plus a $2.50 service charge, and all the seats in the arena cost the same. Not bad, I thought, particularly in light of what I had read about the band's struggles with Ticketmaster in the recent past. Somehow, Ticketmaster Canada had managed to agree to what Ticketmaster in the US would not. Clearly, it was possible for the ticketing giant to keep their service charges at 10 percent of the face value price for tickets, despite Ticketmaster's arguments to the contrary.

In the summer of 1994, the Information, Justice, Transportation, and Agriculture Subcommittee of the Committee on Government Operations convened to discuss an antitrust complaint brought against Ticketmaster by Pearl Jam (*Pearl Jam's Anti Trust Complaint: Questions about Concert, Sports, and Theater Ticket Handling Charges and Other Practices* 1994, 1). The opening statement by Chairman Gary Condit illustrates some of the backstory leading to Pearl Jam's complaint. In 1991, the Antitrust Division of the Justice Department let Ticketmaster purchase its leading competition at the time, Ticketron, and ruled that the purchase did not violate antitrust legislation in place (ibid.). Interestingly, the merger took place a few years before Pearl Jam's formal complaint, but the band would illustrate in their statement and testimony that their problems with the newly enlarged Ticketmaster began soon after their acquisition of Ticketron.

In the statement prepared by Pearl Jam, the band details several examples of their battles with Ticketmaster during their attempts to tour after the huge success of their first album, *Ten*. The first incident was in 1992, when Pearl Jam scheduled a free show in Seattle paid in full by the band. For security reasons, the promoters limited attendance and tickets distributed through an agent such as Ticketmaster, who refused to distribute the free tickets without demanding a $1.50 service charge, resulting in the band contracting instead with the city of Seattle as an alternative (ibid., 15–16). Another show in Seattle, with some of the proceeds going to charity, was affected by Ticketmaster, in that Ticketmaster reneged on an agreement with Pearl Jam to donate $1 of the agreed-upon service fee of $3.25, plus an additional charity contribution by Ticketmaster such that the total donation would reach $20,000, an amount the band would match (ibid.). After this show, the band's statement indicates that they noticed an increasingly hostile and aggressive approach by Ticketmaster when attempting to work with them. Additional arrangements for lower service fees were met with resistance, and Pearl Jam decided to try to distribute tickets without using Ticketmaster. An effort to use the Pearl Jam fan club as a means of ticket distribution for a show in Detroit and the Paramount Box office in New York failed when Ticketmaster served both venues with threats of legal action for potentially violating their exclusive ticketing arrangements with both of these venues (ibid., 17–18). Perhaps the most troubling allegation by Pearl Jam against Ticketmaster was that Pearl Jam's agent in charge of managing concert/tour arrangements received a message from Ticketmaster that "he'd had better watch himself and that if [Pearl Jam] didn't back off he would be run out of the business" (ibid., 18). They sum up their complaint with Ticketmaster as a difference of business philosophy, and suggest that if they cannot work with Ticketmaster, they should be able to work with someone else. They claimed, however, to be unable to pursue an alternative ticket distribution company given the market dominance of Ticketmaster (ibid., 20–21).

The situations that led to Pearl Jam's antitrust complaint were the problems and eventual cancellation of their 1994 tour. During testimony by both Jeff Ament and Stone Gossard of Pearl Jam, the band members revealed that their desire was to be able to offer tickets that cost the consumer no more than $20, total, including any service fees, as they had, according to Ament, actually lost money touring over the last several years (ibid., 28). A base price of $18 dollars, according to the band members, represented the minimum base price they could charge in order to break even or make a limited amount of money per show. In order to keep the total price of the tickets under $20, Ticketmaster would have to honor their request for a service charge of no more than 10 percent of the base price. Ticketmaster was unwilling to agree to this request, and Pearl Jam argued that because of their market dominance, they were unable to successfully find an alternative ticket distributor or another means to sell tickets to potential concert goers that would grant their wishes to both break even or make a small profit touring and keep the ticket prices at no more than $20. The bulk of their complaint is that few alternatives, if any, exist because of exclusive ticket distribution deals Ticketmaster secured with many potential venues. The issue is less about whether or not Ticketmaster has an obligation to honor all requests from bands regarding their service fees, but rather that if bands do not like what Ticketmaster has to offer, there should be a number of other competitors to which the bands can turn for more competitive touring and ticket distribution arrangements.

When dealing with Ticketmaster, Dan Schiller's (2008) work proves insightful. First, the industries of promotion and advertising upcoming musical performances have changed to include fewer promoters/players in the game, and have diversified their ability and strategies to attract larger audiences through a multi-method approach to promotion: the web, television ads, radio ads, and the classic poster ad promoting an upcoming show. Further, the decreasing number of outlets for self-promotion and the full apparatus of touring suffer from increased conglomeration.

Another concern, which almost goes unnoticed during the entire hearing, is the point raised by Stone Gossard on the concerns the band has with booking shows at venues without exclusive ticketing arrangements with Ticketmaster: the challenge of security. He explains this as one of the reasons for their canceling of their summer tour:

> We didn't feel like we could coordinate—because of our dispute with Ticketmaster and feeling really the only way we could tour was to sort of go outside and try to do it on our own, given the amount of time we had and our feelings about security and whether we could actually put on a safe show consistently in these sort of—we would be in outdoor venues probably in fields and stuff, we just felt that it wasn't appropriate and we should deal with this issue first and focus on recording music. (ibid., 28)

This concern with the link between security, open fields as concert venues, and their appropriateness as alternatives to Ticketmaster-only venues would tragically bear itself out in 2000, when nine fans died at an open-field festival during Pearl Jam's set. Since then, Pearl Jam have rarely performed at open-field venues, and have taken to placing seats in the general admission areas near the stage that would normally be left unseated and potentially dangerous.

During the hearing, the Department of Justice allowed Ticketmaster and its representatives the chance to respond to the allegations that they constituted a monopoly of the ticket distribution system and had exclusive contracts with the majority of venues in major cities. Fred Rosen, CEO of Ticketmaster at the time of the hearings, spoke on behalf of the ticket distributor to suggest that not only were they one of several competitors in the ticket distribution industry, they had been turned down by venues to serve as the means of ticket distribution, presumably because alternative distributors were more competitive or offered something Ticketmaster was unable to provide (ibid., 121). Further, Rosen later furnished a report on the 50 largest cities and potential markets in the US and whether or not Ticketmaster had an exclusive distribution arrangement with these venues (ibid., 128–34). The information contained in the list does demonstrate, at least on paper, that at the time of this hearing there were several major arenas in the largest 50 markets that had no exclusive arrangement for ticket distribution. As such, while Ticketmaster may constitute a large portion of the market, there were venues without these exclusive arrangements with Ticketmaster for ticket distribution.

Secondly, Rosen argued that Ticketmaster would lose money if they had agreed to Pearl Jam's requests for a 10 percent service charge on an $18 ticket price and as such declined to agree to distribute tickets for the band's proposed tour. Rosen also suggested that Pearl Jam could meet their goal of a $20 limit for ticket prices desired by Pearl Jam by dropping the base ticket price to $17.50 or $17.75, with service charges in the range of $2.25–$2.50 per ticket. Given that

Pearl Jam argued that $18 was the minimum base price they could set to break even or not lose money as they had on previous tours, this was a clear impasse for both Ticketmaster and Pearl Jam in terms of a working relationship. Lastly, Rosen provides a list of a number of companies considered Ticketmaster competition, including ProTix, The Home Shopping Network, Art Soft, Laser Gate Prologue Select, SofTix, and Sun Micro Systems amongst others (ibid., 120).

After several months of testimony on both sides, the Department of Justice decided to drop the investigation/complaint against Ticketmaster and issued the following statement:

> It is the Plaintiffs['] own allegations in the Complaint which show that they are not best suited to bring this claim against Ticketmaster. If a violation has occurred, the appropriate party is a venue or class of venues and promoters who are the ones who "consume" Ticketmaster's product; they are the ones who would suffer any direct loss if there is uncompetitive pricing in the fee contracts due to Ticketmaster's alleged monopoly power. (*Department of Justice* 1998)

In essence, the law considers venues and promoters to be Ticketmaster's consumers, rather than the audiences. Pearl Jam were deemed to not be the appropriate plaintiffs to bring about the antitrust complaint.

Pearl Jam did not tour that summer and Pearl Jam continued to try to explore other means for ticket distribution, with limited success and an increasing amount of fan resentment for planned and canceled tours—the difficulty and confusion in obtaining tickets through the Pearl Jam fan club and other unconventional means proved frustrating for both fans and the band.

Initially their case against Ticketmaster may seem like an anomaly, particularly since they have resigned to dealing with the concert promoter for shows over the last decade, but I argue that it represents a crucial middle step that feeds directly into their first round of protest with, and endorsement of, the Ralph Nader campaign of 2000. Nader's commitment to corporate responsibility, government oversight of big business and his long career of consumer advocacy dovetail well with the ethical issues at place in Pearl Jam's Ticketmaster battle. As a fan, I found it unsurprising that Pearl Jam would choose to get involved in the 2000 presidential campaign as they did, because of their record of accomplishment. This decision would set the tone for future tours and indicated the band's decision to use their music for explicitly political ends. What I do think bears repeating is that while Pearl Jam have conceded to working with Ticketmaster in recent years, their efforts to keep ticket prices low may have failed but their commitment to protest in and of itself remains constant.

The Third Way: Pearl Jam Endorses Ralph Nader

Pearl Jam commenced their scheduled North American tour in the summer of 2000, supporting the spring release of their album *Binaural*. The album is very much a product of its time, reflected as such by recurring themes throughout the lyrics. "Rival" addresses the Columbine shootings (Manning 2000). "Insignificance" "explores the conflict between their generation's opposing instincts of protest and passivity ... as falling bombs bring death to a small American town, the doomed gather in a bar, dancing while a protest song plays harmlessly on the jukebox," and "Grievance" makes reference to the World Trade Organization riots in Seattle of 1999 (Tannenbaum 2000), the band's current residence, and suggests we "let the song protest." At the time, it may have come across as a throwaway lyric, but if you will pardon the pun, "Insignificance" became incredibly significant, and prophetic, as the tour continued. "Grievance" reflects a generalized disdain with the direction in which the country was headed, another song thatthat would become eerily relevant in the context of an upcoming and important presidential election. Lastly, "Soon Forget" picks up on folk protest tropes and the singer-songwriter model, featuring only Eddie Vedder's vocals while he plays the ukulele, standing as a polemic against materialism (Gallagher 2000). The short ballad is definitely not of the anthem-rock variety, but, as with "Grievance" and "Insignificance," served as vehicles of both protest and presidential endorsement during this tour.

With an important election fast approaching, the band's continued commitment to voter registration remained; but slowly, a clear preference for a presidential candidate emerged. During a concert in Saratoga Springs, NY, fans got a clearer idea of who that candidate was. I attended this concert, and before the show began, the large screens broadcast the music video for "Testify," by Rage Against the Machine (they, however, were not part of the show). The video juxtaposes still images, audio, and video clips to draw compelling comparisons between Al Gore and George W. Bush, presidential candidates for the two major parties during that election cycle. The music video concluded with a clip of Ralph Nader, who emphatically states, "if you're not turned on to politics, politics will turn on you." This video would set the tone for the rest of the tour, with Pearl Jam as endorsers of voter registration, a third party candidate, and in particular, Ralph Nader and the Green Party.

The decision, however, to endorse a candidate was neither swift nor immediate. Although the individual members of Pearl Jam may have made up their own minds on who they would be voting for (and perhaps not the same candidate!), the band initially decided to promote voter *registration* and directing potential voters to resources so as to become aware of the positions of candidates on a variety of issues, rather than publicly endorse a presidential candidate as a band. *Salon.com* detailed the band's initial statements about participating in endorsing a candidate:

> Vedder's decision to support Nader's campaign comes as a surprise to many of
> Pearl Jam's fans. In a July interview in *George*, Vedder and his band mates said

that lending political sponsorship to a candidate was an inappropriate activity for
a rock band. Vedder, in particular, worried that endorsing one candidate might
alienate fans. (Talvi 2000)

Perhaps, within this statement, there lies an implicit reference to Neil Young,
an artist long admired and covered live by Pearl Jam. In "This Note's For You,"
Young criticizes a litany of corporately sponsored music and musicians ("This
Note's For You" 1988). Given this context, however, Pearl Jam's eventual
endorsement of Ralph Nader seems to be the best possible compromise for a set
of artists committed to corporate responsibility and who snub their noses at the
idea of their music being used for commercial ends. Whereas Young compares
politicians to commercial products, Nader's status as a third party candidate in
favor of corporate responsibility, the end of corporate welfare, and the triumph of
the rights of the consumer-citizen, he appears anathema to a consumer product. As
the 2000 tour progressed, Pearl Jam's rejection of both major parties became more
overt onstage. It was clear, however, that the fight for Nader was Vedder's idea
and that the rest of the band agreed to support his decision. As Vedder states in an
interview with *Rolling Stone* in 2003:

> It started as my thing, and they supported me. They figured I was doing my
> homework. It was interesting—one by one, they came around. But the first thing
> Ralph said was, "We are looking for money because we're not taking any soft
> money. We're not taking money from corporations. If there's something you can
> contribute, that would be great." I said, "Not only will I do it, I'll get everybody
> in the band to do it." Then I wrote a check, even before I made the phone calls.
> So I started getting calls: "I heard about this thing, I want to talk to you about
> it." (Fricke 2003)

Additionally, fans were willing to show their dislike of both presidential candidates
at shows. In the *Touring Band 2000* DVD, which compiled video footage and
several songs from various shows during the 2000 tour, Eddie Vedder invited two
fans on stage who had dressed as George W. Bush and Al Gore. The Al Gore
costume featured a suit with money glued all over it, while the George W. Bush
costume consisted of a grim reaper costume, complete with the sickle, and a Bush
mask. The three danced on stage during an extended solo by Mike McCready then
Vedder takes the sickle from the Bush character and pretends to hack them both to
death (*Touring Band 2000* 2000). The real focus on promoting Nader as the better
option required a more concentrated approach, and Vedder volunteered to perform
at several Nader rallies around the country. Notably, it was Vedder alone, without
the rest of the band, that played at these rallies. Vedder explained this decision, and
notably invoked the efficacy of the singer-songwriter folk-protest trope:

> Those [Nader] rallies aren't set up for that. It's better just to show up with a
> guitar and harmonica. They [the band] thought I should carry the weight, which

was fine. This was the campfire of truth—this is where I saw the real stuff coming out. It was so head-and-shoulders above the other rhetoric—it was easy to believe that you were absolutely doing the right thing. I still feel that way. People would say to me, "You know, Nader's not going to win." Hey, I grew up in Chicago—I'm a Cubs fan. I'm used to this. (ibid.)

While Vedder performed a number of Pearl Jam songs at these rallies, the covers performed remain the most poignant in this context. "I am a Patriot," written by E-Street Band member Steven Van Zandt, is perhaps most representative of Vedder's involvement with the rallies.

Given Ralph Nader's status as an alternative to the two-party system, Vedder's performance of the song resonated with the theme of the Nader rallies. When applied to Nader himself, "I am a Patriot" clarifies that while Nader may be very Left-of-center, his policies do not completely threaten capitalism and that a third party in the US is both necessary and possible, as is the case in other democratic nations.

To no one's surprise, Nader did not win the presidency. In fact, many Democrats blamed the Nader campaign for Al Gore's loss, suggesting that votes that would have gone to Gore effectively went in to the garbage can as votes for Nader. Pearl Jam, and Vedder in particular, received criticism from Democrats and fans, blaming them in part for the Bush win. The band may have implicitly acknowledged this possibility, in that they too would have preferred a Gore victory to a Bush victory, with Vedder wearing a "No Bush 2000" shirt in one of the *Touring Band 2000* DVD clips. 2000 closed as a tough year for the band, which faced a Republican president-elect, the fan backlash for their endorsement of Nader, and the continued hangover of the fan deaths at the Roskilde festival. The years between this tour and the next did not prove to be more positive, for the band or the American public at large.

"He's not a leader, he's a Texas leaguer": The "Bushleaguer" Controversy

In November 2002, Pearl Jam released *Riot Act* after a two-year break between albums. Composed in the aftermath of the presidential election won by George W. Bush, the events of 9/11, the deaths of nine concertgoers during Pearl Jam's set at the Roskilde festival, and the war in Afghanistan, the album drew upon these events for lyrical content. "Love Boat Captain" directly references the deaths during the Roskilde show with the phrase "Lost nine friends we'll never know/two years ago today." "Green Disease" continues Eddie Vedder's fight against corporate greed, reminiscent of the theme of *Binaural*'s track "Soon Forget." Most prominently, the album featured the song "Bushleaguer," a blunt and highly critical evaluation of George W. Bush, juxtaposing the last name of the president with the colloquial term for those playing in minor league baseball. This comparison, suggesting the inadequacy and ineptitude of the president, stands out as the most overt form of lyrical protest released by the band.

The song, as released on the album, clearly raised eyebrows, no doubt because Pearl Jam released the album during the build-up to the Iraq War, assumed to become a reality in only a matter of time and welcomed by a large number of Americans. Given this and the continued effects of 9/11 on the American public, criticism of the president was not warmly accepted. It was not the fact that this song was featured on *Riot Act* that caused the most controversy. Instead, it took Pearl Jam's live performance of this song, taken to levels of *spectacle*, which initiated a fierce counter-protest by some fans and the media.

As is generally the case with musical acts, tours support the release of albums. Pearl Jam toured in support of *Riot Act* in the spring and summer of 2003. By this time, the war in Iraq had just begun, and public opinion of the war revealed a divided nation in terms of support for the war effort. The outrage against Pearl Jam's performance of "Bushleaguer" required only its debut at the first show of their tour in Denver.

To understand why the live performance of "Bushleaguer" created such uproar, we need to look at how Pearl Jam performed it live. While I will attempt the most accurate and colorful description of the performance, no account will substitute for actually witnessing it. The song commences, and before Vedder begins to speak/sing the words, he emerges from backstage complete with an ill-fitting silver blazer, a bottle of wine, and a kitschy rubber mask of George W. Bush. While in costume, Vedder alternates between invoking both Michael Jackson and Madonna's signature dances, the Moonwalk and Vogue respectively, and then Vedder starts into the lyrics. When the mask comes off Vedder and places it on the microphone stand, the real show on stage begins. Vedder uses the mask to various ends throughout the tour when "Bushleaguer" is played, alternating between using the mask as a makeshift cigarette holder to forcing the mask to drink Vedder's wine and occasionally simulating foreplay with the mask and stand combination. In general, the performance ends with the mask, in one way or another, ending up on the stage floor.

Pearl Jam performed "Bushleaguer" in Denver, and the reaction was swift and highly critical. Media outlets reported that fans walked out during or immediately after this performance, presumably in protest (Brown 2003). The *Denver Rocky Mountain News* covered the incident the following day:

> One [fan], Kim Mueller, told Denver's Rocky Mountain News: "I wasn't sure if it was really happening. We looked at each other and realized he really did have George Bush's head on a stick and was waving it in the air, then slammed it to the ground and stepped on it." Fan Keith Zimmerman added: "It was like he decapitated someone in a primal ritual and stuck their head on a stick." (ibid.)

Seattle Weekly also reported on the show stating:

Dozens of fans walked out of a Pearl Jam concert after lead singer Eddie Vedder took a mask of President Bush and impaled it on a microphone stand. Several concertgoers booed and shouted Tuesday night for Vedder to shut up as he told the crowd he was against the war and Bush. He impaled the mask during the encore of the band's opening show of a US tour ... During the show, Vedder said, "Just to clarify ... we support the troops. We're just confused on how wanting to bring them back safely all of a sudden becomes non-support," he said. "We love them. They're not the ones who make the foreign policy ... Let's hope for the best and speak our opinions." ("Dozens walk out of Pearl Jam concert after anti-Bush song, remarks" 2003)

It should be noted that only weeks before the condemnation of "Bushleaguer," the Dixie Chicks faced a brutal public reaction for their similar criticisms of George W. Bush at a concert in London. Despite the immediate backlash, Pearl Jam continued to play "Bushleaguer" live at selected shows with all of the theatrics that commanded such negative attention. The back and forth between fans, the media, and the band reached a fever pitch at a show in Uniondale, NY. "Bushleaguer" received a particularly scornful response live at the show. *The New York Times* reported:

When the second encore came around, Mr. Vedder emerged cradling a mask of President Bush, and sang "Bushleaguer," a strong statement of protest: "Drilling for fear keeps the job simple/Born on third, thinks he got a triple." A number of formerly enthusiastic fans responded by making long, low noises that sounded a lot like "boo," and they weren't placated by the remarks that followed. "I don't understand," Mr. Vedder said. "Maybe you like him 'cause he's going to give you a tax cut." A number of people then chanted: "USA! USA!" Mr. Vedder tried a different approach. "I'm with you: USA," he said. "I just think that all of us in this room should have a voice in how the USA is represented." A few people threw things, and the band played two more songs, ending with a cover of Neil Young's "Rockin' in the Free World." As the song faded out, Mr. Vedder reprised the crowd's chant—"USA! USA!"—sounding more defiant than conciliatory. Then he threw down the microphone and walked off. (Sanneh 2003)

The band discussed this reaction on a Buffalo, NY radio station. Mike McCready, lead guitarist for Pearl Jam, said that due to this negative response, the band would not play "Bushleaguer" live again. In their defense, McCready said that he hoped fans would not "misunderstand the meaning behind the song" (Pearl Jam 2003). The band resumed playing "Bushleaguer" only a month or so after McCready issued the statement. In another interview with the *Nashville City Paper*, McCready said he'd rather leave politics out of the performances and concentrate on playing well (Jordan 2003). Clearly, there was tension in the band over what to do with "Bushleaguer" at future shows. I was able to see Pearl Jam perform "Bushleaguer" twice after McCready's statement that "Bushleaguer" had been retired, in both Detroit and Toronto. Interestingly, the Detroit show did not include any of the theatrics, but the Toronto show featured all of the more controversial elements of the performance. Presumably, Canada seemed a safer place to criticize a US president than Detroit, and the performance in Toronto was overwhelmingly greeted with palpable, vigorous support and applause. Pearl Jam guitarist Stone Gossard commented on the change of heart when interviewed by Steve Morse from the *Boston Globe*:

> We still pull the song out at some of our shows ... We don't like to restrict ourselves about what we can and cannot play. Ed hasn't been doing it with the animation of the Bush mask and the theatrics that were associated with it before. Now he allows people to focus more on the song and less on the controversy surrounding it. That's been the right choice at this time for us. Even in terms of the controversy, though, we wanted people to understand that we weren't very excited about the way that George Bush was running the country. That's pretty much something we all believe ... If you believe in something and stand by your words, then ultimately you're going to be fine ... In general, people need to be a little bit more [confident] about what they're willing to do and what they're willing to sacrifice to speak their minds. (Morse 2003)

In lieu of playing "Bushleaguer" even without the theatrics, Pearl Jam opted to play covers of songs by other bands that presented a similar sentiment towards Bush. Creedence Clearwater Revival's "Fortunate Son," decrying the ability for some to avoid the draft because of money, status, and family ties, became a frequent stand-in ("Set Lists and Appearances of 2003–02"; "Set Lists and Appearances of 2003–03"). Pearl Jam also performed "Know Your Rights" by The Clash, with its criticism of the perceived right to free speech re-articulated to become a stinging rebuke of the response by some fans and the media to Vedder's comments during the tour (ibid.). Further, Pearl Jam performed "Soon Forget" frequently, with its critique of corporate welfare, corruption, and greed, perceivably directed at the Bush Administration and its ties to the Enron and Halliburton controversies (ibid.). "Bushleaguer" may have outlived its usefulness, however, as Pearl Jam have not performed the track since 2007, and its last performance was in Europe ("Set Lists and Appearances of 2007") where anti-Bush sentiments were/are unquestionably more pronounced.

It is difficult to pinpoint a single reason for the critical response "Bushleaguer" drew from fans and the media. The response from the media may be easier to explain, in part because of an overwhelmingly uncritical early response to the war in Iraq by networks and individual journalists, for which they would later suffer embarrassment. At the time, criticism of the war, particularly for Fox News, was largely unacceptable by individuals given any sort of pulpit from which to speak and address a captive audience. Lack of support for the war was articulated to a lack of patriotism, or even treachery. Given the pronounced change of attitudes towards the war (and the president, by extension) by most networks, journalists and the general public, "Bushleaguer" might not have drawn the attention it did in 2003 if performed today, and, implicitly, this may also explain why Pearl Jam had not performed it for almost a full two years before the Obama administration took office.

Their vindication as citizens and artists was slow but arrived, as increasing numbers of individuals endorsed their position on the war and president. What remains less easy to explain is the response by fans, though presumably some of their reaction may derive from the overwhelmingly positive media coverage of the war, as I have described above. First, there will always exist a contingent of music fans that want to keep music as entertainment, rather than a conduit for politics. Given this and Pearl Jam's commitment to making public their political views in the concert arena, the "Bushleaguer" incident may have served as a breaking point for fans unhappy with the music-politics articulation, but were willing to tolerate it up until that moment. Second, the format of the "Bushleaguer" performance may in and of itself have turned fans off. As outlined in detail in the literature review, the articulation of music and politics has a history primarily tied to the singer-songwriter and the folk music genre. Given that Pearl Jam performed "Bushleaguer" as an entire band, and in terms of genre the song has few, if any ties to folk or populist themes, it breaks from a well-established form of protest music. This is not to suggest a natural or essential link between folk and protest, but this articulation may remain compelling enough for *these* fans to reject other genres as conduits of protest.

Vote for Change

One year after the "Bushleaguer" controversy and with another important presidential election fast approaching, Pearl Jam decided yet again to tour in response. This time Nader would not be the beneficiary of their endorsement, formally or informally. Instead, in the fall of 2004, Pearl Jam and several other musical acts, including Bruce Springsteen, Steve Earle, and R.E.M., came together as voices of protest from the Left, touring to eliminate the possibility of a second term for Bush. Eddie Vedder explained the decision to not support Nader during this election in a statement to *Rolling Stone*:

> I supported Ralph Nader in 2000, but it's a time of crisis. We have to get a new administration in. All of us who supported Ralph last time should get down on our knees and say, "Can you bow out on October 3rd? We'll get back to the ideals you're fighting for on November 3rd." ("Voices for Change" 2004)

The tour was NOT, however, an explicit endorsement of John Kerry, though there were palpable nods towards supporting a Kerry presidency. As the title of the tour suggests, change, rather than voting for Kerry, was the explicit goal. Rhetorically, this title provides the artists with a degree of flexibility in terms of interpreting its mission and articulating it to their own performances. Change could, and usually did, represent a new president, but change also applied to the policies of Kerry, in that a Kerry presidency should include massive and sweeping policy changes regarding the war in Iraq and Afghanistan, health care, and the relationship between government and big business. Stone Gossard, guitarist of Pearl Jam, stated that the band as a whole decided very early in 2004 that they would play shows in October to promote voter registration and sway voters away from voting in a second term for Bush, and band manager Kelly Curtis contacted other managers and artists closer to October to see what, if anything, they were doing for the upcoming election and if they would be interested in joining a larger tour (*Vote For Change? Part 1* 2008). *Billboard* magazine reported on the formation of the tour as the ambitious work of several prominent music managers:

> First tipped by billboard.biz July 23, the tour is promoted by and benefits America Coming Together, an organization dedicated to mobilizing voters to elect progressive candidates. It is being presented in association with liberal political organization MoveOn PAC. The still-evolving lineup also includes John Mellencamp, Babyface, Death Cab for Cutie, Bright Eyes, Ben Harper, Bonnie Raitt, Jackson Browne, James Taylor, Jurassic 5 and John Fogerty. All artists are donating their services, as are many of the behind-the-scenes players. The list of managers behind the project is nearly as impressive as the artists. Among them are Landau, Bertis Downs (R.E.M.), Simon Renshaw (Dixie Chicks), Coran Capshaw (Dave Matthews Band) and Kelly Curtis (Pearl Jam), who [Jon] Landau calls the project's "guiding light." (Waddell 2004)

As the *Billboard* article underscores, this was not a tour explicitly in support of Kerry, though audiences may have read the tour through this lens. Jon Landau, manager of Bruce Springsteen, explained the decision to not formally affiliate the tour with Kerry:

> "We knew we wanted to stay completely separate from the [Democratic National Committee]," he says. "This is a range of artists with a range of things to say, and we wanted to make sure our platform would remain uncompromised." MoveOn PAC, with 2.5 million members, came on board to both receive and offer visibility. But neither America Coming Together nor MoveOn had anything to do with the creation of the tour, Landau says. (ibid.)

In some ways, the lack of the tour officially endorsing a candidate may appear as a bit of a cop-out, a way for these artists to avoid yet another round of political backlash. Arguably, however, the fact that the tour was not an official vehicle for the Kerry campaign may have worked to its advantage, at least initially, in those formal voting affiliations among the participating musicians requiring only a shared belief that a second Bush presidency was not preferable. Jeff Ament stated that premise of the tour was essentially to get Bush out of office (*Vote for Change?*

Part 1 2008). Rolling Stone reported on the range of political opinions found by those touring with Vote for Change:

> An informal poll of artists on hand the day before the tour announcement revealed that many were registered to vote as Independents ... "I see the divide between Republicans and Democrats as a giant farce," says [Pearl Jam's Stone] Gossard, "because people make liberal and conservative decisions all day long." Gossard is a perfect example: Although he generally votes Democratic, "I'm probably the most Republican guy in Pearl Jam." (Fricke 2004)

Structurally, the tour divided the participating artists into six groups touring in key battleground states such as Florida, Ohio, Pennsylvania, Michigan, and others, with several shows taking place on the same night in different areas of the country (ibid.). The result was a musical blitzkrieg of protest during the last weeks of voter registration.

Eddie Vedder acknowledged the potential for a backlash against musicians participating in the Vote for Change tour, with the events of last year's "Bushleaguer" controversy and the boycotting of the Dixie Chicks (also involved in the Vote for Change tour) on his mind. He stated:

> I read a piece from a musician I respect, Alice Cooper, who wrote that musicians really need to keep out of political discussions ... For one, they're idiots ... For another, when he was a kid and his parents started talking politics, he ran to his room and put on the Rolling Stones and turned it up as loud as he could. And I agree with Alice. I don't think any of us want to be doing this. ... But my problem is that my stereo does not go loud enough to drown out the sound of bombs dropping in the Middle East. (Morse 2004)

For Pearl Jam, the choice of what to play at these shows was a decision made strategically. These shows were not just Pearl Jam shows during a regular tour year, there was to be a method behind song selection with specific consideration given to context. Initially, Eddie Vedder pondered whether it would be plausible to have fans vote in their choices for songs through the band's website, to both democratize the process of creating set lists and to remind fans of what they should be doing in November (ibid.). Vedder mused that "Bushleaguer" remained an obvious choice for the shows, despite the reception it received only a year earlier (ibid.). Given that the audiences at the Vote for Change shows were united by their distaste for a second Bush term in office, if only in this way, the audience reaction to "Bushleaguer" would be less likely to be as hostile as before. Surprisingly, "Bushleaguer" was not the centerpiece of the Pearl Jam sets during this tour, and, in fact, Pearl Jam performed the song once during the tour ("Set Lists and Appearances 2004"). Instead, as was the case with their 2003 tour, cover songs served as a stand-in for the heavy-handed "Bushleaguer." Jeff Ament explained the utility of some cover songs often lies in the ability to make slight alternations to the lyrics to make them more relevant to a specific context (*Vote for Change? Part 1* 2008). Specifically, Ament said that the band learned how to play a number of punk songs written during the Reagan years, and, he states, with slight alterations to the lyrics, one would think they were written about Bush instead of Reagan (ibid.). Some of the punk songs covered included "The American In Me" by the Avengers, "I Believe in Miracles" by the Ramones, and "Bleed for Me" by the Dead Kennedys, all performed with the lyric changes Ament described ("Set Lists and Appearances 2004").

This is an important point to note for the band that had, as previously described, primarily drawn from folk-protest tropes during their own efforts to combine protest and music. To draw from a vastly different genre of music drastically changes the tone, and possibly the shape, of performed protest. Punk has a legacy, much like folk, of articulations to various political movements, but perhaps problematically, many of these articulations are to a generalized distrust of government *a priori* or the abolishment of it entirely. Additionally, punk is less clearly articulated to Left politics than folk music and often finds a comfortable home in both the extreme Left and Right when looking at both the artists' own political opinions and those of their audiences. One need only look at the subgenre of Oi! to see its ties to fascism and Nazism. Even Johnny Ramone of The Ramones, a friend of Eddie Vedder, was a fervent Republican up until his death (Fricke 2003). Clearly, Pearl Jam intended not to eliminate the concept of government nor alter its structure, but distrusted a particular administration and called for an alternative from the moderate Left. As a result, their covers of punk songs fit within the goals of Vote for Change, but doing so successfully rested on the band making very conscious choices about which songs to cover, and making those small lyrical changes to enable their re-articulation to a different political project.

Pearl Jam did not abandon their comfortable folk-protest approach during the Vote for Change tour. During an appearance on "The Late Show with David Letterman," Pearl Jam kicked off the Vote for Change tour with a cover of Bob Dylan's "Masters of War," the song that would define the rest of Pearl Jam's role in the tour. Pearl Jam would also cover Dylan's "All Along the Watchtower," and did so in a particularly rousing duet with Neil Young during their Toledo, OH, show. Young himself covered "All Along the Watchtower" when Dylan was inducted into the Rock and Roll Hall of Fame (*Vote for Change? Part 2* 2008). Apparently, for both Young and Bruce Springsteen, artists who were by no means apolitical but disavowed themselves from party politics and endorsements until very recently, the concerns created by the War in Iraq and the Bush administration pushed these artists to participate in a tour like Vote for Change. Other folk songs covered included James Taylor's "Millworker" and "Don't Be Shy" by Cat Stevens ("Set Lists and Appearances 2004").

Returning to the issue of cover songs, clearly Pearl Jam and Vedder in particular find them useful as instruments of protest, and have used them to this end during each of these tours. Some of the songs have been included on set lists from every tour, and seem at home in each without too much contradiction with the radically different purpose of each tour. "Fortunate Son," for example, appears just as relevant during the Vote for Change tour as it did during the tour in 2003. An exception to this is Van Zandt's "I Am a Patriot," referenced earlier. At several of the Vote for Choice shows, Vedder would play the Van Zandt song solo. As was the case with Al Gore, many Democrats found their respective candidates difficult to swallow and hard to truly support as a good alternative, rather than "the lesser of two evils." Given that the tour was not a Kerry rally, this sort of thing could pass as appropriate without much question.

In total, Pearl Jam played eight shows in 13 days as part of the Vote for Change tour. Despite all of their efforts, and a tour that grossed in the range of fifteen million dollars in *pro bono* revenue (Waddell 2004), the voting public did not unseat a wartime president and Pearl Jam faced four more years of a president they couldn't stand.

Pearl Jam's tours, when seen in light of the outcomes, may beg the question: "Why bother?" For despite Pearl Jam's efforts, Nader did not capture the 5 percent of the popular vote he was aiming for, much less the presidency, and was blamed for a Bush win. Many Pearl Jam fans were alienated, rather than welcomed, by the "Bushleaguer" performance and fired back at the band for this artistic and political choice. Lastly, Vote for Change was unable to secure a Kerry win, and roughly half of young registered voters did not bother to vote (*Vote for Change? Part 4* 2008). All of this reinforces a model of pop politics that: 1) bands build cultural capital; and 2) bands try to spend it politically. I would also suggest that cultural and political capital could become mutually reinforcing, even for "apolitical" audiences.

This is not exactly a glowing track record of success. For any of these tours, it is also difficult to measure "causal effects." There is possible exception: in States featuring Vote for Change shows, the youth vote was 12 percent higher than in previous years (ibid.). Whether this was due to demographics or the Vote for Change tour is unclear. We should consider Pratt (1990) and his statement of the "law of diminishing returns" with larger audiences when attempting to use shows for political ends. These larger shows, according to Pratt's theory, may have shot themselves in the foot due largely in part to their size.

Paying My Dues

> These days, when most people think of [Eddie] Vedder—if they think of him at all—it's as a scowling rabble-rouser who spent the past eight years (and two albums) informing audiences that George W. Bush was not a very good president. It's easy to forget that he was, for a moment, perhaps the biggest rockstar in the world. (Eells 2009, 46)

It always seemed I was around four or five years late to the party (pun intended). Born in the early 1980s, I wasn't yet a teenager when Pearl Jam released their first album *Ten* or their record-setting follow-up album *Vs.* in the early 1990s. Late to the party, or bad timing, I knew only of Pearl Jam through their recordings and the occasional copy of *Hit Parader* magazine featuring dated photos of the band that made them seem eternally youthful and barely recognizable. Bad timing was a factor again when I tried to see them live; between my age and their battles with Ticketmaster resulting in cancelled tours, I wouldn't get to see them live until 1996, long after the death of Kurt Cobain and "grunge," whatever it was, was also long declared dead. The wheels of touring, however, finally had some long-term momentum and seeing Pearl Jam became a ritual I indulged in every second year or so.

The first few times I saw them perform, most of the thrill came from the act of finally getting tickets and seeing them in the flesh, onstage. It was more about saying "I saw them live!" than it was about anything remotely approaching an internal and external dialog about the relationship between their music and their politics, though this would soon follow. In 2000 I finally had the flexibility, age, and money all lined up correctly to permit me to see more than one show a tour. In hindsight, for all my complaints about timing and so forth, it couldn't have been a better year to line up trips to multiple shows. After all, the band had made this tour about more than just social-justice issues, and a historic presidential election would coincide with the conclusion of the tour. Pearl Jam, but more specifically Eddie Vedder, had publicly taken this tour as a means to disseminate their disdain with both presidential candidates Al Gore and George W. Bush, their continued push to register young voters and persuade them to participate, and finally, a not-so-subtle endorsement of Green Party candidate Ralph Nader.

At a show I attended in Montreal in September 2000, Vedder stated that if Bush became the president, the band were all going to apply for Canadian citizenship. This is where I first noticed the schism—the polarizing of fans—but it happened first in an interpersonal setting. After a first-year political science class, I met with a friend on campus to talk about our upcoming plans to see Pearl Jam in Toronto. Nader came up as a topic of conversation … I believe I brought it up first. Despite the social "rules" over discussing religion and politics, I figured this was an appropriate exception. We were Canadians, in Canada, talking about a band with a history of committing themselves to an array of social and political justice issues. I saw no potential tension; the stakes were low for us, and this was a band my friend and I both knew well. I mentioned that I thought what they were doing was a "great idea."

A "great idea." It would be an understatement to state that my academic career would have been different had this endorsement not happened. I was studying political science and music and this collision of events just "felt right." Here was a band I loved, in part because of their music and also because of their commitment to social justice, endorsing a candidate I supported (keeping in mind that as a Canadian citizen, I couldn't vote in the aforementioned election). My friend was also fairly Left-of-center in her political leanings, and given the lack of stakes for both of us, I naturally figured she would agree with my enthusiasm for their presidential turn.

She wasn't. I can't remember exactly how she worded it, but it amounted to a general sense of disappointment with Pearl Jam for, as she put it, "getting involved in that shit." Upon reflection, I had noticed this schism at earlier shows that year, but hadn't recognized it as such. The playing of Rage Against The Machine's "Testify" music video (a critique of both presidential candidates Bush and Gore) at a Pearl Jam show in Saratoga Springs, NY, was met with rather unenthusiastic applause. For a fan base that often defined the very meaning of fandom, this was a palpable shift.

This split in the fan base became most apparent as a fan during the shows I caught during their 2003 tour for *Riot Act*. The "Bushleaguer" issue was front and center at every show, and as I have argued elsewhere, the split over the appropriateness of the music vs. politics collision at Pearl Jam shows lead to an atmosphere of tension and, oftentimes, backlash from this once devoted fan base (Weglarz 2011). While much less apparent at the shows I saw in Canada (Toronto and Montreal), the tension was something tactile at shows in the US. I found myself asking, "Do I clap for that statement? What does the person beside me think of all of this? Do they agree? This could get ugly!" The collective energy of the fans in Detroit and Buffalo felt thick with a combination of worry, fear, and occasionally, but less frequently, fun. It wasn't just the fans that seemed different, Pearl Jam themselves seemed like a band nervously hedging their bets and hoping for a positive outcome. Granted, the shows I saw took place after Pearl Jam declared they wouldn't perform "Bushleaguer" with the theatrics any longer, but when they did perform "Bushleaguer" without them in Detroit, not only was it just not the *same song* in spirit, but Pearl Jam appeared to just sort of plod through it as though it was some sort of performance requirement. This was not the case when they returned to the theatrics for Canadian audiences, and in Toronto, as I stated earlier, they received thundering applause for their full-theatrical version of "Bushleaguer." Not to suggest that the schism wasn't still there at the Canadian shows (as there were a lot of American fans that had traveled to see them) but, truthfully, the band felt looser and seemed to be having much more fun in front of what they perceived to be a more politically sympathetic audience. Instead of boos, "Bushleager," complete with the mask, jacket and other accessories, was greeted with roaring applause and cheering. The doubt and fear from the Buffalo and Detroit shows wasn't present in Toronto or Montreal, or, at the very least, Pearl Jam did a great job of hiding it.

> Once upon a time, [Pearl Jam guitarist Stone] Gossard was a headstrong as the rest of the band ... Now ... they've settled into a sort of middle-aged realpolitik. "Being stubborn, holding on to the core of yourself through thick and thin— there's something to be said for that," Gossard says. "But you're gonna spend a lot of time fighting over a mile of territory instead of opening yourself up to those big moon shots ... Sometimes ... I look back and think, 'I could have been

so much smarter, more helpful. Fuck, I could have had so much more *fun*.'"
(Eells 2009, 46)

Fast forward to 2008. Things aren't all that different from where this anecdote started: there was an important presidential election on the horizon, and I was off to Berkeley to see Eddie Vedder perform at one of the dates on his solo tour. After this long journey of politics, backlash, and both priding and irritating fans, I figured Vedder, with a captive audience, would have something to say about the Obama/McCain election. Midway through the show, he started to drift into discussions of politics in general, and made a point of saying that he didn't think it was right, moral, and/or appropriate for musicians to talk about politics during their shows. For a minute my heart stopped. Had Vedder truly changed his mind? What did this mean for my status as a fan, or my dissertation on popular music and politics? No, this couldn't be happening. I held my breath, trying to parse out what the fallout would be from fans, the press, and so on. How would this newly apolitical Vedder, and, by extension, Pearl Jam, fare with the public?

It was only a second or two that passed, but after Vedder made what I thought was his resignation speech from politics, two assistants unfurled a gigantic "Obama '08" banner and walked across the stage with it, to roaring applause, and a smile appeared on Vedder's face for catching us all off guard. Political Pearl Jam hasn't left us yet.

Conclusion

I have attempted to present the band's perspective on their protest/endorsement actions to argue that their efforts are in fact a good in and of themselves, regardless of which candidate or company they endorsed or protested. Further, I emphasize the importance of *live* rather than *studio* performance to Pearl Jam's aspirations to remain a politically engaged cultural performer, both in terms of actions and motives. Pearl Jam felt that the live arena was the primary means to act as political agents and their actions, however successful or not, reflect their intention to make this focus on the live a political matter, and it is this fact that remains central to why the changing landscape of touring and live performance, with increased concentration, matters to both Pearl Jam and their audiences. For Pearl Jam, the live show is meaningful political theater, a political space worth protecting.

Bibliography

"Brief for the United States and the Federal Trade Commission as Amici Curiae: Alex Campos, et al. v. Ticketmaster Corporation." *Department of Justice*, 1998. http://www.usdoj.gov/atr/cases/f2100/2157.htm.

Brown, Mark. "Concert-goers jam exits after anti-Bush display." *Denver Rocky Mountain News*, 3 April 2003: 53A.

"Dozens walk out of Pearl Jam concert after anti-Bush song, remarks." *Seattle Times*, 3 April 2003. http://community.seattletimes.nwsource.com/archive/?date=20030403&slug=webpearljam03.

Eells, Josh. "Moving Targets." *Spin Magazine*, October 2009: 40–48.

Fricke, David. "Eddie Unabridged." *Rolling Stone Online*, 2003. http://www.rollingstone.com/artists/eddievedder/articles/story/5940075/eddie_unabridged.

Fricke, David. (11 August 2004). "Taking it to the Streets: Artists unite for Kerry with historic Vote for Change Tour." *Rolling Stone Online*, 11 August 2004. http://www.rollingstone.com/news/story/6420236/vote_for_change_taking_it_to_the_streets.

Gallagher, Dylan. "Review: Pearl Jam, Binaural." *PopPolitics: Commentary on Popular and Political Cultures*, 2000. http://www.poppolitics.com/archives/2000/07/Binaural.

Gutmann, Amy. *Why Deliberative Democracy?* Princeton, NJ: Princeton University Press, 2004.

Jordan, Will. "Pearl Jam still rocking in the free world." *Nashville City Paper*, 2003.

Manning, Kara. "Pearl Jam On Columbine-Inspired New Song." *MTV Online*. 2000. http://www.mtv.com/news/articles/1433051/20000419/pearl_jam.jhtml.

McChesney, Robert. *The Political Economy of Media: Enduring Issues, Emerging Dilemmas*. New York: Monthly Review Press, 2008.

Morse, Steve. "Rock Notes; Pearl Jam Stays True to a Tune." *Boston Globe*, 2003: C12.

Morse, Steve. "Pearl Jam takes action on this fall's 'Vote' tour." *Boston Globe Online*, 19 September 2004. http://www.boston.com/news/globe/living/articles/2004/09/19/pearl_jam_takes_action_on_this_falls_vote_tour.

Pearl Jam. Radio Interview by *103.3 The Edge*. Buffalo, NY, 2 May 2003.

Pearl Jam's Antitrust Complaint: Questions about Concert, Sports and Theater Ticket Handling Charges and Other Practices: Hearing before the Subcommittee on Information, Justice, Transportation and Agriculture of the House Committee on Government Operations, 103rd Cong., 2nd Sess., 1994.

Pratt, Ray. *Rhythm and Resistance*. Ann Arbor, MI: University of Michigan Press, 1990.

Sanneh, Kelefa. "Pop Review; Ruffled Feathers Make a Rough Party." *New York Times*, 3 May 2003: B3, 11.

"Set Lists and Appearances 2003–2." *Pearl Jam: Synergy*. http://www.sonymusic.com/artists/PearlJam/fanscene/set2003b.html.

"Set Lists and Appearances 2003-3." *Pearl Jam: Synergy*. http://www.sonymusic.com/artists/PearlJam/fanscene/set2003c.html.

"Set Lists and Appearances 2004." *Pearl Jam: Synergy*. http://www.sonymusic.com/artists/PearlJam/fanscene/set2004.html.

"Set Lists and Appearances 2007." *Pearl Jam: Synergy.* http://www.sonymusic.com/artists/PearlJam/fanscene/set2007.html.

Schiller, Dan. *How to Think about Information.* Chicago: University of Illinois Press, 2008.

Talvi, Silja. "Vedder on Nader: The Better Man." *Salon.com*, 26 September 2000. http://archive.salon.com/ent/log/2000/09/26/vedder/index.html.

Tannenbaum, Rob. "Rebels Without A Pause." *George Magazine*, July 2000.

"Voices for Change." *Rollingstone.com*, 2004. http://www.rollingstone.com/news/story/6487639/voices_for_change.

Waddell, Ray. "Springing into Action: How Five Top Managers Pulled Together Superstar Tour to Unseat Bush." *Billboard* 116.33, 2004: 3, 75.

Weglarz, Kristine. "Lifting the Curse: Pearl Jam's 'Alive' and 'Bushleaguer' and the Marketplace of Meanings." *Transformative Works and Cultures* 7, 2011.

Discography

Pearl Jam. *Binaural.* New York: Epic, EK 63665, 2000.

Pearl Jam. *Riot Act.* New York: Epic, EK86825, 2002.

Pearl Jam. *Ten.* New York: Epic, ZK 47857, 1991.

Van Zandt, Steven. *Voice of America.* Hollywood, CA: EMI, ST 17120 1983.

Young, Neil. *This Note's For You.* Burbank, CA: Reprise Records, 9 25719 2, 1988.

Videography

Charnoski, Rick and Nichols, Coan (Producers). *Vote for Change? Parts 1–4.* 2008. https://www.pearljam.com/activism/vfc.php.

Pearl Jam (Producers). *Touring Band 2000.* Epic, 2000.

Chapter 11
Rage Against the Machine: Militant Poetics

Michael LeVan

> If something deeply affects the order of our collective life and we are taught that
> we have no choice about accepting it when in fact we do, that is a problem for
> democracy. (Lummis 1996, 79)

"Mic check!" shouts Tom Morello, firing up the "people's microphone" so that the nearest in the crowd at the Occupy Wall Street demonstration in Zuccotti Park will chant his words out to those farther away. "MIC CHECK!" confirms the people's microphone. "My first song … MY FIRST SONG … is for all the people … IS FOR ALL THE PEOPLE … who lost everything … WHO LOST EVERYTHING … This is called 'The Fabled City' … THIS IS CALLED 'THE FABLED CITY'."

Standing on a makeshift stage, surrounded by fellow protestors, with just his black acoustic guitar blazoned with the name "Black Spartacus" and a harmonica, Morello launches into his song for the crowd of protestors on 13 October 2011. "The Fabled City" is the title track from Morello's second solo album (2008). Morello recorded it as The Nightwatchman, his solo alter ego. Like all of The Nightwatchman's music, "The Fabled City" evokes political folk anthems from an earlier era of protest music and cuts to the heart of social injustice: "I've seen the fabled city/And its streets are paved with gold/But an iron fence runs round it/ And its iron gate is closed." Within a few weeks, MTV had announced that they had created a special O Music Award (for online and multiplatform music) for the category "Most Memorable #OWS[1] Performance" for his "The Fabled City" performance (Shaw 2011). Soon after, *The Nation* released its *Progressive Honor Roll 2011*, naming Morello Most Valuable Musician (Nichols 2012).

"Dignity has no price/At the corner of now and nowhere/Anywhere/Everywhere/Tomorrow is calling/Tomorrow is calling/Do not be afraid." So ends an untitled poem by Zack de la Rocha, posted 16 November 2011 on the Rage Against the Machine website (www.ratm.com) and "dedicated to the Occupy Movement whose courage is changing the world." Like guitarist Morello, vocalist/lyricist de la Rocha is a member of the hard-hitting political rock band Rage Against the Machine.

---

[1]   On the social media site Twitter, a hashtag (#) indicates a trending topic. Followed by the OWS acronym, "#OWS" indicates trending topic references to the Occupy Wall Street movement. The O Music Award created the category explicitly to honor Morello's Occupy Wall Street performance, particularly its widespread sharing among users of Twitter as an online video.

With Tim Commerford on bass and Brad Wilk on drums, the band has spent much of the past two decades telling people that they in fact *do* have a choice about how we order our collective life and encouraging them to make choices for change.

I first heard Rage Against the Machine in 1992. I was living in Tempe, Arizona, and came across a promotional cassette single from the band's first album. The cassette features two of their best-known songs, "Killing in the Name" and "Bullet in the Head." The cassette insert shows a black and white image of a man on fire, kneeling near a car, the iconic photograph by Malcolm Browne of Buddhist monk Thich Quang Duc. In 1963, Duc burned himself to death in a busy intersection of Saigon as an act of protest against persecution of Buddhists by the South Vietnamese government. A swatch of black across the center of the image on the cassette case contains the band name in red letters in what now looks familiar as an old-time typewriter font. It was obvious before having a first listen that the band name and the emotional content of the songs would be indistinguishable.

I popped the tape in the tape deck of my yellow 1971 Volkswagen Squareback. The stereo was the only equipment in the car that had been upgraded since 1971. The car lacked an air conditioner, was noisy due to the engine location under the back of the vehicle, and we were already into the seemingly endless season of nonstop triple-digit temperatures. The noise of the car, the blasting hair-dryer heat of the Arizona desert, and the boiling political passion of this new band was a perfect mix, and so the two songs became something of a very short and very loud soundtrack for my summer of 1992. Whenever I was barreling through the primal heat of this urban outpost of the Sonoran Desert, I would blast the music against the blast furnace of hot wind coming in through my windows: "You're standin' in line/Believin' the lies/Bowin' down to the flag/You got a bullet in your head." Like the desert itself, Rage Against the Machine is a dry heat of extremes.

The band name Rage Against the Machine is fitting for two reasons. On one hand, it describes the band's acerbic lyrics and its fierce mix of hard rock, rap, funk, and punk. *To rage.* Both music and lyrics pulsate with passion, anger, and demands for social justice and spaces of freedom. On the other hand, raging *against the machine* is an apt description of the political activism of the band and its two most visible front men, Zack de la Rocha and Tom Morello. Rage, as they are known, is an anti-corporate, anti-racist, anti-globalization, anti-empire, anti-control, pro-social justice, pro-labor, radically democratic powerhouse of advocacy and activism. Rage is one of the most explicitly political bands to have ever achieved high-profile status and commercial success.

Rage Against the Machine released just three studio albums of original material: *Rage Against the Machine* (1992), *Evil Empire* (1996), and *The Battle of Los Angeles* (1999). Shortly after breaking up in 2000, *Renegades*, a fourth studio album consisting of covers of progressive and protest songs, was released. The band has been reunited since 2007, touring and playing festivals, but has not released any new studio recordings. Nevertheless, the fan base remains strong, evidenced by a Facebook campaign that propelled their 1992 single "Killing in the Name" to the 2009 "Christmas number one" slot in the UK Singles Chart.

Beyond the music, Morello and de la Rocha have been consistently active in protest movements in support of organized labor, human rights, social justice, anti-imperialism, anti-torture, self-determination, and democracy.

Rage Against the Machine had a quick rise to stardom. Forming in Los Angeles in 1991, the band recorded a demo cassette and, after playing the LA club circuit, quickly found themselves in a contract with media giant Sony Music Group and its subsidiary label Epic Records. The band has an eclectic mix of influences, from The Clash to Public Enemy to Black Sabbath to Afrika Bambaataa. They are known for their funky, hard rock style of music with hard-driving riffs, rap vocals, and crescendos of explosive screaming. Morello is touted as a creative guitarist who is able to mimic the sounds of scratching records and harmonicas with his instrument (he often plays with his hands crossed across the pickups of his guitar, the right hand flicking the pickup toggle switch back and forth while his left hand "scratches" the strings above the pickup). In 2011, *Rolling Stone* magazine honored him as the #26 greatest guitarist of all time. The band had commercial success, with all three albums going multiplatinum in sales. Surprisingly, this was accomplished with some of the fiercest, in-your-face-political, activist music ever recorded.

In many ways, the members of RATM are first and foremost activists. In this sense, their fame and popular success—having sold over 16 million records—can be understood as their medium for consciousness-raising. In another sense, they can be understood as ushering in a new type of public intellectual in the early 1990s. Through music and actions, the band has been a conduit for disseminating messages of critical thought, protest, and causes for justice. They have been inspired by the writings of leftist public intellectuals as well as protest movements across the world. One can get an immediate sense of their depth of political engagement by looking at the books featured in a foldout from the album *Evil Empire* (2006) or on the banner image on the band's website. Those works include Franz Fanon, William Powell, Karl Marx, Noam Chomsky, Howard Zinn, Susan Faludi, Amrita Basu, William Blum, Huey Newton, and Che Guevara. It is nearly impossible to separate RATM's music from their message.

The spirit of activism was forged at early ages for Morello and de la Rocha, both of whom are children of politically active parents. Mary Morello, Tom's mother, was a schoolteacher and founder (in 1987) of the anti-censorship group Parents for Rock and Rap (in opposition to the conservative PMRC, Parents Music Resource Center). Morello's Kenyan father Ngethe Njoroge fought in the Mau Mau Uprising for Kenyan independence from Britain, though he left the family when Tom was a toddler. De la Rocha's mother, Olivia, is an anthropologist, and his father, Roberto ("Beto"), is a visual artist. Beto was a member of the Los Four Chicano artist collective in Los Angeles, and is well-known for his murals and paintings, as well as for his community activism around Dia De Los Muertos festivities in LA. De la Rocha also has family ties to revolution, as his paternal grandfather fought in the Mexican Revolution before immigrating to the US and working as an agricultural laborer (Cuevas 1999). Like Morello, de la Rocha's parents separated when he was very young and he ended up spending much of his childhood in Irvine, California, where his mother earned a doctorate in anthropology at UC-Irvine.

Both men have said they experienced racism and bigotry as biracial children ("Rage Against the Machine" 1999). Morello grew up in Libertyville, Illinois, an affluent, mostly white suburb north of Chicago. He found a noose hanging in his garage when he was 13, which he sings about on the title track for The Nightwatchman album *One Man Revolution* (2007): "On the streets of New York/The cabs don't stop/On the street where I live/They called the cops/Found a noose in my garage/Now how 'bout that" (http://nightwatchmanmusic.com). De la Rocha discusses his firsthand experiences through a place-based dialectic of alternating homes:

> My father was a painter. He made giant paintings in East L.A. He was in this group. They were one of the first Chicano-Art-Groups that exhibited at the Los Angeles County Museum of Art. Living with him helped me to see a lot of things that I normally wouldn't see, if I had grown up in a "perfect" family. He read Mao, did a series of paintings for United Farm Workers and always had some incredible answers to all my questions. I also think that my upbringing as a Chicano in a white suburban environment has a lot of effect on my awareness. My parents separated when I was a year old, and I constantly moved back and forth between them and to very different neighborhoods. From the poor East LA where my father lived and to the college in the rich Orange County where my mother lived, where Chicanos like me normally only would be if they had a broom in their hand or filling baskets with strawberries. There was some large oppositions, that I had to realize and learn to handle, and has probably founded my opinions today. (de la Rocha 1999)

These early experiences inform the first trajectory of Rage Against the Machine activism: anti-racism and social justice. Rage has also advocated critical anti-corporatism, independent media, anti-imperialism, and radical democracy. They have even advocated for activism itself. However, the realization that social injustice is fostered in a system of control—and a contingently produced social order—is what propels the entire aesthetic and politics of the band.

Gaps in "the Sensible"

The political philosopher Jacques Rancière has explored the link between politics and aesthetics as a system of visibility (and audibility) that is distributed or partitioned in society. He defines the political as a demand for equality. Politics comes when those who have no visibility claim it. Rancière writes: "the essence of politics is *dissensus*," which is "not a confrontation between interest or opinions. It is the demonstration of a gap in the sensible itself" (Rancière 2010, 38). This, I believe, gets at the essence of Rage Against the Machine's politics: through sound, language, and emotion, the gaps in "the sensible" burn brightly in dissensus, like an echo of the stoic rage of Thich Quang Duc's self-immolation. Rancière continues: "Political demonstration makes visible that which has no reason to be seen; it places one world in another," commandeering and transforming the interpretive forces of the existing order (ibid., 38).

Rage Against the Machine publicly supports a wide range of anti-racist and social justice organizations, advocates for some high-profile campaigns, and has often played at benefit concerts or other fundraisers for these causes. Whether the Leonard Peltier Defense Fund, The Anti-Nazi League, Fairness and Accuracy in Reporting, Rock for Choice, The Tibetan Freedom Concerts, working in opposition to the 2010 Arizona immigration law, or advocating for the release of Mumia Abu-Jamal, all of their outward activism is first distilled inside their frenetic sound and de la Rocha's lyrics. Though their oeuvre is not enormous, every song is packed with political content and images demonstrating the gaps in the sensible.

Consider "Year of tha Boomerang" from *Evil Empire* (2006). The song is about a young person in school coming to a state of consciousness about how an unjust distribution of the sensible is often reproduced in formalized education. The song likens public education to electroshock therapy, imprisonment, and a generalized disenfranchisement from self-actualization: "Straight incarcerated, the curriculum's a cell block/I'm swimmin' in half truths and it makes me wanna spit." The song also demonstrates the band's engagement with radical political philosophy, as it references seminal postcolonial author Frantz Fanon. The song title "Year of tha Boomerang" reflects a line from Jean-Paul Sartre's preface to Fanon's 1961 *The Wretched of the Earth*: "This is the age of the boomerang, the third stage of violence: it flies back at us, it strikes us and, once again, we have no idea what hit us" (Sartre 2004, liv). The song is representative of a typical Rage composition: heavy funk-rock bass and guitar merges with angry rap-style vocals presenting a story in images of struggle while making references to revolutionary events and figures. As the song continues, de la Rocha expresses despair at the discursive domination of right-wing ideologies, though encouraging listeners to combat anti-democratic oppression by seeking education in political self-actualization: "I grip tha cannon like Fanon an pass tha shells to my classmates/ Aw, power to tha people." The song grooves and churns, building up to a kind of joyous anger as it reaches the chorus, with its crescendo of fist-pumping repetition: "I got no property but yo I'm a piece of it/So let tha guilty hang/ ... /In the year of tha boomerang." The issue at stake for de la Rocha and Rage Against the Machine is to try to reorient a complacency of vision in order to see the ways in which the social orders of race, class, and gender—as well as conditions of global oppression—are coded into mainstream cultural/public discourses. These discourses especially include the content of public education, corporate media, party politics, finance capitalism, organized religion, and consumerism, arguably the six most influential systems of social control.

Rage goes beyond the acknowledgement of what Deleuze and Guattari call the "order-word" function of language as the most basic system of social control: "Language is made not to be believed but to be obeyed, and to compel obedience" (Deleuze and Guattari 1987, 76). They wish to move listeners out of a passive stance of complacency and anomie and into an active position to take control of their collective lives. During the 1990s, Morello hosted a political talk and interview show on Radio Free Los Angeles. In 1996 he interviewed Noam Chomsky about democracy and activism ("On Democracy: Noam Chomsky Interviewed by Tom Morello" 1996). Besides mentioning that Chomsky books like *Manufacturing Consent* are prominent on the Rage tour bus, Morello—who graduated with a degree in Political Science from the Social Studies program at Harvard University—and Chomsky discussed systemic economic inequality, militarism, education, and democracy. Toward the last part of the interview, Morello asks Chomsky a classic Liberal-pragmatic question about social transformation: "What sort of society do you envision as one that would not be based on exploitation or domination and how would we get there from here" (ibid.)? Chomsky's answer would prove to be influential for Morello's own stance on activism and help him understand the potential paradoxes of being a spokesperson for the part without a part. Chomsky responds:

> I don't really understand the question. It's kind of interesting. I'm asked that question constantly in sort of privileged circles. I'm never asked it when I go to talk to poor people. Or say either here or abroad. They tell me what they're doing. Maybe they ask for a comment, but they don't ask how they do it. How you do it is very straightforward: you go out and do it. If you want a more free and democratic society, you go out and do it. (ibid.)

Since then, for Morello, the activism infused in all aspects of Rage Against the Machine (as well as his side and solo projects) is to reveal that there are other ways of looking and doing, and to encourage people to seek out truth and to act upon it. During his "Occupy World Tour," in which he played and spoke at several of the Occupy protest events in the US and abroad, Morello commented on the Occupy movement in ways that clearly echo Chomsky:

> It is a global social justice movement to invert the pyramid of inequality. It's already had great successes in that it has politicized a generation. There are so many young people involved, and so many people who've never been to a protest or demonstration, so many people who are realizing that they are historical agents, that by simply walking out their front door they can have an effect on their country, on their planet. (Baltin 2011)

Likewise, in an interview with the BBC (Cacciottolo 2011), Morello drives the point home in the context of the "Arab Spring" democracy uprising in the Middle

East: It "taught a lesson that all you need to change the world is walk out your door, and change the world."

Rage often attaches specific advocacy causes to their songs in their music videos and during live performances. The song "Freedom," from their self-titled first album (1992), suggests that many militant activists of racial justice are silenced through incarceration, in other words, by institutions of the very system they oppose: "It's set up like a deck of cards/They're sending us to early graves/ For all the diamonds/They'll use a pair of clubs to beat the spades." Tellingly, there is no heart in this deck of cards. The other suits represent racism, violence, and economic exploitation. The hard-grooving riff of the song expresses the missing heart—the passionate pulse of self-determination—evoked in the final primal screams of "Freedom!" The video for "Freedom" is itself a piece of public address about the case of Leonard Peltier, a native American activist and a leader of the American Indian Movement, who was convicted of murdering two FBI agents during a standoff/shoot-out on the Pine Ridge Indian Reservation in 1975. Peltier's conviction has been a focus for Amnesty International and other activist groups over suspicions of unfairness. In the "Freedom" video, footage of the band performing is interspersed with footage of Peltier and other members of the American Indian Movement. Scrolling text presents doubts about the fairness of the trial. Quotes from Chief Sitting Bull provide historical context, and a final statement tells us, "justice has not been done." The video is so full of conviction that it could motivate fans and other viewers of the song to, at worst, develop suspicions of the racial biases of the legal and justice systems, and, at best, to seek out more information about Peltier's case and his defense fund. A major goal of activism is to disseminate information in the form of counternarrative. In effect, the forceful and embodied production of counternarrative—what we might call *militant poetics*—is the raison d'être of Rage Against the Machine.

Militant Poetics

The most concise expression of militant poetics can be found in Rage's iconic song, "Killing in the Name," the track from their first album (1992). The song is explicitly focused on systemic racism in law enforcement and criminal justice in the US. "Some of those who work forces, are the same who burn crosses," de la Rocha quietly begins in repetition, before a more accusatory repetition of "And now you do what they told ya." The song then focuses on the state monopoly on legitimate violence as simultaneously being a legitimation of state-sanctioned racial violence: "Those who died are justified, for wearing the badge, they're the chosen whites." As the song cycles and builds, to the line "And now you do what they told ya" they add, "now you're under control." The song builds more and more through repetition, encouraging listeners to arrive at the revelation of their own submission to the system of control, before finally offering a mantra for resistance in an explosive refrain of "Fuck you, I won't do what you tell me!"

that repeats 16 times in a growing, growling crescendo of, well, rage against the machine.

A second advocacy theme in the music and activism of Rage Against the Machine is critical anti-corporatism, including critiques of corporate media and conservative talk radio, buttressed by advocacy for alternative, independent sources of journalism. On this last point, the band, for example, has played benefits for, and spread the word about, the independent media organization Fairness and Accuracy in Reporting (FAIR). Their song "Vietnow" (1996) focuses on the propaganda machine of AM talk radio and the so-called conservative echo-chamber it helps constitute for public discourse. "Fear is your only god on the radio," de la Rocha seethes, before launching into a critique of conservative rhetoric that relies mainly on a steady stream of manipulations of religion, cultural obedience to power, and shock tactics. Just as Rage levels its critique about a style of fear-mongering rhetoric that combines submission to religious dogma with submission to the interests of political and social power ("the transmissions whippin' our backs"; "Is all the world jails and churches?"; "Terror's the product ya push [...] the sheep tremble and here come the votes"), they also suggest resistance through critical media consumption and the use of counter-media. In "Guerilla Radio," a popular track from *The Battle of Los Angeles* (1999), they further the critique of corporate media as "a spectacle monopolized" at the service of the interests of both major political parties: "They hold the reigns and stole your eyes." Though the band has often been criticized (that is, "called out") for being a part of the very corporate media system they critique (being signed to Sony Music Group), they find no contradiction in being able to disseminate critical media messages widely via a *guerilla use* of corporate media. The song advocates direct action and civil disobedience in pirating the resources of the public airwaves for the dissemination of counternarratives: "It has to start somewhere, it has to start sometime/what better place than here, what better time than now?"

As usual, Rage melds their causes together in the music video for "Guerilla Radio." While the song itself is focused squarely on the propagandistic uses of corporate media, the video, through a parody of Gap commercials, focuses on a blind faith of consumerism, showing ultra-white, yuppie-type bourgeois consumers as mass-produced porcelain copies of each other. The video also emphasizes consumers' blindness to the conditions of production. The video alternates among images of consumers consuming blindly and sweatshop laborers toiling. "Lights out, guerilla radio; turn that shit up!" The band appears in the video in the same pristine white space where the laborers sit at their sewing machines. Wilk's bass drum is emblazoned with the red star symbol of the Zapatistas, and Morello wears something of a Zapatista guerilla uniform while his amp sports the iconic visage of Che Guevara. An ironic red logo reading "rage" appears as a spoof of fashion brands like The Gap. The video can therefore also be read as self-reflexive political awareness of the use of popular music as the soundtrack for consumption and advertising.[2]

"No Shelter" (1998), which was featured on the soundtrack for the *Godzilla* movie, continues the assault on consumerism. The focus is on marketing that co-opts rebellion as a commodity, thus deflating it of its power. By transforming rebellion into the ethos of branding ("Tha thin line between entertainment and war"), a deeper level of social control is maintained by making rebellion appear to be nothing more than a fashion style—and style, as we all know, is fickle and ephemeral, changing as scheduled with the season. At the same time, however, the pervasive culture of brand marketing and what Thomas Frank calls the "conquest of cool" (Frank 1997) serves together as a diversion from the historical and present realities of global exploitation, oppression, militarism, and cultural imperialism. The diversion is bolstered by entertainment media, new media, and advertising alike: "Chained to the dream they got ya searchin for/ ... /There be no shelter here/Tha frontline is everywhere." The irony should not be lost that, once again, the message is delivered via a guerilla use of the very media they are critiquing, showing up on a soundtrack for a Hollywood blockbuster. The video for "No Shelter" alternates among scenes of workers on a 1940s-style assembly line, executives in their boardroom, people in gas masks, images of billboards providing counternarratives about the Hiroshima bombing, poverty, imperialism, Mumia Abu-Jamal, and racial injustice, as well as images of whipping, sensory deprivation, and finally a murder of a youth consumer by a corporate agent of social control.

The band itself experienced the effects of media control when they were censored and kicked off of *Saturday Night Live* in April 1996 after a performance of their song "Bulls on Parade," during which they attempted to hang American flags upside down (a signal of distress) from their amplifiers. The song, from the *Evil Empire* album, is harshly critical of US militarism and the military-industrial complex, placing a focus on the anti-humanitarian and anti-humanist aspects of those industries at the expense of profiteering: "Weapons not food, not homes, not shoes/Not need, just feed the war cannibal animal." The host on *SNL* that night was then-Presidential candidate Steve Forbes, a billionaire Republican pushing a flat tax policy. Just before going on, *SNL* stagehands scuffled with the band to remove the flags, and after the song, the band was ejected from the premises without playing their second number. As Morello stated in a letter emailed to fans, the upside-down flags signified,

[O]ur contention that American democracy is inverted when what passes for democracy is an electoral choice between two representatives of the privileged class. America's freedom of expression is inverted when you're free to say anything you want to say until it upsets a corporate sponsor. Finally, this was our way of expressing our opinion of the show's host, Steve Forbes. ... The

---

[2] Thanks to Mark Pedelty for this observation.

thing that's ironic is *SNL* is supposedly this cutting edge show, but they proved they're bootlickers to their corporate masters when it comes down to it. They're cowards. It should come to no surprise that GE, which owns NBC, would find [our music] particularly offensive. GE is a major manufacturer of US planes used to commit war crimes in the Gulf War, and bombs from those jets destroyed hydroelectric dams which killed thousands of civilians in Iraq. (archived, "Articles/Interviews" 1996)

Even in this sort of defeat, Morello and Rage Against the Machine engage in activism and democratic pedagogy, encouraging fans to write to NBC expressing intolerance of censorship and free expression.

"Bulls on Parade" is indicative of a third trajectory of Rage activism: anti-imperialism and radical democracy. Though inextricably linked with the other two trajectories (racial justice and anti-consumerism), this line of advocacy engages globalization. The deepest and most explicit connection here is with the *Ejército Zapatista de Liberación Nacional* (EZLN), the indigenous revolutionary movement in Chiapas, Mexico. The EZNL is well known among progressive political theorists as a kind of democratic exemplar, with their nonhierarchical network organization, insistence on distributed power, use of new media as a tool of activism, and rejection of neoliberalism. Michael Hardt and Antonio Negri, for example, cite the EZLN frequently as models of autonomy and self-determination of "the multitude" and "the common," a new way of creating democratic life (Hardt and Negri 2004, 2009). As mentioned above, Rage adopts the iconography and flag of the EZLN in their stage show, videos, website, and albums.

De la Rocha has taken several trips to Chiapas to meet the Zapatistas, to listen to their stories and struggles, and to raise money, awareness, and encouragement for them. As de la Rocha explained in an interview, "In February 1996, I visited civil camps for peace, in La Garrucha. There, I experienced the terror the people felt: the intimidation by the soldiers, the isolation in which the communities had to subsist, the military camps located between the houses and the fields." He continues,

> Later I was at La Realidad for the Continental Encounter for Humanity Against Neoliberalism. We realized the importance of dialogue between civil society and the Zapatistas, and we identified with them as a generation. We are a people without a party. We are for a different world where money is not the only exchange value. We are against racist politics in the United States. (Cuevas 1999)

It is unsurprising that the Zapatistas show up frequently in de la Rocha's lyrics. "People of the Sun" (1996) from *Evil Empire*, for example, is about the Zapatista revolution: "since 1516 minds attacked and overseen/Now crawl amidst the ruins of this empty dream." The video for the song explores the roots of the revolution and features imagery of Mexican victims of colonial and government violence, like a worker being buried up to his neck and trampled with horses.

For "Sleep Now in the Fire," from *The Battle of Los Angeles* (1999), the band takes aim at the twin histories of colonialism and imperialism as axes of oppression that have present-day reverberations on the material conditions of contemporary life, as well as for the distribution of poverty and wealth in the Americas: "The nina, the pinta, the santa maria/The noose and the rapist, the fields' overseer/ … /The cost of my desire/Sleep now in the fire." The band enlisted progressive filmmaker Michael Moore to direct the video for "Sleep Now in the Fire," which was shot across the street from the New York Stock Exchange. The video features a spoof of the game show *Who Wants to Be a Millionaire?* called *Who Wants to Be Filthy F#&%ing Rich?* The fake game show presents hapless contestants having no idea how to answer questions like "how many Americans do not have health care?" or about the distribution of wealth in America, or of global poverty—all of which presage the 2011 Occupy Wall Street movement. The video ends with footage of de la Rocha being escorted out of the Stock Exchange before security there locked down its doors. Interview footage of evangelical Republican Gary Bauer plays, as the politician calls the band "anti-family and pro-terrorist." In classic Michael Moore form, the video ends with text placed over footage of the locked-down doors reading, "At 2:52pm, in the middle of the trading day, the Stock Exchange was forced to close its doors. No money was harmed."

The last trajectory of activism I'll discuss is what I think distinguishes Rage Against the Machine from most other political bands, and that is advocacy for activism itself. Not only do all of Rage's songs attempt to inform listeners and move them to political action, but the band encourages a general engagement with political self-determination and activism in a sort of combination of pedagogy and DIY (do-it-yourself) attitudes reminiscent of the punk scene and aesthetic. For example, Morello maintains a website and organization called *Axis Of Justice*, along with Serj Tankian of System of a Down, which has the stated purpose to "bring together musicians, fans of music, and grassroots political organizations to fight for social justice" (*Axis of Justice*).

Rage songs like "Testify" ("We found your weakness/And it's right outside your door/Now testify!"), "Calm Like a Bomb" ("Hope lies in the smoldering rubble of empires"), "Wake Up" ("Fist in the air in the land of hypocrisy"), and "Know Your Enemy" ("Yes I know my enemies/They're the teachers who taught me to fight me/Compromise, conformity, assimilation, submission/Ignorance, hypocrisy, brutality, the elite/All of which are American dreams") all exemplify the general will-to-activist consciousness that propels the band's relentless messages. Speaking with the *New York Times* in October 2011 about performing protest music, Morello states a position that seems unchanged for 20 years:

A lot of liberals and progressives hitched their dreams to [the Obama] administration. I did not. It was a lot easier during the Bush administration. Darth Vader-like presidents make a great target for song writing. But the north star of my music has always been standing up for the oppressed and standing up for the underdog, and in this era, where the gulf between rich and poor continues to broaden, there are a lot of songs that need singing. (McKinley 2011)

The video for "Testify" (1999) was the second to be directed by Michael Moore. It is set as a silent movie in the science fiction genre in which aliens invade earth. The aliens beam down one of their own, who splits into two (one appears as George W. Bush, the other as Al Gore). The video goes on to show, in a style now familiar to watchers of the *Daily Show*'s media critiques, clips of Bush and Gore having identical stances on issues like the death penalty and free trade. De la Rocha growls, "I'm empty please fill me/Mister anchor assure me/That Baghdad is burning/Your voice it is so soothing/That cunning mantra of killing." The video continues with imagery showing campaign contributions coming to each candidate from the same big industries, alongside images of war, oil, immigrants, mass production, citizenship ceremonies, police violence, and highways packed with cars at rush hour. "Mass graves for the pump and the price is set," de la Rocha repeats quietly in the video, with a gas pump nozzle pressed to his temple. The end of the video features footage of Ralph Nader saying, "If you're not turned on to politics, politics will turn on you." This critique of the two-party system in US politics hit full force at a free concert Rage Against the Machine held across the street from the 2000 Democratic National Convention. The concert was publicized as a protest against the false choices of the two-party system, and it ended prematurely with the crowd being dispersed with pepper spray, tear gas, and rubber bullets. The band's message is clear: people need to become completely invested in democracy, which C. Douglas Lummis defines as "a critique of centralized power of every sort" (Lummis 1996, 25).

When the band broke up shortly thereafter in 2000, Morello, Wilk, and Commerford joined Soundgarden vocalist Chris Cornell to form the band Audioslave. During the 2000s Morello also developed his solo career and labor-activist persona The Nightwatchman, in addition to other projects like Street Sweeper Social Club. De la Rocha collaborated on several musical projects and formed a new band, One Day as a Lion.

Since reuniting in 2007, Rage has maintained its provocations for justice. The band played protest shows at both major US political party conventions in 2008. While headlining the Reading Music festival in the UK in 2008, the band began their show hooded and wearing orange jumpsuits like detainees at Guantanamo Bay. In 2010, de la Rocha organized Strikeforce, a wide-ranging musician's boycott against the state of Arizona and its controversial immigration legislation. In 2011, Morello played and spoke during the labor protests in Madison, Wisconsin, and later that same year played at several Occupy sites in the US and in Europe. Writing about the Madison event for *Rolling Stone*, Morello, now 47, sums up his continued activist commitment: "I've played hundreds of protests. I've marched on dozens of picket lines. I've strummed my guitar at innumerable demonstrations. I've been arrested more times than I'm willing to put in print in support of striking workers" (Morello 2011). At the end of 2011, Dark Horse comics began releasing *Orchid*, a future dystopian comic book about social justice, extreme inequality, human trafficking, and savage corporatism penned by Morello. Each issue comes with a download code for a soundtrack song for the issue recorded by Morello.

New York Times reporter David Carr perhaps best captures the political effect of Rage Against the Machine. While covering the band's concert in Minneapolis, during the 2008 Republican National Convention, Carr writes,

> Rage has millions of fans whose ardor has not been diminished by the band's not putting out a record in eight years. The group's insistent calls to action, in song and from the stage, still fall on receptive ears. Some of its hard-core fans are less prone to buying T-shirts than engaging in the kind of civil disobedience that sometimes ends in tear gas. (Carr 2008)

That their rhetorical energy and activist message has not faltered over two decades is a testament to their belief that music can inspire political engagement through untamed tongues, unrestrained instruments, and an unwavering fight for justice.

Bibliography

Axis of Justice. http://axisofjustice.net.

Baltin, Steve. "Tom Morello Returns to Occupy L.A." *Rolling Stone*, 26 October 2011. http://www.rollingstone.com/music/news/tom-morello-returns-to-occupy-l-a-20111026#ixzz1hwBTZuQb.

Cacciottolo, Mario. "Tom Morello: Providing the Soundtrack to a Rebellion." *BBC News*, 10 November 2011. http://www.bbc.co.uk/news/entertainment-arts-15670249.

Carr, David. "At Both Conventions, A Band Sounds Anarchy." *New York Times*, 5 September 2008. http://www.nytimes.com/2008/09/06/arts/music/06rage.html.

Cuevas, Jesus Ramirez. "Zack de la Rocha Interview." *Frontera* 8, 1999. http://www.musicfanclubs.org/rage/articles/frontera.htm.

de la Rocha, Zack. Interview with *Propaganda*, 1999. http://www.musicfanclubs.org/rage/articles/prop.htm.

Deleuze, Gilles and Félix Guattari. *A Thousand Plateaus: Capitalism and Schizophrenia*. Translated by Brian Massumi. Minneapolis, MN: University of Minnesota Press, 1987.

Frank, Thomas. *The Conquest of Cool: Business Culture, Counterculture, and the Rise of Hip Consumerism*. Chicago: University of Chicago Press, 1997.

Hardt, Michael and Antonio Negri. *Commonwealth*. Cambridge, MA: Belknap Press, 2009.

Hardt, Michael and Antonio Negri. *Multitude: War and Democracy in the Age of Empire*. New York: Penguin, 2004.

Lummis, C. Douglas. *Radical Democracy.* Ithaca, NY: Cornell University Press, 1996.

McKinley, James C. "Q and A: Tom Morello Offers 'a Record of Rousing Hopelessness'." *New York Times Arts Beat Blog*, October 18, 2011.

Morello, Tom. "Frostbite and Freedom: Tom Morello on the Battle of Madison." *Rolling Stone*, 25 February 2011. http://www.rollingstone.com/politics/news/ frostbite-and-freedom-tom-morello-on-the-battle-of-madison-20110225#ixzz1hw4WeRCe.

Nichols, John, "The Progressive Honor Roll 2011." *The Nation*, 9 January 2012. Also at http://www.thenation.com/article/165314/progressive-honor-roll-2011.

"On Democracy: Noam Chomsky Interviewed by Tom Morello." *Chomsky.info: The Noam Chomsky Website.* http://www.chomsky.info/interviews/1996summer.htm.

"rage: Articles/Interviews." 17 May 1996. http://musicfanclubs.org/rage/articles/snl.htm

Rage Against the Machine. http://www.ratm.com.

"Rage Against the Machine: Party for your Right to Fight." *guitar.com.* 1999. http://www.guitar.com/articles/rage-against-machine-party-your-right-fight.

Rancière, Jacques. *Dissensus: On Politics and Aesthetics.* Edited and translated by Steven Corcoran. London: Continuum, 2010.

Sartre, Jean-Paul. Preface to *The Wretched of the Earth* by Frantz Fanon. Translated by Richard Philcox. New York: Grove Press, 2004.

Shaw, Lucas. "MTV Honors Tom Morello with Occupy Wall Street Award." *Reuters*, 31 October 2011. http://www.reuters.com/article/2011/10/31/idUS86633844620111031.

Tom Morello: The Nightwatchman. http://nightwatchmanmusic.com.

Discography

Nightwatchman, The. (Tom Morello). *One Man Revolution.* New York: Epic, 82796 67546 2, 2007.

Nightwatchman, The. (Tom Morello). *The Fabled City.* Los Angeles: New West, NW 5040, 2008.

Rage Against The Machine. *Evil Empire.* New York: Epic, EK 57523, 1996.

Rage Against The Machine. "Killing in the Name"/"Bullet in the Head." New York: Epic, catalog # ZAT 4842, 1992 [Limited edition promotional pre-release cassette tape single].

Rage Against The Machine. *Rage Against The Machine.* New York: Epic, ZK 52959, 1992.

Rage Against The Machine. *Renegades.* New York: Epic, EK 85296, 2000.

Rage Against The Machine. *The Battle of Los Angeles.* New York: Epic, EK 69630, 1999.

Index